CAMBRIDGE TEXTS AND STUDIES IN
THE HISTORY OF EDUCATION

General Editors

A. C. F. BEALES, A. V. JUDGES, JOHN ROACH

EDUCATION AND SOCIETY IN
NINETEENTH-CENTURY NOTTINGHAM

IN THIS SERIES

Texts

Fénelon on Education, edited by H. C. Barnard

Friedrich Froebel, a selection edited by Irene Lilley

Matthew Arnold and the Education of the New Order, edited by Peter Smith and Geoffrey Summerfield

Robert Owen on Education, edited by Harold Silver

James Mill on Education, edited by W. H. Burston

Samuel Hartlib and the Advancement of Learning, edited by Charles Webster

Thomas Arnold on Education, edited by T. W. Bamford

English for the English, by George Sampson, edited by Denys Thompson

T. H. Huxley on Education, edited by Cyril Bibby

Studies

Education and the French Revolution, by H. C. Barnard

The Rise of a Central Authority for English Education, by A. S. Bishop

Public Examinations in England, 1850–1900, by John Roach

Education and Society in Nineteenth Century Nottingham, by David Wardle

OTHER VOLUMES IN PREPARATION

EDUCATION AND SOCIETY IN NINETEENTH-CENTURY NOTTINGHAM

DAVID WARDLE

Head of Education Department
Padgate College of Education

CAMBRIDGE

AT THE UNIVERSITY PRESS

1971

Published by the Syndics of the Cambridge University Press
Bentley House, 200 Euston Road, London NW1 2DB
American Branch: 32 East 57th Street, New York, N.Y.10022

Library of Congress Catalogue Card Number: 71—154512

/ ISBN: 0 521 08206 4

Printed in Great Britain by
William Clowes & Sons Limited
London, Colchester and Beccles

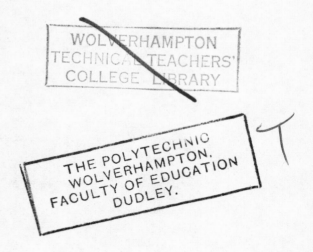

CONTENTS

CONTENTS

ACKNOWLEDGMENTS

In its original form this work was presented as a Ph.D. thesis to Nottingham University, and I wish to thank Mr R. B. Grove for his guidance at this stage. The preparation of this thesis was made much easier by the generous help of Mr A. H. Cryer, who gave me the benefit of his great knowledge of the minutes and reports of the School Board and the Local Education Authority. In the task of shortening and revising the original typescript for publication I have received most valuable assistance from Professor A. V. Judges, editor of this series. I particularly wish to acknowledge my debt to my wife for her help and encouragement at every stage of the work.

Map of Nottingham in about 1800

1 University College
2 Mechanic's Institution
3 Workhouse
4 Hospital
5 Standard Hill

6 Castle
7 St Nicholas's Church
8 High Pavement Chapel
9 St Peter's Church
10 St Mary's Church

INTRODUCTION

This study of the history of education in Nottingham has two principal aims in view:

(*a*) To study the inter-action between education and society at a time when a system of education was in process of development, this within an area large enough to form a recognizable unit, yet small enough for the investigation to be conducted in some detail.

(*b*) To suggest possible points of contrast between the findings of a specific local study and those revealed by the history of education in the country as a whole.

Nottingham differed from some of the great Victorian towns in being a centre of some historical importance; it was a provincial capital and social centre in the seventeenth and eighteenth centuries. But its development in the nineteenth century was characteristic of the industrial towns of the day. Large, overcrowded slums developed and the town was prominent in working class unrest, especially during and immediately after the Napoleonic Wars, and in the Chartist period. Fergus O'Connor was indeed elected Member of Parliament for the town in 1847. The living and working conditions of the poor of Nottingham were reported upon unfavourably and at length by official and unofficial observers. On the credit side organized charity was vigorous, producing many specific subscriptions for the relief of hardship as well as permanent institutions like the General Hospital, the Lunatic Asylum and public dispensaries.

In the sphere of education all the main developments of the nineteenth century were represented in Nottingham. The voluntary agencies, Anglican and Dissenting, were active in elementary education, and one of the earliest Sunday School Unions was formed in the town. The School Board led a vigorous existence and was at the centre of the dispute over the provision of 'secondary' education in higher-grade schools, which was an important reason for the passing of the Act of 1902. The town is credited with the establishment, in 1798, of the first adult school in the country, and, rather more justly, with playing a leading part in the university extension movement.

Also in adult education the flourishing Mechanics' Institution was only one of a number of societies founded to meet the desperate need of the Victorian town for facilities for rational recreation. Three endowed schools, founded in the eighteenth century or earlier, developed in very different directions in the nineteenth century. Secondary education was provided by these, and to a far greater extent, by a number of substantial private schools, some of which struggled intelligently with the problem of producing a curriculum suited to the requirements of the day. The establishment of University College, Nottingham, provided a focus for several contemporary educational movements – the training of technologists and technicians, the liberal education of the middle class, the political education of working men, and the higher education of women.

The emphasis of this work is upon the social rather than the political history of education. The history of education in general has concentrated attention upon the provision of schools on a national scale. Thus great importance has been attached to the activities of the government and of nationwide associations like the National Society and the British and Foreign Schools Society. But, as R. L. Archer pointed out in *Secondary Education in the Nineteenth Century*, this has produced a one-sided and inadequate view of the development of education. Even in those fields such as elementary education, where the public agencies did play a significant part, official sources merely record what the authorities decree shall be done and what action has been reported. Such reports may or may not be accurate. They may not even be relevant since much of the most interesting part of a school's work may lie outside their scope. On the other hand concentration upon the national scene may lead a historian to give undue importance to controversies which attracted the notice of Parliament but were of rather little importance for the schools themselves. For example, the sectarian quarrel which dominated the national educational scene from the time of Bell and Lancaster until at least the First World War was considered by some contemporary writers to be a politicians' quarrel of little concern to teachers and school-children.[1]

A local enquiry may help to explain why educational development took the form it did. Whatever the situation may be at the present time, in the nineteenth century reform in education was very rarely

[1] See e.g. R. D. Roberts (ed.), *Education in the Nineteenth Century*, Cambridge 1901, pp. 54–5; H. B. Philpott, *London at School*, Fisher Unwin, 1904, p. 102.

initiated by government action. An Act of Parliament or an administrative ruling came as the conclusion of a long process of agitation and lobbying, and even an official enquiry was only ordered when the government came under pressure too strong to ignore. If one is to understand the course of educational history it is necessary to know why Members of Parliament and other influential people were asking particular questions at a particular time. To do this one must probe behind the Parliamentary debates to seek out the questions which were exercising the minds of teachers, parents, school managers and parliamentary voters. It is hoped that as a result of the detailed study of a well-defined community it will be possible to examine the local origins of the larger movements of opinion which led to national developments in education.

1
THE INDUSTRIAL REVOLUTION

There has been much controversy about the nature and extent of the changes brought about in England as a whole by the Industrial Revolution, or series of revolutions, but as far as Nottingham is concerned, there can be no doubt that there were two developments which altered, in a relatively short time, the whole appearance of the town and the life of its inhabitants. The first of these developments was a rapid rise in population, and the second the concentration of the bulk of the inhabitants on the hosiery and lace industries. It is not possible, of course, to name a date and say that in that year the Industrial Revolution began in Nottingham. The population of the town rose steadily throughout the eighteenth century, and hosiery was one of its chief occupations since Restoration days. What is certain, however, is that the process of development accelerated very sharply in the second half of the century, and the changes became so great that they were changes of kind rather than of degree.

At the beginning of the reign of George III Nottingham was the principal town in the hosiery trade, but it was also a provincial capital, centre of the social life of the local nobility and gentry, many of whom had their houses in the town. Furthermore it was an important market town, with two market places, and the burgesses maintained a keen interest in the preservation of the town fields on which they enjoyed rights of common. By the end of the reign, the town, with a population swollen to more than four times its previous size, was an industrial centre, with more than 40 per cent of the population engaged in lace and hosiery, while the business interests of the hosiers and lace manufacturers reached out into a ring of surrounding villages which were, in all but administration, part of the town.[1]

In the course of these developments Nottingham suffered from the same teething troubles that afflicted the rising industrial towns

---

[1] Most of these villages have since been absorbed by the modern city, notably by the Borough Extension Act of 1877, when Lenton, Bulwell, Basford, Radford and Sneinton were taken in.

all over England, aggravated by certain peculiar circumstances, the combination rendering the poorer parts of the town, by 1845, 'but one great public nuisance'.[1] In order to examine these troubles it is intended to describe Nottingham as it was about 1750, and then to give an account of the changes which occurred in the next fifty or sixty years. It will then be possible to form an appreciation of the condition of the working class in the new town, and of the size of the problem which faced the educational pioneers of the early nineteenth century. One of the by-products of the Industrial Revolution was an outburst of educational activity far more intense and widespread than any previous similar movement, and this activity led, eventually, to the establishment of a national system of elementary education.

By the standards of the day Nottingham was a large town, coming in the second rank of provincial centres. The population, estimated at about 6,500 in 1700, had risen by Deering's time (1740) to 9,890, and by 1779 to 17,791.[2] Bristol, the second town of England, Manchester, Liverpool, Norwich, Birmingham and Sheffield were the only towns which were significantly larger, and of these only Bristol had many more than 50,000 inhabitants. Hull was a little larger than Nottingham and Leeds about the same size.[3] The small size of these towns is important because it meant that the townsman was by no means as divorced from rural life as he has since become, and his life was materially affected by his having one foot in the country. In the middle of the eighteenth century Nottingham had about ten thousand people, and the nearness of the country to the eighteenth century town would be emphasized by the fact that towns then occupied a far smaller area than a modern town of the same population.

The site of the town had not been enlarged to any considerable extent since medieval times, and the boundaries followed, in all essentials, the lines of the old fortifications, long dismantled. In modern terms the town extended from Chapel Bar in the west to Carter Gate in the east, and from Parliament Street, in the north,

---

[1] *Second Report of the Commissioners for Inquiry into the State of Large Towns and Populous Places.* 1845. App. Part II, p. 253.

[2] The two last figures may be accepted with some confidence. Deering is regarded as a careful writer, while the figure for 1779 was arrived at by a house to house census, financed by subscription among local gentlemen.

[3] G. D. H. Cole, in Turberville (ed.), *Johnson's England*, Oxford, 1933, vol. I, p. 203.

to the Leen. Badder and Peat's map, published in 1744, shows that there was a little ribbon development up the Derby Road towards the future Canning Circus, and some buildings on the north of Parliament Street in the Trinity Square area, but with these small exceptions the whole of the built up area lay within these limits.

To the east a patch of low-lying ground lay between the town and the adjacent hill where the village of Sneinton stood. On the west was the castle and the private park of the Duke of Newcastle. Otherwise Nottingham was surrounded by common land subject to the rights of the burgesses – the Meadows, Sand Field, Clay Field, etc. In the mid-eighteenth century these large open spaces, amounting to 1,120 acres in all, provided pleasant recreation grounds for the citizens, but as the population increased they presented a serious problem. The area of land available for building was 876 acres and it was impossible to increase this to any significant extent until the general enclosure act of 1845.

Nottingham was, therefore, small and compact; from the centre, about where Bridlesmith Gate joins Victoria Street, five minutes brisk walk would take a man out of the built-up area in any direction. But even this small area was not crowded with houses. Gardens and open spaces abounded, there were several orchards and small fields, and several substantial areas were hardly developed at all. Broad Marsh and Narrow Marsh, the scenes of some of the worst nineteenth-century overcrowding, were almost empty.

Nottingham was evidently a pleasant place to live for those who had the time and money to take advantage of its amenities, and it is significant that a considerable number of the nobility and gentry had houses in the town, some of which – the Castle itself, Willoughby House, Newdigate House and Lord Howe's house on Castle Gate – are still standing. The Castle was a principal seat of the Duke of Newcastle, who was generally thought of as being the 'Lord of the Manor', and who also owned Thurland Hall, another of the great houses of the town. The Nottingham Date Book records that in 1750 eleven gentlemen in the town kept their own coach or chariot, 'besides a considerable number who kept chaises and chairs'. Two packs of hounds were kept within the town, one for stags, and the other, kept by the Honourable Rothwell Willoughby of Willoughby House, for hares. In November 1764

The Right Hon. Lord Byron, Master of His Majesty's Staghounds, turned out a fine stag on the Nottingham Race-course, amidst thousands of spectators. The noble animal ran thirty miles in less than three hours, over a very rough country, and crossed the Leen, the Erewash, and the Trent. It was taken in attempting to cross the Soar, in the presence of nearly fifty horsemen.[1]

This anecdote indicates both the intimate connection of the town with the surrounding countryside, and the character of Nottingham as a social centre for the local gentry. By the end of George III's reign this class had left the town, and there was even a tendency for some of the wealthier businessmen to move out; John Smith Wright, a banker, who was to take a great part in the various educational movements of the early nineteenth century, for example, lived at Rempstone, some ten miles south of Nottingham. This movement of the wealthy classes into the country was not, of course, a phenomenon confined to the Nottingham area; the late eighteenth and early nineteenth century was a time of very widespread building of country houses, but it is likely that the increasing overcrowding of the town hastened the flight of these families to less congested quarters. Certainly Nottingham lost its character of a provincial capital at this time.

Life in the old Nottingham was not without its drawbacks. Faced by the squalor of the slums of nineteenth-century industry, writers have sometimes assumed rather too readily that the pre-industrial revolution population lived in a golden age. There was a dark side to life in the 'garden city' of the eighteenth century which must be balanced against the spaciousness which contrasted so attractively with the almost unbelievable over-crowding of the town of the 1840s. Wylie in *Old and New Nottingham*, quotes a little rhyme about the old town :[2]

> I cannot without sin and shame
> Commend the town of Nottingham.
> The people and the fuel stink,
> The place is sordid as a sink.

He then makes some more specific criticisms.

The Trent lanes, especially in winter, were dirty and disagreeable; the lower part of the town near the Leen Bridge almost impassable . . . The fragrant odour from the premises of fell-mongers, curriers and tanners was dispersed over the town; in Bridlesmith Gate nothing was heard save the perpetual beating of iron and the blowing of bellows, the Market

---

[1] E. T. Field, *Date Book of Nottingham*, 1884, part II, p. 63.
[2] Wylie, *Old and New Nottingham*, Longmans, 1853, p. 44.

Place was only partly paved, and woe to the poor woman who went a-marketing on a rainy day; St Peter's Church was bounded by a bog, through which the people threaded a perilous path during the day on a plank with a handrail, and into which they not infrequently fell on those nights unblessed by a moon; St Peter's Churchyard was a swamp; and from Lister Gate to the Leen was a journey fraught with exceeding danger, and not to be entered upon without prolonged and serious consideration.

It is possible that Wylie's gloomy picture is a little overdrawn. His comments on the tanning industry are an anachronism, although this had formerly been an important trade in the town. In 1750 there were only four curriers, two fell-mongers and three tanners in business,[1] although it might be argued that these establishments could raise a sufficiently 'fragrant odour' in a small town. The presence of four 'soap boilers' cannot have improved the quality of the atmosphere. However this passage does draw attention to the fact that even by the low standards of Victorian days, eighteenth-century Nottingham was lamentably deficient in public services and utilities. The streets were badly paved and dangerous; they were unlit until 1762, and then the oil lamps used were declared to be 'nearly useless'. Water was first laid on in 1696, but it was another hundred years before the supply could be considered at all adequate, and not until the time of Hawksley, about 1825, were most houses supplied with piped water. The General Hospital was founded in 1781, the Lunatic Asylum in 1818, the General Dispensary not until 1831. The only public schools were the Free Grammar School and the Bluecoat School. The Corporation took little interest in the condition of the town until almost the middle of the nineteenth century after the Municipal Corporations Act of 1835 and the revelations of various enquiries of the 1840s forced its hand. In its torpor the Corporation behaved in the manner traditionally associated with eighteenth-century corporate bodies, although its composition was untypical, being predominantly Whig and Nonconformist.[2] The only sanitary authority in the town was the almost moribund Mickletorn Jury, a medieval survival which held an annual turn to take cognizance of public nuisances. Fines were levied on the perpetrators of nuisances but no attempt was made

[1] Field, *Date Book*, 1884, part II, p. 7. The tanning business was at its peak in the late seventeenth century.

[2] Cf. R. A. Church, 'Social and Economic Development of Nottingham in the Nineteenth Century', Ph.D., Nottingham, p. 1.

to prevent the repetition of the offence, and, according to the 1845
Commission, the levying of fines was done in a haphazard manner:

These fines are collected when the parties are willing to pay them,
and are not enforced when due resistance is made. The court takes
no evidence, hears no arguments, nor carries in any of its proceedings
the most remote resemblance to a legally constituted and competent trib-
unal ... This is the only body which asserts to have any special local
authority of a sanitary nature.

Of course it is true that the lack of proper streets, drains and water
supply was of less importance when Nottingham was a small town
in which the people had plenty of elbow room than when it became
a large, tightly packed, industrial centre. In this, as in so many other
directions, it was the rapid rise in population which altered the
situation. What had been picturesque, or at worst irritating in a
small country town became a serious nuisance and possibly dangerous in an industrial city with a population five times greater.

The trade of the town was already dominated by hosiery, the only
other considerable occupation being malting. Hosiery was, and
remained for over a century, almost entirely a cottage industry
organized by about fifty large 'putters-out' and a number of smaller
men who ran their business from warehouses, most of them in
Nottingham itself. In 1739 there were about 1,200 frames in the
town and 1,800 in the surrounding villages, and it was estimated that
4,000 people in the area were dependent on hosiery, either directly
as knitters, or in the ancillary trades – frame-smiths, setters-up,
sinker makers, etc. Malting was a smaller affair; yet there were forty
establishments in the town, paying, together, an excise of £1,000 per
year. The other businesses in the town were all concerned with
domestic needs, and they call for no particular comment, except that
the number of masters engaged in any one line suggests that most
men were working on a very small scale. There were, for example,
65 butchers, 40 bakers, 30 barbers and 52 tailors. The population
at this time was rather fewer than 10,000 people, but there can be
no doubt that many of these tradesmen must have depended on out
of town trade among those people who attended the markets. It is
a comment on the recreations of the day that there were 41 inns and
91 'ale or pot houses' selling the Nottingham ale which enjoyed a
high reputation at the time.

The feature which emerges from a study of Nottingham's trade
structure is the dangerous dependence on the prosperity of one

staple occupation. In the absence of any alternative work a depression in hosiery caused almost universal hardship. When the depression was prolonged, as it was in the early nineteenth century, suffering could be very severe. Here, as with public health, the nineteenth century did not bring a new problem to Nottingham, but an old one immensely enlarged because of the vastly greater number of people involved.

From the middle of the eighteenth century the rise in Nottingham's population accelerated sharply. Table 1 illustrates this. Where possible the number of houses in the town has been included, and the figures are given for separate parishes. Two small extra-parochial areas are included in the totals.

The essential features of this table are easily grasped. In 1750 some 10,000 people lived in the town; a hundred years later there were 58,000. The number of houses rose from about 2,000 to 11,891. It will be noticed that while there is a continuous increase in population throughout the period, the rise accelerated sharply between 1821 and 1831, when 3,300 houses and 10,000 people were added, and that there is a very marked slowing down in the last twenty years. The sudden burst of the twenties coincides with the lace boom of those years which will be discussed later,[1] but the slowing down of the increase after 1831 introduces that peculiar feature of the Nottingham housing problem represented by the common land which hemmed the town in on every side except the west, where the Park, in private hands, completed the ring. The area of the town available for building was 876 acres in 1750, and so it remained until after the General Enclosure Act of 1845 which opened the 'Lammas Lands' and the Meadows for development. A series of attempts was made to enclose these lands throughout the eighteenth and early nineteenth centuries, but always foundered on the opposition of the members of the Corporation, who, as burgesses, enjoyed rights of common which they were most reluctant to give up. When a committee waited upon the Council in 1806 to suggest a scheme of enclosure they were met with a blunt reply which exactly revealed the Corporation's attitude to its responsibilities:[2]

---

[1] See below, p. 15.
[2] Quoted by Gray, *Nottingham Through 500 Years*, Nottingham, 1960, p. 150, Mr Gray notes a number of similar examples of the Corporation's opposition to enclosure.

this hall consider themselves in a peculiar manner the Guardians of the
Rights and Privileges of the Burgesses of Nottingham and do therefore
declare their firm purpose and Resolution to oppose any Inclosure of the
Fields and Commonable Lands within the Manor of Nottingham which
shall not appear . . . manifestly to tend to the immediate and permanent
advantage of the Burgesses enjoying a right of Common thereon.

The Corporation's attitude in this matter was not unique; on the
contrary it seems to have been based on the accepted principle of
eighteenth-century local administration. Professor Cole observes[1]
that:

the eighteenth century Municipal Corporation was, indeed, and considered itself as being, far less an organ of local government in the
modern sense than an institute for the management of a corporate
property. Membership of this privileged body had come to be regarded
almost as a property right, and the property of the Corporation almost
as belonging to its members as individuals rather than to the town.

Unfortunately the question of the enclosure of the Commons was
one in which the interests of the burgesses were directly opposed
to those of the townspeople as a whole. The long term effect of the
refusal to enclose by agreement in the late eighteenth century is hard
to determine and will be considered later,[2] but the immediate effects
were obvious and disastrous.

Since the commons were closed to development the population
could only increase by filling up the open spaces inside the town,
and, as the larger and more immediately suitable sites were taken,
desperate measures were needed to meet the rapidly increasing
demand for accommodation. Gardens and orchards vanished under
blocks of back-to-back houses, the low-lying, marshy land along the
Leen was taken for building, although it was liable to flooding and
received the drainage of the rest of the town, and the town assumed
the two features which so struck nineteenth-century investigators
– appalling over-crowding, and the jumbling together of prosperous
tradesmen's houses with teeming slums. There were limits, however, to the number of houses which could be packed in to this
limited area even by the most resolute jerry-builders, and eventually
the rise in the town's population slowed down simply because no
more people could be squeezed in.

[1] Cole in Turberville *Johnson's England*, p. 205.
[2] See below, p. 20–1.

TABLE I. *Population of Nottingham 1700–1885*

Date	Population		Houses
1700		*c.* 6,500	
1740		9,890	2,041
1779		17,791	3,191
St Mary's	12,837	2,314	
St Peter's	2,452	446	
St Nicholas's	2,502	431	
1795		*c.* 22,000ᵃ	
1801		28,861	4,997
1811		34,358	6,497
St Mary's	27,371	5,238	
St Peter's	2,839	529	
St Nicholas's	3,823	730	
1821		40,505	7,576
St Mary's	32,712	6,105	
St Peter's	3,361	626	
St Nicholas's	4,117	845	
1831		50,727	10,896
St Mary's	39,539	8,637	
St Peter's	5,220	1,097	
St Nicholas's	5,447	1,152	
1841		53,091	11,495
St Mary's	41,135	9,034	
St Peter's	5,605	1,259	
St Nicholas's	5,424	1,202	
1851		58,419	11,891
St Mary's	45,729	9,324	
St Peter's	5,832	1,232	
St Nicholas's	5,846	1,218	

ᵃ F. M. Eden, *The State of the Poor*, 1795. This estimate seems rather low in view of the result of the 1801 census; perhaps 25,000 might be a better approximation.

The figures which show the population by parishes demonstrate this process at work in detail. St Peter's parish which included the unattractive Leenside area, lagged behind the other parishes until the 1820s when it filled rapidly, the number of houses almost exactly doubling in twenty years. From 1841, however, the population was stable; the parish was full and there was simply no more building land available. By 1831, in fact, the whole town had reached saturation point. In the ten years from 1831 to 1841 the population of Nottingham increased by only 4·8 per cent, one of the lowest rates in the country. By comparison Leicester increased by 25·2 per cent, Hull by 26·3 per cent and Derby by 38·6 per cent. The increase in the next decade was rather greater, but a particularly unhealthy tendency is noticeable when the census figures for that period are examined. Nottingham had not been greatly troubled by the tenement problem; however mean many of the houses might be, they generally accommodated only one family. The cellar dwellings familiar in Manchester and London did not exist in Nottingham to any significant degree. In 1811, for example, the 7,201 families in the town were housed in 6,497 houses. Between 1841 and 1851, however, only 396 houses were built, while 5,328 people were added to the population. In 1841 there were, on the average, 4·62 persons per house in the town; the newcomers were arriving at the rate of 13·32 per fresh house.[1]

The decline in the rate of increase of the population was, in fact, an illusion springing from the artificial separation of Nottingham from its suburbs by the ring of common land. It is impossible to consider the development of Nottingham at this time without taking into account the parallel expansion of Sneinton, Radford, Bulwell and the other villages, most of which have since been absorbed by the city. As the town filled up, these villages received the overspill of people and industry and expanded with astonishing rapidity. A Directory of 1844 gives figures for the population of some of the suburban villages which illustrate this process.[2]

TABLE 2. *Population of Nottingham suburbs 1801–41*

	1801	1811	1821	1831	1841
Lenton	893	—	1,240	3,077	4,467
Radford	2,269	3,446	4,806	9,806	10,817
Sneinton	558	967	1,212	3,567	7,709
Arnold	2,768	—	—	4,054	4,509
Beeston	—	—	1,534	2,468	2,807
Basford	2,124	—	—	6,305	8,688
Bulwell	—	—	—	2,611	3,157

[1] *Second Report of the Commissioners ... State of Large Towns and Populous Places*, 1845, Supplement, p. 104.

[2] S. Glover, *History and Directory of the Town of Nottingham*, Nottingham, 1844, p. 7.

The increase in population was the most striking change which occurred in Nottingham at this time, but it was accompanied by important industrial developments. These were concerned with the hosiery and lace industries which were to be the staple trades of nineteenth-century Nottingham. Hosiery had been one of the chief interests in Nottingham since Restoration times, but in the period from 1760 to 1827 it lost its pre-eminent position. The number of frames in use rose rapidly, but there was not a corresponding increase in prosperity. At this period there was no industrial revolution in the hosiery trade; the business expanded, but without significant technical developments, and the industry remained organized on a domestic, man-powered basis, the absence of machinery and factories being remarked by every investigator. The first Nottingham hosiery factory, Hine and Mundella's, was not opened until 1851, and throughout the early nineteenth century the industry remained in a state of stagnation and decline. Unfortunately framework-knitting was an easy trade to enter as the degree of skill involved in most branches was not high, and no great outlay of capital was required. A frame could be hired from a hosier in return for a weekly frame rent, and, since technical advances were rare, it remained in use almost indefinitely. The hosiers had no reason to restrict the number of frames employed, since the frame rent was charged regardless of the amount of work the knitter found to do. The result was that men continued to enter the trade, although there was a decreasing expectation of making a decent living by it, a situation aggravated by the acute difficulty of finding any alternative employment in a district dominated by only two allied trades. Dr Church points out[1] that between 1812 and 1844 the demand for the products of the framework-knitter remained stationary while the number of frames in the country increased from 30,000 to 48,000. In the same period, piece rates, as a natural corollary, fell by 33 per cent. Hosiery is a trade particularly liable to the alternation of boom and slump at the best of times, but the story of the trade at this time is one of steady decline with infrequent partial recoveries, and long depressions involving severe hardship for stockingers and their families. Processions by starving stockingers were a regular feature of years of bad trade, and although individuals made creditable attempts to ameliorate the sufferings of their less fortunate fellow citizens, it is hardly surprising to discover a considerable readiness

[1] Church, 'Social and Economic Development', pp. 39, 41.

on the part of some of the framework knitters to resort to violence when less drastic methods failed to achieve any relief. Nottingham enjoyed an evil reputation – by no means undeserved – for rioting and violence, particularly at elections when the conduct of the 'Nottingham lambs' became a by-word. The presence of a permanently depressed and under-employed class of stockingers may have done much to perpetuate this situation. By 1815 hosiery had lost its position as the principal occupation of the town. It still employed 19 per cent of the working population, but it had been overtaken by the lace trade, which found work for 27 per cent. No other industry came near to rivalling these two, the next most important being building, employing 6 per cent.[1]

The lace trade had a very different history in this period. The first patent for making bobbin net on an adapted stocking frame was taken out in 1777, and it was followed by a host of modifications, none of which, apparently, achieved any commercial success. For some time, although the expansion of the trade was rapid, it was held in check by the high fees charged by the patent holders. In 1823 the main patents fell in. A spectacular boom followed with all classes of people rushing to make their fortunes in the new business. Wages in this boom were high, a journeyman lace-maker being able to make £4 to £7 per week, and premiums of as much as £60 were given for instruction in the use of machines. Machine makers shared the general prosperity. Setters-up charged £20 for adjusting a six-quarter machine, a job which could be completed in two or three weeks. Forgers could command £5 or £6 per week, and the makers of bobbins and other accessories received high wages. Smiths from Birmingham and Sheffield and watch and instrument makers from all over the country were drawn into Nottingham to make up for the acute shortage of frame and accessory makers.

The boom of 1823 to 1825 was merely a spectacular example of the particularly violent fluctuations to which the lace trade was liable. Lace was very vulnerable to the vagaries of fashion, and, in contrast with hosiery, underwent a rapid technical development, which had the effect, very frequently, of rendering all existing machinery obsolete. In 1833 and 1834, for example;

so complete was the despair . . . of ever making narrow and slow machinery again profitable that from 500 to 600 machines were then broken up.

[1] *Ibid.* p. 204.

Many were thrown piecemeal out of the upper rooms, in which they were worked, into the street, not being thought worth the trouble of being carried down the stairs, though they had cost a few years before several hundred pounds apiece, and were still in good working condition.[1]

These causes, together with the normal nineteenth-century trade cycle, and occasional difficulties due to dislocation in the supply of raw material led to recurrent ruinous slumps in which lace workers frequently suffered great hardships. But, in contrast with the stockingers, lace makers could earn good wages when business was brisk.

An important difference between the lace and hosiery trades lay in the larger scale of organization which existed in the newer industry. Lace machinery was initially expensive, and the frequent modifications made a considerable amount of capital necessary for business to be carried on. As larger machines were introduced the use of steam power spread – the destruction of machines mentioned above was caused by this innovation. From early days, therefore, there was a tendency for lace making to be done in factories. These were generally very small, and it was a common thing for the power of the factory's engine to be hired out to a number of small masters working in the same building, but even this represented a greater degree of concentration than was achieved in hosiery at this time. It must be emphasized that this applied only to the actual making of the lace; the various processes of finishing were still largely carried out in small workshops and private houses.

These, then, were the two basic changes which occurred in Nottingham in the period roughly covered by the reign of George III – a rapid and dramatic rise in population, accompanied by an alteration in the structure of business, involving the apparently permanent stagnation of the staple industry, and its partial replacement by a new, if closely allied, trade. From a small market town and administrative centre, still retaining a sufficiently rural character to be considered a desirable social and sporting centre by the local gentry, Nottingham became an industrial town, with its attention concentrated on trade and commerce, and hemmed in from the open country on three sides by a ring of large industrial villages, looking to Nottingham as the centre of the industries on which their economy depended. These changes brought problems with them. Not

---

[1] Glover, *History and Directory*, pp. 121 ff.

all of these were new problems, many were old ones inflated to new proportions by the vastly increased size of the population they affected. In the next chapter an attempt will be made to describe the new Nottingham of the early nineteenth century, and to look more closely at these problems, particularly where they affected the lives of children.

2

NOTTINGHAM IN THE EARLY
NINETEENTH CENTURY

The first fact which emerges from an investigation of the life of the poor in Nottingham is that for most people it was extremely short. The average age at death for males in Nottingham in 1845 was 20 years and 5 months and for females 23 years 9 months, about seven years below the national average in each case.[1] These figures, however, do not tell the whole story, because of the great variations between the prosperous, relatively healthy districts and the impoverished working class districts. When the figures are given by wards the picture becomes more clear (Table 3).[2]

TABLE 3. *Mortality in Nottingham, by wards*

Ward	Death rate per 1,000	Mean age at death	Birth rate per 1,000	Children dead before 4 years %
Park	19·5	29·3	25·7	28·8
Sherwood	20·1	24·3	28·5	31·8
Castle	23·2	23	33·2	33·9
Exchange	25·3	22·4	31·9	39·7
St Mary's	26·5	21·3	39·9	35·3
St Ann's	27·9	19·2	35·86	42·3
Byron	30·9	18·1	37·86	44·5

The essential feature of these figures is the appalling infant mortality; in substantial areas of Nottingham children had a less than even chance of reaching the age of five years. And there was little improvement in the next twenty years. Figures were given to the Children's Employment Commission of 1862 which show the same dreadful loss of child life, and the same contrast between the best and the worst parts of the town. In Park Ward 98 out of 734 recorded deaths were of infants under one year of age, about 13·3

[1] *Second Report of the Commissioners ... State of Large Towns and Populous Places*, 1845, App. part II, p. 255.
[2] J. D. Chambers, *Modern Nottingham in the Making*, Nottingham Journal, 1945, p. 12.

per cent. In St Ann's Ward the number rose to 558 out of 2,138, nearly twice the proportion; while in Byron Ward nearly a third of all deaths, 501 out of 1,517 were of infants. The situation may be summed up by saying that in the working class quarters of the town a child was as likely as not to die before his fifth year, and that his chance of growing up into a healthy adult was correspondingly low.

Two factors in particular contributed to this state of affairs – housing conditions and ignorance of proper methods of child rearing. By 1830 five people were living where one had lived seventy years before, the natural advantages of the town's position had been dissipated and its character as a garden city entirely lost. In 1845 it was reported[1] that

faults of construction are accompanied by a marshy foundation, overcrowding, and every combination of injurious circumstances so as to render some parts of Nottingham so very bad as hardly to be surpassed in misery by anything to be found within the entire range of our manufacturing cities.

Nottingham's peculiar problem arose from its surrounding ring of common lands and gentlemen's estates which was unavailable for building. The greatly increased population had to be crowded into the existing boundaries of the town, and gardens and other open spaces were bought up and built upon in a totally unplanned manner. These circumstances led to the houses being built in hollow blocks of irregular shape. Most houses looked out, not on to a street, but on to a court, often wholly enclosed and approached only by a narrow tunnel. Privies for the whole block stood in the court, which was drained by an open kennel running down the centre. No public facilities existed for clearing the privies so that the tenants had to enter into contracts for their clearance with 'muck majors' who sold the nightsoil to farmers and market gardeners as manure.

By these building methods a surprising degree of over-crowding was achieved in the poorer parts of the town. Several quarters had a density of population exceeding 450 persons to the acre, and in one area a density of 568 to the acre was reached. Such over-crowding was a first-rate danger to public health in itself, but unfortunately much of the new working class housing was built in low-lying areas which were inadequately drained, and had hitherto been considered unsuitable for habitation. Under these conditions it was

[1] *Second Report of the Commissioners ... State of Large Towns and Populous Places*, 1845, App. part II, p. 250.

impossible to prevent the spread of epidemic disease, and severe outbreaks of cholera occurred in 1832, 1848, 1853 and 1865. The epidemic of 1848 was a major factor in frightening the Corporation into reluctant activity towards ameliorating the conditions in poorer quarters. These quarters were very extensive. Of 11,000 houses in the town in 1845, 8,000 were built back to back. At the most conservative estimate 40,000 people inhabited these houses.

Life in the Nottingham slums had one or two redeeming features. After the work of the noted engineer Thomas Hawksley in the 1830s there was a water supply which was considered unusually good by the standards of the time. Before his day most of the poorer houses bought water at a farthing per bucket of three gallons, or a halfpenny per bucket if the water had to be carried any distance.[1] By 1845, however, all but about a thousand houses were supplied with piped water. About seventeen gallons per person per day or eighty to ninety gallons per house were allowed, and the price varied from 5s. per year on a house of £5 rent per annum to 60s. per year on a house of £100 rent.

One evil which Nottingham was largely spared at this period was the subdivision of houses into tenements. Engels[2] speaks of 7,862 cellar dwellings in Liverpool containing 45,000 people and mentions that in an investigation of 2,800 families in Bristol 46 per cent occupied one room. By contrast the Nottingham houses, cramped and squalid as they were, were generally occupied by only one family, and it was only in the 1840s that tenement dwellers began to appear in any numbers. In 1845 the General Enclosure Act was passed which made it possible for building to take place upon about 1,000 acres of common land, and this tended to ease the pressure upon accommodation, although it was not until the 1860s that the former common land was generally built over.

The enclosure of the commons was not altogether an advantage. The old town, however insanitary and squalid, was small in area, and the inhabitants could, by an easy walk, reach fields where they could amuse themselves in games and picnics. Contemporary witnesses make it clear that very general use was made of these amenities, especially in late summer and autumn, after haymaking. In *The Age of the Chartists*, J. L. and Barbara Hammond ask

---

[1] J. D. Chambers, *Modern Nottingham*, p. 110.
[2] Engels, *The Condition of the Working Class in England in 1844*, Allen and Unwin, 1952, p. 36.

whether 'a bad slum in Nottingham with open fields nearby which could be used for games in summer might be preferable to a less bad slum in Manchester, surrounded by other slums'.[1] It is hard to strike a balance in such a case, but no doubt the open air and the recreations offered by the common lands did something to offset the congested conditions of the working class area.

But when all mitigating circumstances have been taken into account life in the slums of Nottingham, for adult or child, can only have been wretched and precarious. The conclusion of the 1845 report on large towns was that 'in such quarters it is hardly possible that a family can preserve, for any term of years, either decency, morals or health'.[2] It is hard to see any reason for dissenting from this verdict.

The second great factor in producing the terrible infant mortality rate of the period was the general ignorance or neglect of rational methods of child-rearing. This ignorance was repeatedly emphasized by contemporary investigators and was blamed on the lack of domestic instruction in schools, and, perhaps with greater justice on the absence of any training passed on from mother to daughter. This, of course, was not a condition peculiar to Nottingham, but the great demand for women's work in the area meant that neither mothers nor daughters had much time for domestic training, or even for running a home.

The two particular abuses which attracted criticism at the time were putting children out to nurse, and the administration of opiates to babies. Women who were working at lace or hosiery could not afford the time to look after small children and it was therefore the general custom either to put babies out to professional baby-minders or to leave them with young girls who were hired to look after the baby and to do some needlework in their spare time. Girls of six or seven years, or even younger were thought to be quite old enough for this employment. In either case a charge of about 2s. per child per week seems to have been customary, which, in the case of a baby-minder would cover any food which might be provided. It was the opinion of the Nottingham coroner in 1862 that many mothers resorted to baby-minders because they 'wanted to be rid altogether of an incumbrance'.[3]

---

[1] J. L. and B. Hammond, *The Age of the Chartists*, Longmans, 1930, p. 114.
[2] *Second Report of the Commissioners ... State of Large Towns and Populous Places*, 1845, App. part II, p. 251.
[3] *Children's Employment Commission*, 1862, 1st Report, pp. 242–3.

Whether children were put out to nurse or kept at home they were frequently dosed with opiates in order to quieten them so that they would not disturb their mother's work. Godfrey's Cordial was the most popular of these and was sold in great quantities by apothecaries. It was made of laudanum dissolved in treacle at the rate of two or more teaspoonsful per quart, and the coroner of Nottingham, in evidence to the Children's Employment Commission of 1842, mentioned a case of a local chemist who made up into cordial thirteen hundredweight of treacle in a year. Another shop sold a gallon of laudanum a week and others 'many gallons in the year'.

The practice was described in 1842 by a chemist from a densely populated part of Nottingham;[1]

they begin with the syrup of rhubarb and Godfrey's mixed together; then they go to Godfrey's pure, and then to laudanum as the effects become by habit diminished. Half a teaspoonful of equal parts of Godfrey's and rhubarb is the dose to begin with; very soon this is increased to two teaspoonful; these doses . . . are given three times a day. When the pure Godfrey's is used, about one teaspoonful is given, and they will go on to two teaspoonsful, and then they begin with laudanum. This is at first administered in five drops thrice a day, and it is increased to twenty drops; does not think that this is exceeded . . .

Chemists and doctors who gave evidence before commissions of enquiry produced examples of children who had died either from overdoses of drugs or from the long-term effect of addiction. They also reported that the use of opiates was as general in the 1860s as it had been twenty years before.[2] All these witnesses criticized the parents, to whom they attributed part at least of the blame for the ill-treatment of children which their evidence revealed. Undoubtedly parents showed almost universal ignorance of proper child care, much carelessness and thoughtlessness, and some deliberate cruelty. But if they are to be fairly judged, one must take into account the intensely depressing effect of their long working day, their wretched housing, and their bleak future. Much laudanum and opium was taken by adults, and this, together with the drunkenness of which observers frequently complained, suggests that many people were seeking an escape from the ever present worries about unemployment and an old age spent in the workhouse. Probably the habit of driving children to work when trade was good and money

[1] *Children's Employment Commission*, 1842, 2nd Report, Witness No. 187.
[2] *Ibid.* 1862, 1st Report, p. 241.

relatively plentiful sprang from the urge to cash in on the good times in anticipation of the bad times which must follow.[1]

The children who survived the dangers of infancy usually went to work in lace or hosiery. The lace industry dominated the economy of the town throughout the nineteenth century with hosiery as its only serious rival. The surrounding villages, several of which were incorporated in the borough in 1877, were largely concerned in particular branches of hosiery. Domestic service took a fair number of girls; only shops and the various service industries made any other significant contribution to the employment market.

The processes which went into the manufacture of lace may, for our purposes, be divided into two groups, on the one hand lace making, and on the other the various processes together known as finishing. Most of the men in the industry were employed as makers, and they were assisted by a substantial number of women and children, but there were far more finishers than makers; it was estimated in 1862 that there were 8,000 to 10,000 children and young women employed in lace finishing in warehouses alone in Nottingham.[2] A similar situation obtained in hosiery where the knitting was done by men who were assisted by a large force of women and children, most of whom were engaged in different forms of needlework. Hosiery continued until well into the second half of the century to be organized on a domestic basis, single masters or small workshops being the rule, the different processes being co-ordinated by hosiers who gave out work from their warehouses which tended to congregate in Nottingham. In contrast lace making, originally a domestic trade, was early affected by the factory system. In 1842 the tendency for lace making to become factory based was already marked, and one witness before the Children's Employment Commission of that year stated that 695 machines owned by small men had ceased work in the previous six years, many of the men having moved into factories. By 1862 virtually all lace making was done in factories, and steam-driven machines, the exception twenty years earlier, were universal.[3]

The lace factories were very small; a typical hand-powered factory contained between six and fifty machines, and few of the

---

[1] For further evidence on child care see D. Wardle, *English Popular Education, 1780–1970*, Cambridge, 1970, pp. 46 ff.

[2] *Children's Employment Commission*, 1862, 1st Report, p. 182.

[3] *Ibid*. 1842, 2nd Report, App. part 1, pp. 2, 3, and 1862, 1st Report, p. 236.

steam-powered factories were much larger. It was not at all unusual for a factory to contain both hand and steam-powered machines, and in some concerns there was a curious system whereby the machines were owned by various masters who rented space and sometimes steam power from the proprietor. These factories presented a problem to those who wished to introduce reforms in conditions of work, since it was difficult to apportion responsibility for any infractions of regulations.

The hours worked by lace and hosiery makers varied enormously. Steam factories had some sort of standard day because of the necessity to use the engine while it was working. Usually the engine ran from 4 a.m. to midnight, except on Saturday when it stopped at 8 p.m.; to make up for this some engines ran all through Friday night, and in some factories the engine ran all night every night except for one hour for cleaning. Two shifts were commonly worked in such factories, giving a day of ten or eleven hours. Where hand machines were used, either singly or in factories, the hours of work were left entirely to the men, who were paid on piece-work rates, and contemporary witnesses were unable to suggest a useful average. Two facts do emerge, however. First, the general custom, until well into the second half of the century was for independent workmen at least to celebrate 'Saint Monday', which meant that no work was done on Sunday or Monday, and that work was often done at half pressure on Tuesday. This old custom of the hosiery trade was taken over by lace, and it only died slowly as factories became more general. To make up for 'Saint Monday' men would often work from Friday morning through to Saturday night, a practice very hard upon the children who assisted them. Second, hours of work fluctuated violently throughout the year due to differences in the volume of trade, and this meant that workers of all ages might be involved in two, three or more hours of overtime every night for weeks or months at a time. Overtime was often popular with children, because, by prescription, overtime pay was their perquisite, the rest of their wages, less perhaps a halfpenny or a penny, going to their parents.

The work done by children in Nottingham was rarely particularly unpleasant or dangerous, by comparison with conditions in the Potteries, for example, or in mining areas. There are no accounts of large numbers of children being crippled or deformed by their work, as was the case in many industrial areas at the time. Neither does there appear to have been a great deal of deliberate cruelty and ill-treatment. There were certainly many cases of casual ill-usage, but this seems to have been largely confined to the independent masters and small workshops where conditions were far worse than in the large factories and warehouses, where the proprietors adopted a relatively enlightened policy. But this is not to say that life was pleasant for working children. They suffered very severely from the long working hours, particularly the 'winders' and 'threaders' who had to tend the machines of the lace makers. The many thousands of girls who were employed in various kinds of needlework, were engaged from a very early age in close, sedentary work, often in a fetid, airless atmosphere, which affected their eyesight and posture, and frequently caused internal complaints. In general it was the girls who suffered most, since they had domestic duties on top of their other work.

Children began work very young. The variation was so great that no average figure is very useful, but it may be said that it was the exceptional child who was not working by the age of eleven. Most started much earlier; seven or eight was a common age to begin, and, particularly in hosiery, children of three to five years were quite frequently employed. It was usual to start work with independent masters or in small workshops and to proceed, at perhaps twelve to fourteen years, to larger establishments, which rarely employed very young children. This was one of many directions in which the larger proprietors adopted a more enlightened line than the small firms. Wherever a child worked, however, there was one constant factor – the lack of any genuine training or prospects. Children were used for the simple repetitive tasks now usually performed by machinery, and if they wished to learn a trade had to start again at perhaps fourteen years. Apprenticeship was moribund and very few apprentices were taken either in hosiery or lace. Further, the frame-work knitter was entering a chronically depressed and over-manned industry in which he had little hope of making a decent living.

Since Nottingham was so completely dominated by lace and hosiery, it is possible to give a fairly comprehensive picture of children's work in the town. A very common job, particularly for boys, was threading. This consisted of threading the needles on a lace-making machine with thread from bobbins which had been charged by another group of workers, usually girls and women. There were about 1,800 needles to a machine, and with two or three boys at work the process took three hours; as a rule there was one threader to every three machines. The average age for commencing threading was about 8½ years, and a number of boys went from threading to minding a machine at fourteen or fifteen. Pay varied according to age and skill from 2s. to 8s. per week. In many cases the boys were hired by the makers individually rather than by the proprietors, but the proprietors of the better managed concerns employed the children themselves, and this was thought to be preferable from the boys' point of view.

The feature of this job which was so injurious to children was the long period spent at work. The time actually on the machine was not excessive by the standards of the time – seven to ten hours was normal; but the machines 'came off' at odd intervals during the working day so that it was necessary to keep the threaders on the premises whether they were employed or not. If a machine came off late at night the threaders would be at work until the small hours of the morning, and then would be expected when work began again, only three or four hours later. In spite of the well-known fact that the children were idle for a good part of the working day, in no case was any provision made for rest or recreation. Much improvement would have been effected if shift work had been arranged as was usual with the men, but in only one factory was this done. Two other factories had two sets of bobbins and carriages, which allowed the threaders to prepare in advance for a machine coming off, and avoided night work, and a few others had regulations which prevented the threading of machines which came off after a certain time at night, but these were very much in the minority. Most threaders were not employed by factories but by independent workmen, and their position was worse still. One man did not provide enough work for a threader, so that a boy was generally employed by two or three masters. This made it more than ever likely that he would be called up at all hours of the day and night, and where the masters lived any distance apart very real hardship could and did result.

The number of people, both adults and children, engaged in lace finishing greatly exceeded the number employed in lace making, and the conditions were, on the whole, much worse. Finishing included various processes which may be taken together since they all involved some kind of needlework, and, together with similar processes in the hosiery industry these employed many thousands of women and girls. The great majority worked in small workshops, perhaps six to ten girls under a mistress who took in work from a warehouse. By 1862 there was a tendency for work to be concentrated in warehouses, but this had not gone very far and even the warehouses were quite small. The largest in the town only employed 450 people, and the majority employed less than 100.

Conditions in the workshops were bad. Most of them were simply private houses into which as many children as possible were crowded. It was remarked in 1845 that 'in comparison with these wretched places factories are elysiums'.[1] Examples were found where 67 cubic feet and 90 cubic feet of air space were allowed per child; it was noted by comparison that the War Office allowed 500 to 600 cubic feet per soldier in barracks.[2]

The particular features of the lace finishers' work which attracted criticism were the youth of the workers, the long hours and the sedentary and cramping nature of the work. It was the regular practice for girls to start work at home or in a workshop somewhere between five and eight years and to go on to a warehouse at eleven or twelve; as a rule warehouses would not take younger children than this, and some refused to take children at all. Four consecutive witnesses before the 1862 Employment Commission gave the start of their working lives as $5\frac{1}{2}$; 'before she was six'; 'before she was five and could not reach the door'; and 'about five'.[3] The hours were long, and outside the large warehouses very irregular. The usual day in the large firms was 8 a.m. to 6 or 7 p.m., and it was usual to pay anything after 7 o'clock as overtime. An hour was allowed for dinner and half an hour for tea. The busy times of the year were February to July and September and October, and it was common for overtime to be almost continuous at these periods, when work regularly continued until nine or ten o'clock. In the workshops hours were longer, a twelve or thirteen hour day being customary, and eighteen hours being not uncommon when business was brisk. There was a distinct improvement in the matter of hours of work between 1842 and 1862 when the average day was perhaps two hours shorter and overtime restricted to about two hours.

[1] *Second Report of the Commissioners ... State of Large Towns and Populous Places*, App. part II, p. 251.
[2] *Children's Employment Commission*, 1862, 1st Report, p. 184.
[3] *Ibid.* 1862, 1st Report, pp. 221 ff.

Several witnesses in 1862 definitely stated that they never worked after 9 o'clock.

Wages were very low. Children started at 1s. to 1s. 6d. per week and the average for a girl of twelve might be 2s. 6d. to 3s. Of 96 girls who attended St Mary's Sunday School in 1842 only one earned more than 5s.[1] Adult women did not do much better and several witnesses before the 1842 employment commission stated that it was impossible to earn a living wage at lace finishing. There seems to have been little improvement by 1862.

In hosiery all the abuses of the lace industry were to be found, but to an exaggerated degree, due chiefly to the chronically depressed state of the trade. Boys began winding bobbins for the framework knitters at nine or ten, earning 2s. 6d. per week, and were introduced to knitting themselves at twelve or thirteen. The worst hardships, as usual, fell upon the women and girls who were engaged in 'seaming' or sewing up the garments, and part of the blame for this was attributed to the observation of 'Saint Monday', which led to extremely long hours late in the week. A woman called Mary Thorpe gave evidence to the 1862 Employment Commission which speaks for itself.[2]

Little children here begin at stitching gloves when very young. My little sister, now 5½ years old, can stitch a good many little fingers. [This girl began at 3½ years of age.] She used to stand on a stool so as to be able to see the candle on the table. I have seen many begin as young as that, and they do so still . . . Children younger than seven but not younger than six are kept up as late as that [i.e. 11 or 12 p.m. on Friday]. Mothers will pin them to their knee to keep them to their work, and if they are sleepy give them a slap on the head to keep them awake . . . little girls of eight or so often go out to nurse a baby, and they have to stitch while the baby is asleep during the day, and they are kept to stitch after the baby is put to bed.

One point of considerable importance emerges from this section, apart from the evidence about the lives of the children themselves. Industry in Nottingham was organized on a small-scale basis, and this made the task of legislating for reform and enforcing the legislation extremely difficult. Legislation could be made to apply to the factories and warehouses, but these provided employment for only a small proportion of the children, and it was agreed on all sides

[1] *Children's Employment Commission*, 1842, 2nd Report, pp. 64 ff.
[2] *Ibid*. 1862, 1st Report, p. 265.

that they were relatively enlightened in their treatment of employees. The worst abuses were found in small workshops or in the treatment of children by their own parents, and neither was likely to be reached by legislation on the scale sanctioned by nineteenth-century political ideas. The cure was found, not in controlling the conditions of children's labour, but in requiring all children to be at school. The 'school board man' in enforcing school attendances was the most effective instrument in abolishing abuses in child employment.

One of the features of life in the early nineteenth century which strikes any modern observer was the lack of recreational facilities for any except the monied classes. Occasional activities drew very large crowds. The first recorded cricket match of importance was played in 1771 between teams from Nottingham and Sheffield and the game rapidly became popular as a spectacle, on one occasion drawing a crowd estimated at 10,000 persons. Cock fighting and bull baiting only slowly died out as opinion turned against them and there were prize fights and foot-races. The annual horse races held in July were an excuse for general celebration as was Goose Fair in early October.

But there were no regular means of recreation which would provide alternatives to public houses and ale shops. The old rural sports, suitable when Nottingham was a small market town were no longer practicable and the new athletic sports such as football were not properly organized until the end of the century. Indoor entertainment, unless home-made, was virtually non-existent. Perhaps the main reason for the failure of the numerous temperance campaigns of the period was their failure to offer an attractive alternative to drink. The fact is that drink, seconded by drugs, gambling and violence formed the staple entertainments of working-class Nottingham. There were 152 inns and ale houses in the town in 1795 and 193 in 1850. The periodic drunkenness of lace and hosiery workers was taken more or less for granted, and drug taking was common in the poorer parts of the town. It is hard not to sympathize with the inhabitants of the slums if they did try to forget their miseries with the help of drink or drugs. The squalor of their lives and the long hours of grinding toil, together with the hopelessness of any improvement must have made resistance to drunkenness very difficult.

Nevertheless, there was a brutality about the attitude to life of many people which one usually associates with an earlier period.

The punishment of criminals was a signal for festivity. The last exposure in the pillory took place in 1808 and the last public whipping in 1830, but enormous crowds attended executions until the middle of the century. In 1844, at the execution of a man named Saville for a notorious murder, the crowd was so great that it got out of hand and many were precipitated down a steep and narrow street called Garner's Hill, where seventeen were killed in the crush. It is a comment upon the public attitude towards suitable entertainment for children that fifteen of the dead were under twenty years, the youngest only nine years old.

Laissez-faire was carried to an extreme in moral and legal matters. Elections of all kinds were marked by flagrant bribery and every species of sharp practice, but, although cases were freely reported in the press, the reports expressed no moral indignation except when partisans of the other side worked some unusually successful stratagem. The Corporation notoriously interfered in parliamentary elections in the Whig interest, to such a degree that after the election of 1802 the County magistrates received the right to interfere in the exercise of justice in the town due to well-founded complaints that the town magistrates refused to defend Tory candidates and their supporters from violence. There was no improvement in the conduct of elections until the very end of the century. Bribery was still almost universal in the early School Board elections, when votes could be bought for the cost of a pint of ale, although some determined voters insisted upon the higher price of a whisky. The *Nottingham Journal* commented about the election of 1870 that 'Certainly the process of electing a school board for Nottingham has shown the necessity for one if it has shown nothing else.'

Rioting and violence were an accepted part of life. Several factors contributed to this state of affairs, of which the habitual drunkenness of many of the poor was only one. Boredom and lack of rational means of recreation no doubt made people only too ready to enjoy the excitement of a riot, and the small area of the town made it easy for news of trouble to be passed round. The rapidly rising population provided a large pool of personnel ready to join in whether they had any interest in the quarrel or not. Most men worked at home or in small workshops and it was simple to down tools and join in, while the mass of virtually uncharted slums made escape easy if the military, or in later days the police, were pressing. Fluctuations in trade led to serious unemployment so that there was often a large body of men ready to work off their bitterness at real or imagined grievances in attacks on persons and property. Stockingers, in particular had a perpetual feud with hosiers over piece-work rates which was quiescent when trade was good, but flared up savagely on occasion. The lack of police made rioting easy since there was no means of preventing a riot short of calling in the military which was only done in the last resort since it generally meant loss of life. A police force was formed in 1836 which eventually brought about an improvement, but it was at first too weak to control a determined mob, and on one occasion found itself besieged in an inn-yard during an election riot.

But perhaps the fundamental reason for the endemic riotousness of the period lay in the absence of any direct way by which the ordinary man could make his opinions known to the authorities. Lacking the suffrage, people were in the habit of expressing their views by organizing large meetings and processions, and almost every local or national event of any significance was greeted in this way. These processions could be very large; one which occurred in 1819 was counted as being 5,057 strong, and others were described perhaps with some exaggeration, as having 15,000 or 20,000 members. Such affairs frequently got out of hand, as might be expected. Like the modern 'protest march' they provided a cover for all kinds of irrelevant activities. The most famous case, but by no means an isolated one, accompanied the rejection of the first reform bill by the House of Lords in October 1831 when the Castle and Colwick Hall were destroyed and an assault upon Wollaton Hall was repulsed by a garrison of miners armed with cannon.

It is impossible to detect any coherent political programme behind the rioting; it seems to have been possible to assemble a mob for any purpose, political or otherwise. The most consistent cause was an increase in prices, and the butchers' stalls near the Market Place were looted on at least five occasions between 1788 and 1800. Major food riots took place as late as 1854 and 1857. In the 1790s occurred much brutal 'rabbling' of suspected Jacobins, even the Mayor being attacked in 1793. He, however, after remonstrating with the mob, met them in their own spirit and put them to flight with a discharge of his blunderbuss, killing one man and wounding five. The riots which invariably accompanied elections had no political significance; they were looked upon rather as sport than fighting, although damage to persons and property was common enough. Nottingham had a well-deserved reputation for the violence of its elections and perhaps the worst riots occurred as late as the 1840s when Fergus O'Connor was one of the members for the town. His meetings habitually turned into battles in which every kind of weapon was used, including private troops of cavalry.

The endemic rioting and violence are significant because it is impossible to comprehend the size and difficulty of the nineteenth-century educational problem unless it is appreciated how thin was the veneer of civilization in even a large and relatively well governed town. The Hogarthian nature of Nottingham elections is a reminder of the immense forces of anarchy which were only with difficulty controlled by weak authorities. An appeal to blows was still the obvious way to resolve an argument, and, as with corruption in elections, there was as yet no considerable body of opinion to condemn the habitual resort to violence.

With the Corporation uninterested in social problems, and resort to the Poor Law considered a disgrace, the ordinary man depended for support in hard times upon charity and self-help, and the late eighteenth and early nineteenth centuries were particularly prolific in both of these. Subscriptions for the assistance of the families of unemployed workmen in times of slack trade were a normal procedure, and individual men showed considerable generosity. General Napier was of the opinion that the work of William Rowarth, the Mayor, and Ichabod Wright in relieving distress in 1840 did much to avert the threat of violence in the Nottingham area at that time.[1] Not all the appeals were for local charities. In 1793 a play was performed for the benefit of widows and orphans of those killed in the war which had just begun,[2] while in 1830 5,000 francs were raised for the families of those who had suffered in Paris 'in the cause of liberty during the glorious three days of the second French Revolution'.[3]

All these subscriptions were raised to meet temporary needs, but towards the end of the eighteenth century a large expansion occurred in the number and size of more permanent charities. Along with this expansion went an important change in the method of raising funds

[1] A. C. Wood, *Chartism in Nottingham*, Transactions of the Thoroton Society, 1955, p. 57.
[2] *Nottingham Journal*, 15 June 1793.
[3] White, *Directory of Nottingham and Nottinghamshire*, Nottingham, 1864, p. 92.

for benevolent objects. Nottingham had not been devoid of charitable institutions in earlier days; in fact the number and extent of such endowments drew the approving notice of more than one observer, but these charities were nearly all individual foundations based upon a legacy or similar contribution from a single benefactor. In this way the town had become rather well provided with almshouses, which, in 1844, accommodated 180 inmates with 32 further out-pensioners.[1] The charities which were founded in the late eighteenth and early nineteenth centuries were of a different type, for this may be called the great age of the public charity. The procedure followed by the sponsors of an appeal was nearly always the same, the nature of the charity necessitating certain minor alterations in some cases. A public meeting, well advertised, was the usual start of the campaign so far as the general public was concerned, although one must assume that much private canvassing preceded this. The Mayor was frequently in the chair at the initial meeting, at which a committee was appointed. The same names appear repeatedly on these committees. In the first few years of the nineteenth century no committee was complete without Mr Francis Wakefield, who was prominent, to name only two examples, in the establishment of the General Hospital and Sunday Schools. Mr Wakefield's son, Thomas Wakefield, was later equally active although his public career ended with his bankruptcy. William Rowarth, at least two generations of Oldknows, and William Felkin also did more than their share.

The first public meeting was invariably extensively reported by the Press, usually with a lengthy leader recommending the charity to the public. A subscription list was opened, and the progress of the contributions well publicized. Those members of the nobility who had local connections, and the surrounding gentry always headed the list, often with very substantial contributions. Subscribers of stated sums were sometimes allowed certain privileges once the institution was working. At the General Hospital, for example, subscribers of £100 or five guineas per year were allowed to recommend six in-patients and twenty out-patients a year, while those who contributed ten guineas or one guinea per year could recommend two in-patients.[2] Wherever possible definite stages in the progress of the charity – the laying of foundation stones, etc. – were marked by celebrations which served to revive public interest.

[1] Glover, *History and Directory*, p. 94.   [2] *Ibid.* pp. 104 ff.

Large sums of money were raised by these methods, but the real difficulties of the organizers began when the charity was established and the costs of maintenance had to be met. The great weakness of the system of organized charity lay in the decline in enthusiasm which followed the initial burst. All charities, especially those whose success was difficult to measure, suffered from a falling off of subscriptions and donations which not infrequently proved fatal. Charity sermons, bazaars, processions and every other form of advertising were used to attract funds, but sooner or later most charities found themselves working on very reduced incomes. Educational charities, which by their nature, could not produce spectacular results, were especially liable to this loss of income, while hospitals, which could publish lists of patients cured, and whose necessity was obvious and tangible, found less difficulty.

The first large public charity to be formed in this way was probably the Bluecoat School in 1706, but the great age of such charities really began with the establishment of the General Hospital in 1781. This was supported by a vaccination institution in 1805, a lunatic asylum in 1812, and the Nottingham Dispensary in 1831. The usual methods of public subscription were used in 1819 when a scheme was floated to finance the emigration of framework knitters and their families. The Duke of Newcastle, who also largely supported the hospital and dispensary, headed the subscription list with £500, and about 300 families were assisted to emigrate to the Cape. Some years later the local historian, J. Orange, introduced a plan to provide quarter-acre allotments in order to make working men rather less dependent upon industry. Some success was achieved, but mainly in suburban villages. In Nottingham itself land was too scarce and expensive for the plan to be practicable.

The period which was so fertile in organized charity also produced a great deal of collective self-help. The natural reaction of the people of the time, when faced by a problem beyond the abilities of one individual, was to form an association, which was generally founded and supported in very much the same way as the charities which have already been considered. If the advertisements in the newspapers may be taken as a guide, the period of the Napoleonic Wars was the great age of these 'associations' which were formed by every social class and for every conceivable purpose. Perhaps the most common were the local associations for the prosecution of criminals which existed in every town and village at a time when there was virtually no police force. Some of these were large affairs like the Nottinghamshire Association which comprised most of the nobility and gentry of the County;[1] others were far smaller, and their lists of subscribers consisted almost entirely of small farmers, tradesmen and framework knitters. An example was the 'association of Charles Pierrepoint and his tenants for prosecuting horse stealers and others', whose members were drawn mainly from the Gamston area, although individual members came from Sneinton, Thoresby, Gedling, Cotgrave and Stoke Bardolph. This association, like others, offered a regular tariff of rewards to non-members who were responsible for the apprehension of criminals who preyed on its members. For the arrest of a housebreaker ten guineas was offered, a footpad was worth seven guineas, a horse stealer five guineas, and so on down the scale to ten shillings for a gate breaker.[2] These were attractive rewards when two thirds of the stockingers in Nottingham were earning less than ten shillings a week.

Most associations were largely composed of men of some substance, but the mutual benefit idea was firmly rooted among the working class, and Friendly Societies were numerous in the town. When the growth of these societies began is not known, but they were flourishing by the 1790s when there was some sort of central co-ordinating organization known as the 'Club Mill' to which a number of societies belonged. At Whitsun 1793, 400 members of twelve societies affiliated to the 'Club Mill' marched in procession to a service at St Peter's Church with a large banner inscribed 'the Club Mill for Public Good', and accompanied by a military band.[3] According to Eden,[4] writing in 1795 there were then 51 Friendly Societies in Nottingham, and their membership was restricted to 41 or 51 members, What benefits these clubs provided is not anywhere stated, but it may be assumed that arrangements were made for giving the members a decent funeral, and there may well have been sickness and unemployment payments. All the societies met at inns, so it is likely that there was a convivial side to their activities, but it must be remembered that inns were, in those days, the only places in which working people could meet. The Poor Law returns of 1807 show that there were then 61 Friendly Societies with 2,091 members,[5] so that the size of the individual societies seems to have

---

[1] *Nottingham Journal*, 8 October 1791.   [2] *Ibid.* 23 July 1791.
[3] *Ibid.* 18 May 1793.   [4] Eden, *State of the Poor.*
[5] *Records of the Borough of Nottingham*, vol. VIII, pp. 35–6.

remained constant since Eden's time. An interesting detail is that one of the societies existing in 1807 was for women, but unfortunately no information about the activities of this or any other Friendly Society appears to have survived.

These societies did not exhaust the efforts of the working people at mutual support. In 1818 the Nottingham Savings Bank was established, moving to a new building on Smithy Row in 1837. To some extent this was a charitable institution, since it was founded with the assistance of a number of distinguished patrons in an attempt to encourage the working man to save against hard times. It was a favourite contention of moralists and philanthropists that working men added to their troubles by their refusal to put money by when work was plentiful, and it must be said that events like the lace boom of the 1820s gave the critics some ammunition. The Friendly Societies provided a means of savings, of course, and there was an interesting development in the suburbs of Hyson Green and Carrington in the 1820s when working men formed building societies in which members contributed £70 by installments to build for themselves. These small organizations, however, tended to lack permanence and security for savers, and the Savings Bank provided a more substantial and well backed concern which gave workmen the opportunity to save.

The general picture which one gains of Nottingham in the early nineteenth century is of a town suffering from all the problems of rapid, unplanned growth, complicated by the lack of efficient local government. The working class quarters of the town were squalid, insanitary and disease ridden, and many of the inhabitants ignorant, rough and lawless. Politics were characterized by intimidation and corruption. But the picture was not without promising features. There were clear signs of a stirring of the public conscience about evils which had long been ignored or tolerated. Methods had been found of organizing and stimulating the charitable impulses of the individual so that more effective assistance could be brought to those in distress. The need for an expansion in educational provision existed, and the machinery was there for a start to be made on such an expansion.

3

THE PROVISION OF VOLUNTARY SCHOOLS

Before looking in detail at the provision of schooling by voluntary agencies it is necessary to attempt an answer to two questions. Why were influential people in the late eighteenth and nineteenth century so concerned to promote public charity? And why was so much attention paid to charities with an educational purpose?

First, there was the manifest need for action. Hosiery was entering its long decline, and the violent fluctuations in the lace industry caused spasmodic unemployment. Much hardship was also caused by wartime conditions and by the postwar depression. The rapid increase in population made the sufferings of the poor more obvious; in the crowded new town not even the most self-centred person could ignore the effects of unemployment or epidemics. But, under the influence of the religious revival generally referred to as Evangelicalism, self-centredness was becoming unfashionable and was being replaced by a sense of social responsibility. A new seriousness was apparent in religious observance, and with it went a readiness to condemn, and to work to remove, evils which had hitherto been regarded as ineradicable. This frame of mind was by no means confined to people who accepted the particular religious beliefs of the Evangelicals.

To social conscience was added fear. The period of the industrial revolution was one of relatively rapid social mobility. To some the new opportunity for social advancement was one of the most encouraging features of the age, but to others it seemed that society was breaking up. To such people it was absolutely necessary that the social hierarchy be preserved by inculcating in the lower orders habits of subordination and order. Their point of view was reinforced by the appearance of the new phenomenon of an urban working class increasingly conscious of its political identity and inclined to adopt or produce political programmes which were indubitably subversive of the existing structure of society. With the French Revolution before everyone's mind the 1790s were a period of acute anxiety on this account. After 1811 came the Luddite

37

disturbances followed by the long-drawn troubles of the post-war period when radical propaganda was particularly active.

Under the circumstances it was natural enough to turn towards education as an agent of social and political discipline. It was hoped that education could cure the 'idleness and dissoluteness of youth' and encourage devotion to religion and loyalty to government and employer. But a new definition of education was adopted. For at least four centuries the characteristic educational agency had been apprenticeship, and schooling had served merely a preparatory function for most of the townspeople. Apprenticeship declined sharply in the eighteenth century, leaving education in the hands of the schoolmaster by default. In the nineteenth century, indeed, there was an increasing tendency to look upon the work of the school as a crusade carried on in the face of the hostile influence of the home and the workshop, an attitude quite unintelligible to earlier periods.

Sunday schools in Nottingham came as part of one of the periodic waves of concern about the moral condition of the youth of the town. Throughout the 1780s there was a lively correspondence in the local papers suggesting remedies. One writer remarked that 'it is on all sides admitted that the idleness and profligacy of the lower Ranks is becoming extremely alarming',[1] while another pointed out that the 'sole amusement' of 'too many of our youths . . . consists in idle dissipation or tumultuous conversations, which only corrupt the morals, weaken the intellectual powers, destroy the constitution, and bring on a lassitude of both body and mind, while the latter continues in a state of ignorance and the former of imbecility'.[2]

In the autumn of 1784 the plan of establishing a Sunday school went through the usual stages of public meetings and subscription lists, and the school opened in Exchange Hall in January 1785. Although the movement began as an inter-denominational venture it was not long before individual churches and chapels organized their own schools, the town school being allowed some sort of primacy for a number of years. The first of the town school rules touched upon a problem which was to dog the movement throughout its history. The rule ran: 'No child shall be received or continued unless he or she shall come to school with clean linen, washed hands and face, and hair combed'.[3] Unfortunately the effect of this was

[1] *Nottingham Journal*, 20 November 1784.   [2] *Ibid*. 29 April 1786.
[3] *Ibid*. 30 October 1784.

to bar from the school, children who might be deemed to be most in need of assistance. And this was the burden of one of the most frequently made criticisms of Sunday schools. The Children's Employment Commission of 1842 was particularly critical on this score,[1] and some fifty years later the organizer of a ragged evening school remarked: 'the quaint but pathetic reason they give for not attending school is "they won't have us in, for we ain't got no clo'es nor shoes".'

In the early days the teachers at the town school were professional school teachers who were paid at the rate of one penny per week per child. It is not certainly known when the use of paid teachers was given up, but unpaid volunteers provided assistance almost from the start. It is a guess, but no more, that the Methodists, whose class system was based upon voluntary leadership, originated unpaid teaching. It is also likely that the Anglican schools gave up paid teaching when they were reorganized in 1801 after a period of decline.

For twenty years after the establishment of the first school the Sunday school movement made rather fluctuating progress. Sectarian rivalry was sharpening in this period, making co-operation difficult, but the net result was probably to increase provision rather than otherwise. By 1802, although the town school declined, other schools were certainly being run by Methodists, Church of England, General Baptists, Particular Baptists, and Independents. A local newspaper claimed that 1,863 children were attending Sunday schools, and it is clear that the movement was firmly established.

A new wave of enthusiasm for elementary education rose in the early years of the nineteenth century, and the Sunday schools were criticized for their slow development. In particular it was felt that a higher degree of organization and co-operation was needed. The result was the establishment of the Nottingham Sunday School Union in April 1810. Significantly its founding coincided almost exactly with the establishment, as a result of the same dissatisfaction with the achievement of Sunday schools, of the first monitorial schools,[2] in which part of the 'teaching' was entrusted to some of the older pupils. The Union was almost entirely a Nonconformist affair, although Church schools did occasionally enter. It was

[1] *Children's Employment Commission*, 1842, 2nd Report, App. part i, p. 37.
[2] See pp. 44 ff.

energetic and successful, producing its own hymn book which ran through four editions by 1816, and running its own book depot for many years, although this was a less successful venture.

With the establishment of the Union the Sunday school movement may be considered to have reached maturity and it remains to attempt some assessment of its work. In the first place the provision of schools was very extensive. Tables 4 and 5 illustrate the development of the movement in the middle of the nineteenth century, perhaps the great age of the Sunday school. Table 4 is from Dearden's Directory of 1834, Table 5 from the enquiry undertaken by Mann in connection with the 1851 census. The figures should not be taken too literally. There are too many round figures in Dearden's list and there is at least one serious mistake in his figures, other evidence suggesting that the return for St Mary's School was at least twice the real figure.

TABLE 4. *Attendance at Sunday schools in Nottingham 1834*

Church of England		General Baptist	
St Mary's	570	Stoney St	500
St James's	800	Broad St	179
St Peter's	250		
St Nicholas's	120		679
	1,740	Scotch Baptist	126
Catholic	143	Congregational	66
Unitarian	240	Friends	100
New Methodist		Arminian Methodist	130
Parliament St	366		
Mansfield Rd	203	Particular Baptist	
Kingston Place	102	George St	370
	671	Independent Hill	155
Primitive Methodist			525
Canaan St	310		
Canaan St (adults)	305	Independent	
Cross Lane	154	Castle Gate	234
	769	St James's St	166
		Friar Lane	300
Wesleyan Methodist		Fletcher Gate	180
Halifax Place	386		880
Hockley	190		
St Ann's	200		
Woodland Place	150	Total attendance	6,995
	926		

TABLE 5. *Sunday schools in Nottingham 1851*[1]

Denomination	Schools	Total attendance	Boys	Girls
Church of England	11	3,583	1,741	1,842
Independents	4	861	382	479
Baptist	8	1,581	689	892
Friends	2	184	62	122
Unitarians	1	466	236	230
Wesleyan Methodists	2	763	274	489
New Methodists	2	503	193	310
Primitive Methodists	2	630	268	362
Wesleyan Association	1	213	53	160
Undefined Congregations (Protestant)	3	142	142	—
Roman Catholic	2	411	164	247
Total	38	9,337	4,204	5,133

Nevertheless these lists provide material for a general comparison which casts some light upon the progress of the movement. The number of children in the schools continued to increase, but the leadership of the movement had shifted. In the early days the initiative lay with the Dissenters, and various writers have criticized the Church for its negative attitude towards the schools.[2] The returns for 1834 give some support to this criticism, especially since there is good reason to suppose that the figures were inflated. By 1851, however, Anglican activity had expanded and accounted for most of the increase in accommodation since 1834. This phenomenon will be encountered in other contexts. The Church in Nottingham entered a period of vigour in the 1830s when several new churches were built, St Paul's, Holy Trinity, St Matthew's and St John's for example, and there was a new interest in the provision of Sunday and day schools as well as some experiments in adult education. By contrast the record of the Dissenters in this period was less impressive and one is left with the impression that their educational efforts had passed their peak.[3]

In attempting to assess the work of the Sunday schools it is necessary to avoid confusing two aspects of their activity – the

[1] Mann, *1851 Census, Education*, B.P.P., 1852–3, vol. xc. Table S, p. cxc.
[2] E.g. S. D. Chapman, *Evangelical Revival*, pp. 43 ff.; J. L. and B. Hammond, *Age of Chartists*, p. 195 note.
[3] Cf. below, pp. 54 ff.

academic and the social. The standard reached in academic work was extremely low. It may be stated as a rule that a pupil who attended a Sunday school at all regularly would learn to read, but that only the exceptional child learned anything more. Returns from schools to the 1842 Children's Employment Commission may be summarized as follows:[1]

	No.	Partial knowledge	Yes
Reading	9	44	124
Writing	111	30	37

Of 22 individual children interviewed by the Commission, one could neither read nor write, 16 could read and five could write. These were the only children recorded as attending Sunday school only. One problem in this connection is that children who attended day schools invariably attended Sunday school as well, making it difficult to assess the individual contribution of Sunday schools. So far as other subjects were concerned, the Employment Commission again provides a depressing but definite answer:[2]

As regards any general information, even of the most limited kind, such as the situation of Scotland, the names of the four quarters of the globe etc., I do not think that more than a dozen of those whom I questioned, including it must be remembered, a large number of young persons between 13 and 18 years of age, had any knowledge at all upon the subjects.

The work, therefore, was confined to reading and Religious Education in the great majority of cases. But even in these subjects the standard achieved was low. Of the reading it was remarked:[3]

But of those who could read, only a very small proportion did so otherwise than in a most mechanical and imperfect manner, plainly evincing by this and by the answers they gave that they felt no interest in what they read, and, in by far the greater number of cases that they did not comprehend either the meaning of many of the words or the sense of the entire passage ... in the vast majority of cases this exercise consisted of nothing but the monotonous and usually discordant utterance of articulate sounds, in

[1] *Children's Employment Commission*, 1842, 2nd Report, App. part 1, pp. 65 ff.
[2] *Ibid.* App. part 1, p. 35.
[3] *Ibid.*

which it was palpable the mental faculties had no share further than was necessary for the use of eyes and tongue.

The verdict on Religious Education was no more cheerful:

It is especially to be deplored that, notwith-standing the instruction in the existing schools is, with few exceptions, exclusively limited to Religious Knowledge, a most awful ignorance was generally evinced upon this, the most important of all subjects.

There is no need to look far for the reasons for this state of affairs. The hours of attendance were inadequate for much progress to be made. It is true that it was possible for a pupil to attend for 15 or 16 hours a week if he joined the evening classes, but in fact hardly anybody did so. Evening schools, in the first half of the century, were an aspiration rather than a reality; in 1842 only three witnesses from Nottingham were definitely stated to have attended evening schools. The six hours or so of Sunday attendance included two church services, and it was notorious that attendance was extremely irregular. Under these circumstances the curriculum was inevitably restricted, but there is little evidence that a wider curriculum would have been adopted if it had been practicable. As Mann observed in 1851:

It is not for the sake of imparting secular instruction that 318,000 members of the various Churches voluntarily every week assume the teacher's office; but for the purpose of inculcating religious truth and exerting a religious influence. If the children in the Sunday school are taught to read, it is only for the purpose of removing an impediment to the grand design.[1]

Furthermore the schools suffered from the reverse side of one of their great advantages. They always enjoyed a remarkably good staff/pupil ratio. Ten pupils per teacher was a fair average,[2] and the teachers included men and women of substance and education, but they were amateurs and made little or no attempt to study the art or craft of teaching:

The Sunday school teachers, who have by their unpaid and most meritorious services conferred the deepest benefits on the community, must yet as a body be regarded as not duly qualified for the highly important office they have undertaken. They have not generally paid any attention to the subject of education as a thing requiring in itself to be studied . . .

[1] Mann, *1851 Census*, p. lx i   [2] *Ibid*. p. lxxvi.

they are selected . . . rather on the grounds of moral and religious conduct than of any peculiar fitness for the office of teaching.[1]

On the other hand the Sunday schools were well organized to exert a social and religious influence, for the teacher, usually a layman and often near in age to the pupils, could bring a personal and direct influence on the small class. Sunday schools did not reach the lowest stratum of the population, but among the more respectable families of the working classes their influence was strong, and it has to be remembered that they were often fighting a lone battle since it is unlikely that more than half of the children of the poor made any significant attendance at day schools until the second half of the century.

But the Sunday school movement had one result which, although accidental, was of major social importance. This arose from the opportunity provided by the schools for co-operation and friendship between different social classes. Every class of society was engaged in the work; teachers were drawn from the gentry, the commercial and industrial aristocracy, tradesmen, artisans and operatives, and the schools provided a common ground upon which people could meet without the barriers raised by the relationship of hosier/stockinger or proprietor/operative. This may have helped to damp down inter-class bitterness; Carter writing the history of the Nottingham Sunday School Union in 1860, thought that this was the case. It certainly brought members of the more prosperous classes, men and women, into contact with poverty and helped to spread some knowledge of the problems and miseries of the poor. It is probably more than mere coincidence that many of the men most active in the founding and maintaining of day schools and other philanthropic institutions were, or had been, Sunday school teachers.

The same combination of religious, political and philanthropic motives which led to the establishment of Sunday schools in the 1780s influenced the founders of elementary day schools 25 years later. However, certain special factors caused day schools to be added to the existing Sunday schools.

Between 1784 and 1810 the population of Nottingham almost doubled, and the evils which had disturbed the founders of Sunday schools became correspondingly more serious. About 1810, too, the

[1] Mann, *1851 Census,* p. lxxi.

trade of the town, which had flourished spasmodically since the beginning of the century took a prolonged downturn, and the combination of social and political unrest, never entirely hidden in Nottingham at that time, burst into the open, Luddism being one of its manifestations. No doubt the long war, quite apart from its effect on the economy of the town, helped to upset the balance of society, and democratic ideas, driven underground by the anti-Jacobin riots of 1793 and 1794 and subsequent legal persecution, still smouldered to break out again under the stress of unemployment and its accompanying distress.

Leaving aside the Sunday schools, there were four public day schools and an unknown, but large number of private schools. The Free Grammar School provided for about 50 boys, the Bluecoat School for 60 boys and 20 girls and High Pavement School for 40 boys and 24 girls. None of these were elementary schools in the sense that Lancaster's or Bell's schools were, and they were never considered as providing accommodation for the poor at this period. A small school connected with St Mary's Church provided for a few children; this was founded some time prior to 1713 and was still functioning a hundred years later, but almost nothing is known about it. Altogether, therefore, public schools provided places for 180 to 200 children, and nearly all of these were in schools which were not intended for children in need of the rudiments of education. The vast majority of those children of the poor who attended school at all went to private venture schools which were extremely numerous. Fees at such schools were not high, threepence to sixpence per week at the cheapest 'common day' schools, but it will be seen that there was, to all intents and purposes, no provision for day schooling of those children whose parents were unable or unwilling to pay a fee.

The first monitorial school in Nottingham was opened in July 1810 in a room in Wool Alley off Barker Gate, from which it moved to a cotton mill in Broad Marsh a few months later. It was on the Lancasterian plan, and was always referred to subsequently as the Lancasterian School. The aims of the institution were set forth in an advertisement in the local newspaper, which invited subscriptions.[1]

There should be no individual amongst us of any situation incapable of reading and writing or unacquainted with the first principles of arith-

[1] *Nottingham Journal*, 28 July 1810.

metic. If we connect with teaching to read and write, the correcting of bad dispositions, and the . . . introducing of good ones, accustoming the rising generation to habits of cleanliness, subordination and order; teaching them to fear God and to respect all men, it is manifest that the interests of religion and society must be very greatly promoted.

At first the Lancasterian School was an all-party venture supported by Churchmen and Dissenters alike, but in December 1810 a dispute arose over the appointment of a teacher, and the school became a Dissenting institution. This dispute turned out to be a blessing in disguise, since the Church interest felt it necessary to establish their own school, which they did in January 1811. The quarrel was, in fact, a very temporary affair, and both sides saw the establishment of two schools rather than one as an excellent thing.

Almost immediately a girls' school was opened which came to be called the 'Girls' School of Industry'. In some ways this was a reversion to the seventeenth-century idea of a spinning school; it was avowedly vocational in its aims, more attention being devoted to domestic training than to academic work, and it was not organized on Lancasterian lines, the monitorial system not being adopted until 1824. The thinking which led to the establishment of this school is clearly illustrated by the first annual report,[1] which indicated that the only academic achievement aimed at was reading. In practice even the teaching of reading, at least in the early years, was very much subordinated to the needlework side,[2] and the girls were chiefly employed in the 'providing of child-bed linen and other articles of clothing for the poor, at a lower rate than can be afforded by other means.'[3] The first balance sheet of the school illustrates the order of priorities, the salary of the mistress being exceptionally low even for the period.

RECEIVED	£	s.	d.
Subscriptions, donations, etc.	105	3	0
Clothing, bed-linen, etc., sold to the poor cheap	90	11	0
PAID			
Salary to mistress	14	6	0
Rent, fire, cleaning	9	7	0
Pinafores, workbags, needles, stationery	18	7	4½
Materials for work	103	19	0

[1] *Nottingham Journal*, 7 March 1812.
[2] G. Wilkins, *A Letter ... to the Rev. J. Burnett Stuart*, London, 1822, p. 18.
[3] *Nottingham Journal*, 7 March 1812.

The burst of enthusiasm for popular education which produced the Lancasterian School, the Boys' National School and the Girls' School of Industry was of rather short duration, and for fifteen years elementary education in the town stagnated. Subscriptions and donations fell away with a corresponding decline in the number of children educated. This process is most clearly seen in the case of the Lancasterian School, which was peculiarly subject, throughout its career, to vicissitudes of fortune. In 1811 subscriptions amounted to £311 and there were 440 children in attendance; by 1820 subscriptions had fallen to £170 and attendance to 180. From this time attendance never exceeded 234, a high point reached in 1829, and frequently fell below 100 in the recurrent crises which afflicted the school. Few details have survived of the other schools, but their course seems to have been very similar. The National School, planned for 500 pupils, never in fact, appears to have taken more than 250. Investigators in the 1830s credited the school with 570 pupils,[1] but this was an example of the common mistake of confusing the accommodation of the building with the number of children in attendance. The subscriptions of the School of Industry declined from £105 in 1812 to £67 in 1824, when the school was unique in experiencing a revival. The only new public elementary school founded in this period was the Girls' British School, established on Hound's Gate in 1820. This was a precarious institution from the start. Subscriptions were only £55 in 1824, and by 1833 they had fallen to £40. In that year there were 122 children in the school, which was said to be more than for many years.

The basic reason for the schools' decline was the eternal problem of sustaining the interest of voluntary subscribers in any charity after the first excitement, a problem made more acute by the difficulty of producing acceptable records to prove the schools' success. The hospital could publish statistics of patients cured, but there was nothing comparable for the managers of schools to report, and interest in popular education tended to fluctuate sharply and to need stimulation from time to time. Added to this the early 1820s were the years of the great lace boom in Nottingham when wages were high and workmen much in demand, and it was a common experience that interest in education waned in times of prosperity.

---

[1] R. Hopper in a paper presented to the Nottingham Literary and Philosophical Society, *Nottingham Journal*, 13 December 1833. He is followed by Chapman, *Evangelical Revival*.

Under the circumstances the schools were much dependent upon the efforts of individual managers to arouse enthusiasm, and it is very obvious that both the National and the Lancasterian Schools suffered from inept management at this period. The recurrent financial crises which affected the Lancasterian School and the fact that on one occasion the annual subscriptions were never collected, gives an impression of feeble leadership, while the National School suffered from a violent quarrel between the vicar of St Mary's and the vicar of St James's, which reached the stage at which the two clergymen carried on their dispute in privately published letters. The rights and wrongs of the quarrel are not now very clear, but since the two men dominated Anglican affairs in the town their inability to co-operate was a grave drawback to the interests of the school, control of which was one of the points at issue.

In the late 1820s a new start was made to the extension of public elementary education in Nottingham. There was no significant break in this process which reached its peak in a great burst of school building in the 1850s and 1860s. As was so often the case the new wave of interest in education was sparked off by the introduction of a new method of teaching which caught the attention of the public. In this case it was the infant school, on Wilderspin's pattern, which attracted attention and four such schools were established, St Ann's and Rutland Street in 1827 and Independent Hill and Canaan Street in 1829. The first two were Anglican, Rutland Street being an offshoot of the School of Industry. Independent Hill was run by the Particular Baptists, and Canaan Street cannot be attached to any particular denomination.

An interesting feature of these schools is that some of them at least paid their teachers on a commission basis, the teacher receiving a small fixed salary plus the children's fees, which were usually about twopence per week. Their history is difficult to follow since they received little publicity after the first year or two, but Rutland Street and Canaan Street were both still operating in 1870 when they appear in the list of schools compiled by the School Board. Rutland Street alone appears to have received government grant, the others being run at least partly as private ventures. Independent Hill was certainly still in existence in 1844; St Ann's is not mentioned after 1834, but in neither case is it at all certain that they closed after those dates since information on schools before the days of the School Board is invariably fragmentary.

The establishment of the four infant schools was only one result of the revived interest in popular education. The Dissenting congregations founded two new schools, Barker Gate in 1831 and Canal Street in 1835. Canal Street received some assistance from the Corporation, which gave the site and £100, while upwards of £2,000 was subscribed by the public for building. These schools represent the last major effort made by the Dissenters in the cause of elementary education. A new building was provided at Bath Street in 1851, but this replaced Canal Street, so it was not a new venture, while the few schools founded in the 1860s were small and financially insecure from the start.

But as the Dissenters lost interest the Catholics began to provide schools and the Church of England, after a long period when its efforts had been rather perfunctory, got into its stride, making good use of the government building grants, available after 1833. The first Catholic school was opened for girls in 1828 in an old chapel in Stoney Street, and in 1834 a boys' school was added in Bell Yard, off Long Row, a particularly crowded area. Their first school building was erected in Kent Street in 1841, and by 1870 schools, some with two or more departments, existed at Kent Street, George Street, Derby Road and Narrow Marsh.

The Church of England effort started rather slowly, but gathered momentum. A girls' National school was founded in 1835. It was in a good building, but the scarcity and high price of land made it necessary to place it in the corner of a disused burial ground, which formed the somewhat macabre playground for the children. In this respect, however, it may be considered fortunate since other schools had no playground at all, and the Canal Street school was built over a public sewer, and, in 1845, was reported to be subsiding into it.[1] An infant school was established at St Paul's in 1840 to serve the fearfully overcrowded area between Broad Street and Lower Parliament Street. A boys' National school was added to the girls' in 1845, and then began a large amount of new building connected with the establishment of new parishes which was proceeding rapidly at that time. Trinity and St John's schools appeared in 1847, St Mark's in 1850, St Peter's and St Matthew's in 1855, St Nicholas's in 1859. A ragged school was founded in 1854 and, at about the same time, a number of branch schools were set up by existing institutions –

---

[1] *Second Report of the Commissioners ... State of Large Towns and Populous Places*, 1845, App. part II, p. 252.

Mapperley in 1860, Bunker's Hill 1861, Bullivant Street 1866. Four new churches all founded schools in the 1860s – All Saints', St Anne's, St Luke's and St Saviour's.

In order to provide an impression of the progress made, by the voluntary agencies, in providing elementary school accommodation, two lists are given of the schools existing in 1835 and 1870, together with the number of children in attendance. The 1870 list is taken from the report of the Statistical Committee of the School Board, and is the first statistical account which can be argued from in any detail. The 1835 list is compiled from various sources of which the most important are the abstract of returns made to the parliamentary enquiry of 1833 and a paper by R. Hopper read to the local Literary and Philosophical Society in the same year.[1] There are a number of discrepancies between different sources, some of which can be resolved by the use of local directories and annual reports. The list may be taken as accurate regarding the number of schools, and rather less accurate regarding the number of children in attendance.

The figures given above are for the number of children attending the schools, and no account is taken in the totals of whether the schools were considered efficient since the standard taken as acceptable rose rapidly with time, and a school considered inefficient in 1871 would pass as very adequate in 1835.

Between 1835 and 1870 attendance at public elementary schools rose from 2,190 to 7,137. By the later date there were about 12,000 places in these schools for children, and the School Board estimated that if half a dozen schools which were classed as unacceptable were to be improved, there was only a deficiency of 307 places in the town.[2] By comparison with the vast deficiencies discovered in other large industrial towns, Leeds or Birmingham for example, this was a negligible figure, and the Board was able to enjoy a relatively quiet first few years, without the necessity for large-scale building schemes.

This great expansion in educational provision was accomplished by voluntary efforts, generally with the assistance of government grants. To provide school places for every child in the borough was a substantial feat which speaks well for the charity of the day.

[1] *Nottingham Journal*, 13 December 1833.
[2] The grounds upon which the School Board's calculations were based are discussed below, p. 86.

There are, however, two features which call for particular attention.

In the first place the accommodation provided greatly exceeded the number of children in attendance. Taking the town overall, in 1870 the schools were rather less than three quarters full, even if it

TABLE 6. *School provision in 1835 and 1870*

I. SCHOOL PROVISION IN 1835

School	Attendance			
	Boys	Girls	Infants	Year
Church of England				
National Boys', High Cross St	225^a	—	—	1811
National Girls', Barker Gate	—	90	—	1834
School of Industry, Rutland St	—	100	—	1812
St Anne's, Infant	—	—	150	1827
Rutland St Infant	—	—	100	1827
Total	225	190	250	
Dissenting				
Lancasterian Boys', Derby Rd	200^b	—	—	1810
Lancasterian Girls', Hound's Gate	—	122	—	1820
Barker Gate	180	90	—	1831
Canal St	160	110	—	1835
Canaan St, Infants	—	—	120	1829
Independent Hill, Infants	—	—	100	1829
Total	540	322	220	
Roman Catholic				
Girls', Stoney St	—	78	—	1828
Boys', Long Row	165	—	—	1834
Workhouse School	128	72	—	1833
Grand total	1,058	662	470	
= 2,190				

Total attendance	
Church of England	665
Dissenting	1,082
Catholic	243

NOTES

^{a} The attendance at the National Boys' School was constantly given as 570, but the annual reports show that the actual attendance was about 225.

^{b} The numbers at the Lancasterian School fluctuated considerably. When the school was functioning fully about 200 children were in attendance.

2. SCHOOL PROVISION IN 1870[1]

School	Attendance		
	Boys	Girls	Infants
Church of England			
All Saints', Raleigh St	167	90	148
Trinity, North Church St	435	108	176
Trinity Branch, Colville St			146
St Matthew, Talbot St		60	154
St Stephen's, Bunkers Hill	158[a]		158[a]
St Ann's, St Ann's Well Rd	159	80	166
St Ann's branch, Bullivant St			202
St Ann's branch, Mapperley Plains	←——— 45[b] ———→		
St Mark's, St Michael's St	91	50	87
Ragged, Newcastle St	←— 105[b] —→		161
St Mary's, Barker Gate	245		
St Paul's, Cherry St	92	←— 156 —→	
St Luke's, Carlton Rd	130	168	
School of Industry		95	140
St Saviour's, Arkwright St	76		120
St Saviour's branch, Launder St			64
St John's, London Rd	87	44	60
St Nicholas's Castle Rd	115		165
St Peter's, Broad Marsh	60	←— 115 —→	
St Mary's, Plumptre St		94	232
St Luke's branch, Poplar[c]		52	42
St John's (no address)[c]			56
Dissenting Schools			
Christ church, Peas Hill Rd	←——— 97[b] ———→		
British, Bath St	113	75	
British, Derby Rd	156		
British, Hound's Gate	104		
British, Dukes Place	←— 37 —→		18
Wesleyan, Arkwright St	80	65	117
Town Mission, Ragged, Colwick St	←———245———→		
Town Mission, Leen Side[c]			90
Roman Catholic			
Kent St	48		
St John's, George St			126
St Mary's, Derby Rd		94	
St Patrick's, Leen Side		90	
St Patrick's, boys[d]	64		
St Patrick's, infants[c]			40
Workhouse, York St	66[a]	58[a]	

[1] *School Board Minutes*, 31 July 1871.

[continued on facing page]

Grand total

Church of England	5,354
Dissenting	1,197
Roman Catholic	462
Workhouse	124
	7,137

NOTES

a The attendance figures are unavailable and the accommodation is given instead.

b Mixed school.

c These schools were not considered to be efficient by the Statistical Committee.

d These schools were returned as 'can be made efficient'.

is allowed, as was notoriously untrue, that every child on the books of a school was actually in attendance. Most schools were fairly empty, and as a rule only the infant departments showed any over-crowding – parents were more likely to send their young children to school since there was less chance of profitable employment for them. Of the large senior schools only Trinity and St Luke's were really full. This is not a surprising situation; it is exactly what one would expect in a town where the staple industries were noted for their employment of young children, before the days of compulsory school attendance. Nevertheless the emptiness of the schools points to the real failure of the voluntary system in Nottingham; the schools were there, but parents could not be induced to send their children to them. This was perhaps the most pressing problem bequeathed by the voluntary system to the School Board.

Secondly, virtually the whole of the expansion in school accommodation between 1835 and 1870 was the work of the Church of England. Until the 1830s the Church definitely lagged behind the Dissenters in the provision of schools. Most of the new ideas – Sunday schools, monitorial schools, the Sunday School Union – seem to have originated among the Dissenters, and there are grounds for believing that the lead on the Anglican side was taken by the congregation of St James's Church, which claimed to follow a line of 'moderate Calvinism', and was regarded with suspicion by other established churches.[1] Thus, in 1835 the Dissenting day schools provided almost exactly twice the number of places that the Church did. The year 1835 marked the turning point. After then the

[1] Chapman, *Evangelical Revival*, pp. 52 ff.

Dissenting interest in education declined while that of the Church of England flourished. By 1870 the number of children in Church schools had multiplied by nine, while there was no change in the figure for Dissenting schools. Very few British schools were established in the intervening years, and those that were founded led a stunted existence. Duke's Place, for example, had only 55 children in a building which would take 340.

It is very difficult to account in any satisfactory manner for these differences in attitude and effort. The explanation for the predominance of Nonconformity in the early years of the century is clear enough. Nottingham was a Whig and Nonconformist town, at least as far as the leading citizens were concerned, and it was virtually a necessity for taking any public office that a man should attend one of the three leading Chapels, High Pavement Unitarian, George Street Baptist and Castle Gate Independent. Attendance at Dissenting places of worship was far more extensive than at Church. In 1833 a local investigator[1] stated that 5,800 people attended Anglican services and 12,000 attended Nonconformist services. His figures may have been somewhat inflated, but it is likely that the proportions were accurate enough. One would expect Dissenters to take the lead under these circumstances, and this is what one finds. But in the 1840s the whole situation changed. New churches were built, mainly in the new centres of population surrounding the old town, but the overgrown parish of St Mary's was also subdivided. The new churches, perhaps naturally, showed a missionary spirit and established schools, as well as interesting themselves in experiments in adult education, which will be described in their place.[2] Thus the new vigour of the Church in the provision of elementary schools was merely one aspect of a general picture of activity and expansion.

The difficulty is to explain why the Dissenting side withdrew from the struggle just as the Catholics and Anglicans began their greatest efforts. Mr Chapman suggests[3] that there was a halt in their educational programme after the building of Canal Street because, 'this new school was no sooner established than the depression of 1837–42 hit the town with catastrophic results, and all philanthropy was diverted to the relief of distress. The problem of the neglected

---

[1] *Nottingham Journal*, 13 December 1833.
[2] See below, chapter 8, pp. 188–9.
[3] Chapman, *Evangelical Revival*, p. 64.

areas (outside the old town boundaries) was not attacked again until 1849, when the workers of the Dissenters' Town Mission established a Ragged School in Narrow Marsh'. Unfortunately this explanation falls down on two counts. If the Dissenters were unable to provide schools between 1837 and 1842, why did they wait another seven years before opening a Ragged School ? The fact is that the building of Canal Street marked the effective end of the Dissenting effort; there was no question of a temporary lull. Furthermore the Anglican response to the situation was very different, for they opened three new schools, Trinity, St John's and St Paul's at this very period, the first being large schools in new buildings attached to newly established churches. The Dissenting congregations, in particular those which attended the older 'respectable' chapels, seem to have suffered from their position as the local 'establishment' which inhibited their response to missionary activity. By contrast, the Anglicans had the stimulus of representing the opposition and being thus forced into a radical position.

As early as 1836, some of the leaders on the Dissenting side in Nottingham were turning towards the idea of state intervention in education.[1] As the full extent of the educational problem became apparent due to repeated investigations from the 1830s onwards, the Dissenters increasingly looked to government action, despairing of the ability of voluntary efforts, while Catholics and Anglicans redoubled their attempts to provide the schools themselves. In the event the future lay with the system of government control, but the fact remains that for forty years the provision of elementary schools in Nottingham was left almost exclusively to the Church of England, the Catholics being the only other denomination to make a serious contribution.

The period from 1780 to 1870 was the great age of voluntary provision of elementary schools for the poor. It may be thought of as falling into two phases. The first ran from 1780 to 1830, and included the establishment of Sunday schools and of the first elementary day schools. The lead at this time was generally taken by the Dissenters, especially in the provision of Sunday schools. A particular feature of the period was the difficulty experienced by the sponsors of the schools in sustaining the original interest of subscribers. Sunday schools suffered as early as the 1790s from a decline

[1] Chapman, *Evangelical Revival*, p. 64.

in public interest, while all the day schools ran into the same problem. No doubt this had much to do with the preference shown by many sects for the Sunday school, which could be run satisfactorily by a comparatively small number of enthusiastic volunteers on a low budget, while the more expensive day school required a steady and substantial income if it was to succeed.

After about 1830 the voluntary movement entered a new phase characterized by a great effort by the Church of England, supported on a naturally smaller scale by the Catholics, to provide school places for every child in the town. By 1870 this aim had been achieved, the deficiency of places revealed by the School Board's enquiry being negligible. There were, however, serious deficiencies in some of the surrounding villages like Radford, Basford and Bulwell where the local Church lacked the resources available in a large and prosperous town. It remains to consider the work of the voluntary schools, and to consider to what extent they offered an adequate education to the poor children of the town. This task will be attempted in the next chapter.

4

THE WORK OF THE VOLUNTARY SCHOOLS

As was suggested in the previous chapter, elementary schools faced two fundamental problems from which many of their difficulties sprang. These were, first, that children left school too young and attended irregularly, and, second, shortage of funds. Every teacher and investigator complained about the short and irregular school life of elementary school children. The master of the Lancasterian school told the 1842 Employment Commission:

the boys leave school generally at a very early age; on an average they do not remain more than twelve months. At this time the number on the books is 120; in the last twelve months 112 have left the school.[1]

His colleague at the National School concurred and added details:

The boys who attend are from six to ten years of age; there are very few above that age. The number in attendance greatly fluctuates, which witness attributes to this being a manufacturing town. During the last twelve months about 340 boys have on the whole been in the school, so about 120 have gone out. They are withdrawn from the school on the average at about nine to go to work. A large number, however, leave younger to go as seamers and runners. Some have left for this purpose as young as seven. If trade is good the number in attendance is considerably diminished.[2]

Mistresses of girls' schools told the same story:

Finds great difficulty in keeping them sufficiently long. In the last 12 months 166 have been admitted, more than the total number on the books at the present time. The children are withdrawn at a very early age; has known some leave to go to the lace works before six. If the trade of the town is good they lose a great number; if it were brisk now, in a fortnight half the school would leave.[3]

These complaints may be divided under three headings, although the three were closely inter-related. The children left school too

---

[1] *Children's Employment Commission*, 1842, 2nd Report, Witness No. 318.
[2] *Ibid.* Witness No. 319.
[3] *Ibid.* Witness No. 321.

young; their school life was too short; their attendance was spasmodic when they were nominally at school. All three points are amply borne out by the evidence. The Employment Commission of 1842 recorded the names and ages of the children in the top forms of six Nottingham schools.[1] At the Lancasterian school there were sixteen children in the class, two being thirteen, three being twelve and the rest ten or eleven years of age; the average age was $11\frac{1}{4}$ years. This was a better figure than was reached by any other school. At St Mary's girls' school the children ranged from six to thirteen years, the most common age being ten. The other schools reported a similar pattern, $10\frac{1}{2}$ being the average age, but no other school had pupils as old as thirteen. These figures, however, give an unduly optimistic view of the situation since many of these children were monitors, who were encouraged to remain at school by a small payment. At St Mary's school, the only school which returned this information, one third of the top class were monitors, and it is likely that a similar proportion obtained elsewhere. One or two witnesses[2] stated that children who were not monitors left at an earlier age; eight to ten years being considered normal. It must also be remembered that these schools were all relatively large and well-run institutions, and that it was notorious that children left the cheap private schools at an even earlier age.

Progress in raising the age of elementary school attenders was slow and halting. Indeed, in the 1840s and 1850s it was the opinion of Inspectors and other investigators that the situation was, if anything, worsening.[3] As one local inspector remarked: 'We may be educating more, but they are, I believe, younger children and stay with us less time.' It was not until the 1860s that a slight but definite improvement was perceptible in the proportion of older children attending inspected schools. In 1846 an inspector examined an unspecified school in the Midland region and found the following state of affairs:[4]

> 20 pupils had attended less than 1 year
>
> 17 pupils had attended for 1 to 2 years
>
> 10 pupils had attended for 2 to 3 years

[1] *Children's Employment Commission*, 1842, 2nd Report, Witness No. 318 onwards.

[2] *Ibid*. Witnesses Nos. 322, 324.

[3] *Minutes of Committee of Privy Council on Education*, 1846, vol. 1, p. 150; and 1855–6, p. 605.

[4] *Ibid*. 1846, vol. 1, p. 152.

10 pupils had attended for 3 to 4 years
4 pupils had attended for 4 to 5 years
1 pupil had attended for 5 to 6 years
1 pupil had attended for 6 to 7 years

The average attendance at the school was 96, and 88 children had left in the course of twelve months. The average length of stay was 1 year 11 months 2 weeks and 4 days, but this figure was clearly inflated by the one or two children who remained for several years, and who were presumably monitors. No such detailed analysis has survived of a Nottingham school, but the figures agree very well with the estimates of witnesses before the 1842 Commission that the average school life was something over one year. These estimates are also supported by the fact that it was quite an ordinary thing for the number of children entering or leaving a school in twelve months to equal the number in average attendance. In 1846, for example, the Lancasterian school had an average attendance of 154; 149 boys were admitted and 144 left in the year.[1]

TABLE 7. *Percentage of pupils attending inspected elementary schools in the Midland area at different ages*

	1852	1861	1864
Under 7 years	35·44	39·85	35·99
7–8 years	16·38	12·57	12·89
8–9 years	13·80	12·09	11·91
9–10 years	11·60	10·62	11·38
10–11 years	9·55	8·91	10·03
11–12 years	6·52	7·02	7·78
12–13 years	4·00	4·77	5·65
Over 13 years	2·71	4·17	4·37

There may have been a worsening of the situation in the 1840s and 1850s; certainly little or no progress was made. In the late 1850s, however, the schools do appear to have achieved some success in persuading children to attend for a little longer; there is a marked improvement between 1852 and 1861, and this was sustained. The depressing fact is, nevertheless, that, in 1852, more than half the children in elementary schools had attended for less than one year, and only 15 per cent for more than three years; even in 1864 the

1 *Nottingham Review*, 6 February 1846.

TABLE 8. *Length of school life of children in inspected elementary schools*[1]

	1852	1861	1864
Less than 1 year	53·36	37·88	38·73
1–2 years	19·67	23·29	22·19
2–3 years	12·08	15·57	15·26
3–4 years	7·80	10·48	10·22
4–5 years	3·87	6·37	6·71
Over 5 years	3·22	6·41	6·89

proportion of children who had been in school for more than three years was only 24 per cent (Table 8).

It is more difficult to arrive at any accurate estimate of the regularity with which children attended school before the days of the School Board. It can, however, be confidently stated that by modern standards attendance was unbelievably bad. Every witness was agreed that, in the first place, any improvement in trade immediately emptied the schools, and annual reports of schools give ample support to their statements. Thus in 1824, when the lace boom was in progress schools had much reduced attendance,[2] while in 1842, a year of bad trade it was reported that 'never has the school (St Mary's girls') been better attended, and never have the results been more gratifying'.[3]

In this respect some definite progress was made, although not before the 1860s. Figures are available of the number of children at different schools who qualified for capitation grant by attending 176 times in a year, and they show a very significant increase during the 1860s (Table 9). Obviously this increase reflects the fact that more children were being attracted into the schools as well as greater regularity of attendance, but it seems likely that most of the improvement did arise from greater regularity, since the increase in the number of children attending schools in this period, although substantial, was much smaller than the increase in the number qualifying for grant. Even in the 1860s, however, attendance remained very irregular. When the School Board took over an average attendance of 65 to 70 per cent of the children on the roll was normal. Since this

[1] *Minutes of Committee of Privy Council on Education*, 1852–3, p. 683; 1861, App. 1, Table 1; 1864–5, App. 1, Table 1.
[2] *Nottingham Review*, 14 May 1825, 29 October 1825.
[3] *Ibid.* 4 November 1842.

TABLE 9. *Comparative table of number of children qualifying for capitation grant, 1861, 1866*[1]

	1861	1866
Basford	45	148
Beeston	86	169
Carrington	18	63
Hyson Green	97	220
Lenton	191	347
St Peter's	70	286
School of Industry	50	108
St James's (infants)	29	116
St John's	90	161
St Matthew's	60	165
St Mary's	216	477 (including) branches)
St Nicholas's	92	210
Trinity	231	631
Trinity branch	65	90
New Radford	113	332
Sneinton	78	93

represented an improvement, perhaps due to the 'payment by results' system of the 1860s it will be obvious that the attendance of children in the earlier days of the voluntary system must have been irregular indeed.

On the average, therefore, children attended public elementary schools for a school life of between one and two years, which probably finished by the time they were nine years old, and was interrupted by periods of employment when business was good. Under these circumstances it would be absurd to expect the pupils to reach a high level of attainment. There were other factors, however, which aggravated the position.

Elementary schools were chronically short of money. It was calculated in 1845 that the average school in the Midland area overspent its income by an average of £7 per year.[2] This sum appears small by modern standards, but it represented a substantial proportion of the budget of a voluntary school. In 1824 the School of Industry had an income of £67 9s. 6d.;[3] the Boys' National School

[1] *Reports of the Committee of Privy Council on Education*, 1862 and 1866–7, App. 3.
[2] *Minutes of the Committee of Privy Council on Education*, 1846, vol. I, pp. 258–9.
[3] *Nottingham Journal*, 26 March 1824.

in the following year collected £111 12s. 6d.[1] These were relatively flourishing institutions; in 1842 subscriptions to the Girls' British School amounted to only £43 2s. 9½d.[2] Obviously an annual deficit of £7 would soon amount to an overwhelming burden.

The financial problem had two aspects. In a town like Nottingham, which was relatively wealthy and had a long corporate tradition, there was rarely any particular difficulty in founding a school. Trouble began when the school was working and the first enthusiasm had faded; then it became an arduous task to maintain subscriptions. Naturally schools had to exert extreme economy in their running costs, with the result that books were few and were used until they dropped to pieces, furniture was inadequate and rarely replaced, and, most important of all, it became virtually impossible to recruit efficient teachers.

The teacher's salary was far and away the largest single outlay of any school. In 1836 the total expenditure of the new British schools on Canal Street was £131 12s. 11d.; of this sum £120 was spent on the salary of the master and mistress. The Girls' British School spent £62 14s. 3d. of which £40 went to the mistress, while a few years before the National School spent £80 out of £111 12s. 6d. on salaries. Even the best placed schools had to economize on salaries, while less fortunate institutions were quite unable to pay an efficient teacher. Assistant teachers were virtually unknown; there were only two in the Midland area as late as 1854, and it was not unusual for a school to be forced to dismiss an efficient but expensive teacher and replace him by a cheaper man. This occurred at the Girls' British School where the salary was reduced from £40 to £25 and then to £20, and at the Lancasterian School where the reduction was from £90 to £80.

But Nottingham was relatively fortunate in that it was at least possible to start schools even if problems of maintenance arose later. The situation was far worse in the surrounding villages, which were immensely swollen in population but which lacked any administration above parish level. They depended almost entirely upon hosiery and therefore suffered recurrent bouts of grinding poverty, and they lacked any wealthy citizens to give a lead to charitable efforts. By and large they offered a first-class proof of one Inspector's contention that the existing system of building grants meant that schools were

---

[1] *Nottingham Journal*, 14 May 1825.
[2] *Nottingham Review*, 4 November 1842

built where they were least needed.[1] The problems in the way of school building in such areas are illustrated by the case of Basford which applied for a grant in 1844. The government granted £300 towards the £940 required, and the National Society added £250, but in twelve months only £70 could be raised towards the balance from a population of 9,000.[2]

Another problem for elementary schools was the depressing effect on the educational potential of children of life in the slums of an industrial town. The consequences of such an environment were clearly stated by the Inspector for the Midland area in 1845.[3]

No greater error can be made in elementary education than to suppose that, for the education of the poor man's child, nothing more is required than is needed for our own children. In reality the task is infinitely more difficult; our own children, by the contact of their minds with ours, have acquired that familiarity with the resources of language, those habits of thought, and those powers of reason and reflection, and those stores of general knowledge in which the children of the poor are always found to be most conspicuously deficient. All that we need for our children is that technical instruction which cannot thus be indirectly obtained.

The Inspector went on to draw the conclusion that since the education of the poor was more difficult than that of the wealthy, it required better provision of equipment, of teachers, and, in particular, of money.

Until the institution of the pupil-teacher system in 1846 there was not any recognizable career of elementary school teacher, and one of the significant features of the later years of the voluntary period was the appearance of a degree of professional consciousness and solidarity among teachers. It will be convenient in this study to examine the lot of the elementary school teacher as it was about 1840, just before the pupil-teacher system was introduced, and then to look at developments up to the time of the School Board.

In every Nottingham elementary school in 1840 the monitorial system was used.[4] Each school, or department had one teacher who was assisted by a number of monitors chosen from among the older pupils. The schools fluctuated greatly in size, but it was not unusual for the master of one of the larger schools to be responsible for 300

---

[1] *Minutes of Committee of Privy Council on Education*, 1846, vol. I, p. 169.
[2] *Ibid.* 1843–4, p. 290.
[3] *Ibid.* 1845, vol. I, p. 268.
[4] The only exceptions to this rule were the infant schools.

or more pupils. The monitorial system was used even by the most intelligent teachers in spite of the fact that they showed themselves to be fully aware of its weaknesses. At its best the system was a mechanical way of conveying elementary information, but it is obvious that it removed any direct influence which the master might have on the bulk of the school. Unfortunately it also possessed less manifest faults. The master of the Nottingham Lancasterian School pointed out that the most intelligent boys disliked and avoided the office of monitor because it retarded their own progress. Too often the monitors were boys of inferior character who enjoyed a little power, had favourites, and, according to another local teacher, even took bribes.[1]

It was not merely unintelligent conservatism which preserved the monitorial system. In the conditions of the time there was hardly an alternative. The Lancasterian master, noted as an intelligent and enterprising man remarked 'no master can convey an effective education, moral and intellectual to more than 50 scholars'. The numbers in his school varied between 180 and 240, and the children were of every age from the nursery upwards. Until some more efficient method of providing the teacher with assistance could be found, the monitorial system was a necessity. Further, until Stow's introduction of his 'simultaneous' method there was little understanding of the technique of class teaching. The pupils in non-monitorial schools worked separately at their work, taking turns to have their efforts examined by the teacher, and attempts to use this method in the large elementary schools of the nineteenth century led to chaos. It was remarked in 1842 that:[2] 'Several of the schools which I visited were in a state approaching to riotous, and so little control had the masters that it was only amidst incessant interruptions and confusion that the information sought could be obtained'.

The training of teachers was of the most rudimentary kind. The trainee was attached for a week or two to an established school and there 'learned the system' often by sitting in with each class in turn. The master of Nottingham National School was credited in 1844 with having trained fifty teachers in this way. No doubt an important reason for the uncritical retention of the monitorial system long after its defects were well known was the inadequate training which encouraged mindless following of rule-of-thumb methods.

[1] *Children's Employment Commission*, 1842, 2nd Report, Witnesses Nos. 318, 319.
[2] *Ibid.* 1842, App. part I, p. 35.

There is no lack of information about the pay of teachers, but the variations from one school to another were so great that it is difficult to make any useful generalizations about the teachers' position beyond saying that even the best paid were barely on a level with a skilled craftsman. In 1845 the average for teachers in inspected schools in the Midland area was as follows.[1]

Master   £51 15s. 3d. } about half the teachers were provided
Mistress   £28 19s. 0d. } with a house.
Infant mistress   £18   6s. 1d. }

Compared with these figures Nottingham teachers were paid relatively well, especially at Canal Street where the master was paid £105 and the mistress £65 – the highest salary for a mistress in the Midland area.[2] The pay in Nottingham schools at about 1840 is recorded below.

Boys' National   £80 and house
St Mary's Girls'   £47 no house
School of Industry   Mistress – £35
                        Sewing mistress – £18
Lancasterian Boys'   £90 – reduced to £80
Girls' British   Fluctuating £20–£40
Radford National   Master – £60
St Paul's Infant   £30
Canaan St Infant   £13 plus 2d. per child per week

Apparently the mistress at Canal Street was paid on a commission basis at £25 plus fees, amounting to £60 in all.

In the later years of the period of voluntary provision, from 1840 to 1870, important improvements were made in the status and conditions of work of the elementary school teacher. It was during this period that it first began to be realized by those concerned with educational administration that 'the efficiency of a school depends, unquestionably, more upon the efficiency of the teacher than upon any other circumstance',[3] and the foundations of a profession of elementary school teaching were laid.

The most important single step taken to improve the teacher's position was the institution, in 1846, of the pupil-teacher system,

[1] *Minutes of Committee of Privy Council on Education*, 1845, p. 240.
[2] *Ibid.* 1845, vol. II. These figures do not altogether tally with other evidence.
[3] Mann, *1851 Census*, p. xxxiii.

since this solved at a stroke the two problems of recruitment and basic training. The system received enthusiastic support from the Inspectors of the area. In 1851 the Rev. J. J. Blandford, inspector of National schools, wrote;[1]

If there is one part of the present measures in operation for the improvement of the labouring classes more satisfactory and full of hope than another, it is the system of apprenticeship by which a large body of teachers are now being trained . . . I think it would be difficult to find a body of young men and women who have given greater satisfaction, or whose conduct has been more exemplary.

A few years later he repeated his praise of the apprentices, and added some good words for the teachers who were responsible for them, while his Catholic colleague picked out the pupil-teachers at Nottingham for special mention.[2]

The system rapidly became general in Nottingham. By 1851, Trinity, St John's, Lenton and Hyson Green all had apprentices, and St Mary's and the Lancasterian school, by then reorganized as a 'British' school, followed in the next year or so. The first recorded pass by a Nottingham pupil in the Queen's Scholarship was by a Trinity boy in 1851, who went on to Derby Training College. The first collective pupil-teacher examination was held in the town in the same year. In 1861 four boys and three girls passed the Queen's Scholarship.

With the development of the pupil-teacher system went an increase in the number of certificated teachers. In 1855 there were certificated teachers at Trinity (2), St John's (2), Carrington, Hyson Green, Lenton and Sneinton. In 1869 the following schools certainly had certificated teachers. There are certain possibles which are ignored.

All Saints'	St Ann's (2)
Bath Street	Derby Road
New Radford (probably 2)	Old Radford
St John's	St Luke's
St Mark's	St Mary's
St Peter's	Sneinton (2)
St Saviour's	Trinity (at least 2)
Lenton (2)	

[1] *Minutes of Committee of Privy Council on Education*, 1851–2, vol. II, p. 291.
[2] *Ibid.* 1855–6, p. 614.

Not all qualified teachers were of the first calibre. The pupil-teacher system undoubtedly tended to produce teachers who were wedded to rule-of-thumb methods since there was virtually no opportunity for the apprentice to study education beyond the confines of the school within which he worked. In 1862 the Inspector of British Schools in the area observed:[1]

Ranging the schools I have inspected under the headings of 'good', 'fair' and 'indifferent', I find this year, as in former years, the second of these classes far the most numerous. Much of the instruction they exhibit is satisfactory; but it is marked by a constant tendency to fall into a groove.

Nevertheless, this represented a great advance on the situation of 1842. The appointment of a certificated teacher carried a virtual guarantee that a certain level of competence would be reached and no more is heard of the total unsuitability of teachers for their posts. The fact that teachers were certificated also gave them a sense of professional solidarity, and in the 1850s the beginnings of associations of teachers can be detected. The Nottingham and Nottinghamshire Church Schoolmasters' and Schoolmistresses' Association came into being some time before 1860 when it was holding regular meetings.[2] By 1869 the meetings were monthly and a manuscript magazine was compiled. The Association was clearly recognized as possessing some representative status by this date, when it negotiated successfully with the local Church authorities about the publication of the results of the annual inspection.[3]

Some definite progress was made towards raising the pay of teachers to a respectable level. By 1855 the average pay of certificated masters in the Midland area was £87 10s. and of certificated mistresses £57.[4] The number of teachers who were given a house also increased, and, so far as Church schools were concerned at any rate, it was the rule in Nottingham for schools to have one, and sometimes two, houses attached. At some time in the 1860s it became the custom for teachers to be paid a fixed sum plus a share of the government grant; there is no exact information about when this change occurred, but it seems reasonable to suppose that it followed the introduction of the Revised Code. Certainly, by 1870 it was so

---

[1] *Minutes of Committee of Privy Council on Education*, 1862, p. 99.
[2] *Nottingham Journal*, 27 April 1860.
[3] *Ibid.* 16 April 1869.
[4] *Minutes of Committee of Privy Council on Education*, 1855–6, pp. 430–1.

general as to be taken over by the School Board without question. The first pay scale of the School Board, issued in 1875, is interesting for two reasons. It illustrates the substantial rise in salary which had occurred since the 1850s, and also the big differences between the pay offered in urban and rural schools. The Nottingham Board paid its masters £110 with one third of the gross government grant; mistresses received £75 and one quarter of the grant. By contrast the village of Ruddington, four miles from Nottingham offered its master £70 and one twentieth of the grant. One other interesting feature of the Board's scale was that it allowed for increments so that a master's pay could rise to £130; this appears to have been an innovation.

It will be noticed that no mention has been made of the pay of assistant teachers. This is because they were virtually unheard of in this period. In 1861 there were 416 certificated teachers in the Midland region and only 11 qualified assistants. In Nottingham there is a possibility that Trinity School, considered a show school – the head was a member of the first School Board, an unusual honour for a teacher – may have had two assistants in 1869, but the authority, a local directory, is dubious. No other cases occurred before 1870.

In 1842, Joseph Aldridge, master of the Nottingham National School, summed up the attainments of his pupils by saying that the majority of boys who left his school could read the New Testament, but not the Old, and write on slates.[1] This agrees very well with the evidence of other witnesses before the Employment Commission and also of the Inspectors, although it should be added that a pupil who stayed for any length of time would probably gain some rudimentary knowledge of arithmetic – then generally referred to as accounts. Girls were nearly all taught sewing and knitting, and Religious Education was so much a matter of course that it never figured on the lists of subjects which the schools claimed to teach. Most schools had a senior group of pupils who had stayed longer than the rest, and an attempt was made to teach them extra subjects, of which grammar, geography and history were the most usual.

The one universal subject, apart from Religious Education, was reading, which was taught in an inefficient and mechanical manner,

[1] *Children's Employment Commission*, 1842, 2nd Report, Witness No. 319.

leading to dreary, unintelligent results. The Inspector of National schools remarked in 1846:[1]

Considering that 'teaching to read' is the principal occupation of our National schools, that it is a drudgery begun with the first opening of the intelligence of the child, and continued without intermission until the last day it passes in the school, it is to me very wonderful that so inadequate a result is obtained.

He went on to estimate that half of the pupils left school unable to read.

It was the Inspectors' custom, in preparing results, to divide readers under four classes. The first class read 'letters and monosyllables'; the second 'simple narrative'; the third read 'in the Bible', and the fourth class read 'books of general information'. Thus only the fourth class could be said to be fully competent, and the results of the elementary schools fully bore out the gloomy assessment of the Inspectors. In 1847, of 12,786 children in inspected National schools in the Midlands, 2,891 could read 'in the Bible', and 651 could read 'books of general information'. The Nottingham schools did not even reach this standard.[2]

TABLE 10. *Reading standards in Nottingham schools, 1847*

School	Present at examination	Letters and monosyllable	Easy narrative	Holy scripture with ease	Books of general information
Arnold girls'	65	23	9	2	—
Basford boys'	70	28	27	17	—
Basford girls'	86	21	37	28	—
Carrington boys'	72	16	16	26	14
Lenton boys'	113	22	65	17	9
Lenton girls'	62	19	34	8	1
St Mary's (Nottingham) boys'	88	17	32	19	—
St Mary's (Nottingham) girls'	129	41	72	12	—
St Mary's (Nottingham) infants'	182	160	24	8	—
Radford boys'	67	26	33	11	—
Radford girls'	38	14	14	10	—
Sneinton mixed	137	81	41	7	—
	1,109	468	404	165	24

[1] *Minutes of Committee of Privy Council on Education*, 1846, vol. I, p. 162.
[2] *Ibid.* 1847–8, vol. II, Report of the Rev. J. J. Blandford.

In other words, of 1,109 children only 24 were fully literate, and more than half of these were from the Carrington school, which was noted at this period for its efficiency.

It is possible to gain a more detailed picture of the progress made by the children in reading by examining the type of reading book used in the schools. An example of an early reading book of this period, has survived, which was compiled by a schoolmaster from Wilford, just across the river from Nottingham.[1] It must have been popular, since it reached its nineteenth edition in 1816, and it well illustrates the meticulous subdivision of material and the procession from simple to complex, which was so typical of the monitorial system. It also casts some light on the meaning of 'simple narrative', as used by the Inspectors. The children began by learning the alphabet, assisted by small woodcuts to illustrate each letter – A for ant, B for bell and so on. From the alphabet children graduated to monosyllables, reading long lists of two letter sounds;

ab	eb	ib	ob	ub	
ac	ec	ic	oc	uc	
ba	be	bi	bo	bu	by
ra	re	ri	ro	ru	ry.

Syllables of three letters followed;

act	asp	box	cur	dog	fin
ark	bob	cry	doe	fur	gut.

Then the pupil reached the stage of reading simple narrative. Astonishing ingenuity was shown by the author in producing paragraphs, consisting entirely of monosyllables, which made sense of a kind, and which often were designed to convey a moral message;

A net may rot if you let it lie in the wet, and do not set or put it by in the air to dry. Do not cry, but dry up the eye if one is nigh. Hit not the eye or toe of him who is thy foe.

Good boys will not play with bad lads for fear they be led to be as bad as they; for good boys may soon be made bad lads, by play-ing with such as are bad boys.

> Don't hurt a bird, or duck, or frog,
> Or lamb, or cock, or cat, or dog;
> But be you kind and shew your love
> To all, and you will gain much love
> From men, and from the God above.

[1] Local History section, Nottinghamshire County Library.

If the results obtained in reading were disappointing, those for writing were far worse. The majority of boys, and considerably fewer girls, learned to write on slates, and many progressed as far as writing on paper, but the ability to write, in almost all cases extended only as far as copying; composition was virtually unknown.

The results of the 1847 inspection of Nottingham schools illustrates the situation (Table 11).[1] It will be seen that no single child attempted composition on paper, and that there was a significant difference between the attainment of boys and girls. In all the boys' schools but one all boys were writing in one way or another, but only 141 out of 380 girls were doing so.

Even in the 1840s writing was not always considered to be an essential subject, and in Dissenting schools it was customary to charge extra fees for children who wrote on paper. At the Lancasterian school the fees were 1d. per week, or 1½d. if writing was taken, while at Canal Street 1½d. and 2d. was charged.[2] The fees at Lenton National School were also graduated from 1d. to 3d. per week, but it is not known whether the range of fees was related to the subjects studied; sometimes the fee was increased with the age of the pupil.

TABLE II

| School | Present | Writing on slates | | | On paper | |
		Copies	Dictation	Composition	Copy	Composition
Arnold girls'	65	2	3	—	9	—
Basford boys'	70	8	3	—	11	—
Basford girls'	86	14	—	—	15	—
Carrington boys'	72	14	24	—	54	—
Lenton boys'	113	35	26	4	56	—
Lenton girls'	62	24	8	—	19	—
St Mary's boys'	88	33	9	—	14	—
St Mary's girls'	129	7	4	—	6	—
St Mary's infants'	182	23	—	—	—	—
Radford boys'	67	44	22	—	23	—
Radford girls'	38	14	6	—	10	—
Sneinton mixed	137	64	—	—	8	—

[1] *Minutes of Committee of Privy Council on Education*, 1847, vol. 1. Report of the Rev. J. J. Blandford.
[2] Glover, *History and Directory of the Town of Nottingham*, 1844, p. 102.

Most of the better schools at least attempted to teach their older pupils something beyond the three 'R's. At Nottingham National School there was a senior group of about 30 boys, in 1846, who were studying geography and grammar, and who had taken their arithmetic beyond the rudiments. The position was very similar at Lenton, where history was added, and at Carrington. At Arnold, on the other hand, nothing beyond the three 'Rs' was attempted. The value of this extra work was dubious. The children were totally lacking in any sort of background into which to fit the information with which they were presented, and it is very doubtful how far they achieved any real understanding of the subjects they nominally studied. The capacity of the teachers to proceed beyond the three 'Rs' was also suspect and the textbooks, where they existed, were nearly if not wholly useless.

Thus the standard reached in elementary schools was abysmally low; little was done above the three 'Rs', and what little advanced work was done was of very doubtful value. Many of the pupils, perhaps most of them, left school without even an efficient knowledge of the rudiments. The progress made before the days of the School Board in raising the standard of work was not impressive. Considering the definite improvement in the quality of teaching, this is rather disappointing, but it must be remembered that it was only in the 1860s, perhaps as one of the more happy effects of 'payment by results' that much headway was made in increasing school life and regularity of attendance. It is probable that there was, in fact, some improvement in the level of work in the rudiments. This is hard to tell because expected standards tended to rise inconspicuously so that work which was roundly condemned in 1870 might have been thought very acceptable thirty years before. The fact remains, however, that throughout the period the work of the schools was overwhelmingly in the three 'Rs', and that, as late as 1870, the amount of work done in additional subjects was negligible.

In 1854 the Inspector for the area produced some figures which showed how few children did any work outside the three 'Rs' (Table 12).[1] His report also suggests the miserably low standards that were reached. 2·14 per cent of the pupils had progressed in their arithmetic as far as fractions and decimals, and only 4·3 per cent were working in proportion and practice. 60 per cent of the children

[1] *Minutes of Committee of Privy Council on Education*, 1854–5, p. 497.

TABLE 12. *Percentage of children on registers of National schools learning different subjects*

Geography	54·97
Grammar	28·0
Sewing	18·87
History	10·52
Drawing	0·93
Mensuration	0·21
Algebra	0·18
Geometry	0·03

were in the first four rules, and 11 per cent were doing no arithmetic at all.

There were very great differences between the level of attainment in different schools, both as regards the basic work and the extra subjects. On the whole boys' schools did better than girls', but there were substantial variations over and above the sex difference, due to more efficient teaching, or greater resources. A few examples will illustrate the situation (Tables 13, 14 and 15).[1]

In 1873 the local Inspector, Mr Capel Sewell wrote a letter to the chairman of the School Board, which gives some information about

TABLE 13. *Trinity boys' school, 1854*

Present 216		
Reading	Letters and monosyllables	75 boys
	Easy narrative	77
	General information	40
Writing	On slates from copy	88
	On paper	103
Arithmetic	Four rules and below	120
	Proportion and practice	7
	Fractions and decimals	0
	Algebra, geometry, etc.	0
Extra subjects	Geography and grammar	141
	History	87
	Vocal music	141
	Linear drawing	73

This was considered to be a good school and had an unusually large number of children doing advanced work. The master was Mr Thurlow who acquired a local reputation for efficiency.

[1] *Minutes of Committee of Privy Council on Education*, 1848–9, Report of the Rev. J. J. Blandford.

TABLE 14. *Lenton boys' school, 1854*

Present 135		
Reading	Letters and monosyllables	28 boys
	Easy narrative	52
	General information	10
Writing	On slates from copy	38
	On paper	73
Arithmetic	Four rules and below	52
	Fractions and decimals	13
Extra subjects	Geography	83
	Grammar	59
	History	27

This may be taken as an example of a school which was run efficiently and secured good, if not enthusiastic, reports. With Trinity it was among the earliest to introduce pupil-teachers.

the condition of the elementary schools at the time when the School Board took over.[1] He made it clear that no dramatic change had occurred in the previous twenty years. Even in the three 'Rs' the pass rate at the annual examination was only 54 per cent for boys' schools and 50 per cent for girls' schools, although this rate was much exceeded in the best schools. To make the report even more depressing he pointed out that only 15 per cent of the children who were examined sat for the standard corresponding to their age. Fifty-seven per cent were one year too old, 26 per cent two years too old, and 9 per cent three years too old.

TABLE 15. *Hyson Green boys' school, 1854*

Present 55		
Reading	Letters and monosyllables	25 boys
	Easy narrative	14
	General information	0
Writing	On slates from copy	7
	On paper (15 were not writing)	27
Arithmetic	Four rules and below	12
	No advanced work	
Extra subjects	History	15

This was a poor school which earned a series of bad reports at this time. It will be seen that the curriculum was in effect confined to reading and writing.

[1] D. Wardle, 'The Work of the Nottingham School Board', M.Ed. Nottingham, 1961, pp. 56 ff.

If the achievements of the children in the three 'Rs' were un-impressive, the results of teaching in more advanced work were more depressing still (Table 16).

TABLE 16

In Boys' departments		
8 departments presented	137 in geography	82 passed
4 departments presented	60 in history	41 passed
3 departments presented	50 in grammar	27 passed
5 departments presented	136 in literature	126 passed
1 department presented	67 in physiology	35 passed
In Girls' departments		
3 departments presented	28 in geography	15 passed
3 departments presented	44 in history	39 passed
3 departments presented	28 in grammar	11 passed
3 departments presented	49 in literature	45 passed
1 department presented	11 in domestic economy	9 passed

There were, in 1873, about 10,000 children attending school in Nottingham and it cannot be said that this state of affairs represents a very serious attempt at advanced education. Of course it need not be supposed that every child who studied history or geography sat the examination as a specific subject, but there is little evidence of any considerable advance in this direction since the 1850s. It is, indeed, possible that the introduction of 'payment by results' caused a contraction of advanced work after 1862, but the evidence does not permit of any definite statement on this head.

A feature of the work of the elementary schools which has not attracted much attention was the amount of work done for the children out of school hours. This work was limited, of course, by the chronic shortage of funds experienced by all schools, but enough was done to make it apparent that teachers did not restrict their efforts to the classroom.

It was the universal custom to hold an annual treat at each school. These varied in character. In 1846 the boys of the Lancasterian School went to a circus, but the usual treat was a mass picnic, the Forest or the riverside being favourite venues. The school generally marched in procession to the site accompanied by friends and rela-tions, and often cheered on by one of the school bands of which there were at least two or three. Old Radford National School had a drum and fife band which played at the annual festival of the Bluecoat and St Peter's schools in 1855, when about 400 children marched to the scene 'with the usual profusion of artificial lace banners, garlands and devices in coloured eggs and flowers, characteristic of the Bluecoat processions'.[1]

The treat was occasionally combined with a public examination of the school to which the public was invited in the hope of raising subscriptions. Thus, in June 1855 the British School, Bath Street, 'was gaily decorated with suspended garlands formed of lilac and laburnum which diffused a most refreshing odour', while the scholars were examined 'upon various topics, history, geography, natural productions, mineralogy, vegetable products indigenous to the Southern and Northern latitudes etc'. The children were then fed with tea and plum cake – the staple diet at these functions.

These celebrations had various motives beyond the simple one of giving the children a treat. The advertisement given to the school's activities helped to raise funds, while the hope of qualifying for the treat encouraged children to attend regularly. A small sum was always set aside for prizes which also encouraged attendance. One girl who gave evidence before the Employment Commission of 1862 remembered that she 'got a many little pictures and once a doll for being a good girl and minding her lessons'.[2]

Throughout the period an increasing number of schools established libraries. In 1835 only the National School had one for certain, but they became more common, and in 1859 the local Inspector particularly noticed that the number of libraries was on the increase. One of the most valuable aspects of the work of the Sunday schools was the provision of libraries. In 1835 there were twelve Sunday schools in Nottingham and others in the suburbs with libraries, and the Union gave assistance to schools which wished to equip themselves in this way. No doubt the selection of books was carefully censored, but these libraries represented virtually the only invitation to children to read anything at all. Since all day school pupils also attended Sunday schools, it is likely that a fair number of them benefited by these efforts, especially since they would tend to be the best readers in their Sunday schools.

[1] *Nottingham Review*, 10 August 1855.
[2] *Children's Employment Commission*, 1862, 1st Report, p. 269.

Various schools had their own particular methods of providing their scholars with amusement or assistance, often no doubt, with the additional motive of encouraging regular attendance. Evening schools were fairly common, and often had a social side to them. Two or three schools also had clothing clubs. The schools which interested themselves particularly in these extra-curricular activities were, as might be expected, the ragged schools, which deserve separate treatment.

The foundation of ragged schools followed the discovery that the ordinary elementary schools were not drawing their pupils from the lowest strata of the population. The report of the 1842 Children's Employment Commission made particular mention of this and recommended that there should be an extension of the ragged school system. In Nottingham, the suggestion was taken up with some enthusiasm for within a few years, Anglicans, Dissenters, and Catholics all established institutions of this type.

The Church of England ragged school was established about 1847, and shortly afterwards moved into new buildings complete with a teacher's residence, on Glasshouse Street, a strategic position in one of the poorest areas of the town, very near the workhouse. At first the institution was a Sunday school, but the organizers wished to extend its sphere of usefulness, and in 1852 a day school was added.

As was to be expected, the welfare work of the school received much emphasis. In 1855 the annual report noted that anonymous donors were paying for meals for the day school twice a week, and also for the evening school. Upwards of 200 children were benefiting from this and the committee were planning to feed the children every day. The food was apparently appreciated, and the Mayor, who was Chairman of the annual meeting, quoted the remark of a parent to the teacher:[1]

You sent home my girls last night because they was so little. They had scarcely anything to eat all day, and they were talking of the bread and butter and coffee they should have in the evening, but they came home without and I had nothing to give them, so they went supperless to bed.

This pathetic little anecdote reveals the desperate poverty against which the founders of the school were struggling, and the value of

[1] *Nottingham Review*, 23 February 1855.

the assistance that such institutions were able to give. The little girls, longing for the bread and butter and coffee, are a reminder of the grim existence of the poor, even at a time when, nationally and locally, trade was good, and there was relatively little discontent.

The activities of the ragged school were by no means confined to day and Sunday schools. Several evening classes were held, intended mainly for boys and girls too old to be included in the ordinary schools. The ages given in the annual report for 1855 were 10 to 18 years for boys, and 10 to 24 years for girls, but there is no saying how many pupils attended for any length of time. The school did, however, make very determined efforts to keep in touch with its old scholars, and to encourage them to walk in the right path after they left the school. In 1860 thirty old pupils who had held a job creditably for twelve months attended a ceremony to be presented with 'beautifully embossed cards of merit',[1] and old pupils also were invited to the annual treat, which was regularly attended by 400–500 children.[2] The most ambitious scheme for the benefit of the old pupils was the 'Female Home and Industrial Institution' which was established ten years after the original foundation of the school. The committee were aware that the most difficult moral problems relating to those who left their school applied to girls, and so they proposed, in 1855, to establish an industrial school for

young females, who having spent years in their schools, and being without qualifications for domestic service, find it impossible to obtain suitable situations, and are, in consequence, exposed to the most serious temptations to an evil mode of life, an exposure to which more than one or two have already fallen victim.[3]

The funds necessary for opening the institution were soon raised, and thirty girls were accepted. There are no contemporary records of the nature of the work, but at the beginning of the twentieth century the inmates, whose number had by then risen to forty, took a three-year course in domestic subjects with the accent on the duties of a maid.[4] The institution had some financial difficulties in its first ten years, which is not surprising since it cost £450 per year to run, being, therefore, one of the most expensive educational charities in the town. In 1865 there was a debt of £250, but a bazaar

[1] *Nottingham Review*, 10 February 1860.
[2] *Ibid.* 17 August 1860.
[3] *Ibid.* 18 May 1855.
[4] R. Mellors, *Men of Nottingham and Notts*, Nottingham, 2nd ed. 1924, p. 15.

raised £209, and the cost of the building had been paid off, so that the institution succeeded in reaching a more secure position.[1]

The Dissenting Ragged school, known as the 'Town Mission' was in the field earlier than its Anglican opposite number, and opened in 1839. It does not seem to have run a day school, however, before 1859, when it moved into new buildings on Colwick Street,[2] near Sneinton Market. Until that time it contented itself with Sunday and evening schools. The Catholics ran their school on George Street as a ragged school, the teaching being carried out by nuns, but it is not known when the school was opened for this purpose.[3]

A particular feature of the work of the ragged schools was their attempt to use the school as a social centre through which to influence the parents and families of the pupils. No details have survived of the work of the Catholic School, but both the Town Mission and the Nottingham Ragged School had mothers' meetings and working mens' associations, beside adult evening and Sunday classes, libraries and penny banks. The mothers' meetings were largely concerned with the manufacture of cheap clothing which was sold to the members at below cost price, but there was also a social side. At the Ragged School there was a weekly 'concert and improving talk', accompanied by the inevitable tea and plum cake. The records of the Penny Bank run by the Town Mission reveal the poverty of the congregation and the difficulty which the lowest classes experienced in saving. 460 members deposited £210 12s. 5d. in a year, but they withdrew £218 11s. 8d., and the balance at the end of the year was only £40 5s. 9d.[4]

The workhouse was a massive building in York Street, and it always had a large number of children in residence; in 1844, according to Glover's Directory, there were 256, and there were 124 in 1871. It was Glover's opinion that the workhouse children were better treated than the children of the poor who lived outside 'their clean and healthy appearance is the admiration of all who contribute to their support; indeed they enjoy superior advantages to the generality of the children of the poor out of the house, for they have plenty of wholesome food, warm clothing, are comfortably lodged,

---

[1] *Nottingham Review*, 3 February, 1865.

[2] *White's Directory*, 1864, p. 145; *Nottingham Review*, 31 March 1865.

[3] The ragged school is mentioned by Wylie, *Old and New Nottingham*, Longman, 1855, p. 144.

[4] *Nottingham Review*, 31 March 1865.

and well disciplined'.[1] Glover, who invariably included more detail than any other contemporary writer on Nottingham, made a note of the prescribed dietary, and it will be seen that, if the food was unbalanced by the standards of a modern dietician, there was no prospect of starvation.

Breakfast and supper. Each man 7, and each woman 6 ounces of bread, and 1½ pints of milk porridge thickened with fine flour, morning and night.

Dinners. Sunday, Thursday. Men 7 and women 6 ounces of beef and unlimited potatoes.

Tuesday. Pudding of suet and fine flour. Men 16, women 14 ounces.

Wednesday, Saturday. Broth, in which carrots and other vegetables are boiled – an unlimited quantity, and bread, men 7 ounces, women 6 ounces.

Monday. Irish stew – unlimited.

Friday. Pea soup – unlimited but no bread.

Some special allowances were made for the sick and aged, but it seems that children ate on the same scale as adults.[2]

In his report for 1850 the government inspector of workhouse schools observed[3] that the results achieved in the three R's in these schools were better than those from ordinary National schools. In the more advanced subjects, on the other hand, the reverse was the case. This suggested that, while the workhouse teachers were generally less knowledgeable than those in National schools, the regular attendance and strict discipline of workhouse schools made them more efficient in a limited field.

A serious problem that applied to every workhouse school, was that the children were kept segregated in the school, had very little contact with the outside world, and were inadequately prepared for life on leaving the house. Industrial training was apparently difficult to organize, as the certified industrial schools found a little later, and it was generally entirely ignored. Where it was attempted, and Nottingham and Bedford workhouses were mentioned as examples of institutions where most was done in this line, it generally concentrated excessively on one or two trades. At Nottingham, for example, 40 boys learned shoemaking and tailoring, and although

---

[1] Glover, *The History and Directory of the Town of Nottingham*, Nottingham, 1844, pp. 64–5.

[2] It may be of interest to compare this dietary with that offered 40 years later by the Day Industrial School. See chapter 5, p. 113.

[3] *Minutes of Committee of Privy Council*, 1848–50, pp. 77 ff.

the Inspector commended the guardians for their efforts to organize training, he was not very happy about the result.

Though, however, this kind of industrial training is undoubtedly better than none, it does not appear to me calculated to be our sole, or even our principal resource. Firstly on account of the danger of over-stocking the market with shoemakers and tailors; and secondly because those trades being of a sedentary character and carried out in a close, confined atmosphere, cannot be conducive to the health and vigour of a class of children usually suffering from the effects of hereditary poverty, and shut up every day for several hours in an ill-ventilated schoolroom.

The problem of finding suitable industrial training was never solved. In 1862 Nottingham workhouse still gave instruction only in shoemaking and tailoring, but was still unusual in that it did anything in this line at all. Apart from four boys at Basford who were engaged in tailoring, none of the 103 boys at Basford and Radford workhouses had any form of training,[1] and the Inspector took the view that this system was incapable of further development.

The training of girls presented fewer problems: 'as the making and mending of the clothing and linen of the house afford them a constant and appropriate occupation. They are always employed for two hours of the afternoon in sewing and knitting, and become, in some places, accomplished needlewomen'.[2] Other domestic work was also done by the girls, so that the workhouse was performing, to some extent, one of the educational functions most emphasized by writers of the day, that of preparing girls for service and housekeeping. The chief difficulty with the girls, apparently, was to keep them apart from the female adult paupers who were looked upon by masters and matrons as containing the worst moral elements in the house.[3] The Inspector observed approvingly about the Nottingham institution that, 'the workhouse, admits of the complete separation of the children from the adult paupers'. In no part of the description of the workhouse is there any mention of the possibility of family life for the paupers; rigid separation of sexes and ages was insisted upon. Although it was probably true, as the Inspector asserted, that a high proportion of the children in the workhouses were orphans or deserted, there were, no doubt, a number to whom life in the house meant compulsory separation from their parents and families.

[1] *Minutes of Committee of Privy Council on Education*, 1848–50, p. 124.
[2] *Ibid.* p. 83.   [3] *Ibid.* p. 83.

5

ELEMENTARY EDUCATION UNDER
THE SCHOOL BOARD

The first Nottingham School Board was elected on 29 November 1870, and the event was of some importance since it marked the appearance of the first local authority with any specific responsibility for education. The original intention of the framers of the 1870 Education Act was that school boards should fill in the gaps left by the voluntary system, and in its early years this was precisely what the Nottingham School Board aimed to do. As time passed, however, the Nottingham Board, along with the boards of other large towns, found itself, more by force of circumstances than from any clearly formulated policy, taking an increasingly ambitious view of its responsibilities. By 1903 it was operating as a local education authority, with interests in secondary technical and adult education as well as in elementary education, which was its legitimate field of activity. The work of the Board in secondary and further education is treated separately; in this chapter attention is concentrated upon the ordinary elementary schools.

The School Board originally had 13 members, increased to 15 in 1877 when a number of suburbs were added to the town. These suburbs had their own school boards until that date. 97 people sat on the Board, in all, and it was always dominated by the business and professional classes, with clergymen in a great majority; no less than 28 of the members were in orders. There was usually a member of the working class on the Board, but rarely more than one, and it was only in the 1880s that working men were elected without the support of one or other of the main parties. Women were eligible for election, and six sat on the Board, the first, Mrs Cowan, being elected in 1883. The only local person with a national reputation in the educational field was Dr J. B. Paton, principal of the Congregational College, and father of a high master of Manchester Grammar School. He never stood for election to the Board, but exercised much influence, especially in adult education.

The violence of political controversy fluctuated during the School Board era, and four well marked periods can be distinguished. Until about 1875 party strife was intense and elections to the Board were fiercely contested, but this was followed by a quiet period, when at least one election was settled by a compromise, and others aroused little enthusiasm. In 1889 there was a revival of the 'Voluntary' party accompanied by an intensification of party and sectarian strife, until 1895, when the Liberals were returned to power. After this peace reigned until 1903, with another uncontested election in 1898.

The two main parties were those which respectively favoured and opposed the voluntary schools. Party labels varied from time to time, but it will be convenient to refer to them as 'Denominational' and 'Liberal' parties. The term 'Liberal' should not be taken to imply any necessary connection with the Parliamentary party, and the name was not generally adopted until 1886.

Two other groups elected representatives to the Board, the Roman Catholics, and the 'working men'. The Catholics never attempted to secure more than one seat, and could usually be sure of success in this limited objective, since all Catholics were urged to 'plump' for their candidate, which meant giving him all their votes rather than distributing them among several candidates.[1] The Catholic member was usually regarded as an ally of the Denominational party, and it was by establishing an arrangement between the Catholic and Church of England groups that the Denominational party was able to win the elections of 1889 and 1902.

In the early years of the Board the Liberals usually ran one or more 'working man' candidates, but it was not expected that they would show much originality or independence, and there is no evidence that the Liberal policy was influenced by the alliance. The Liberal view was very fairly put in 1870 by the Rev. Francis Morse, who was, in fact, a moderate Denominational:[2] 'moreover they thought that the working men, being parents of children who would attend Board Schools, might have a knowledge of the wants of their important class, and could give good information to the Board'. There was no sign at this period of a working-class movement with a distinct policy of its own. In 1889, however, John Peacock, who had

---

[1] A voter in a School Board election was allowed as many votes as there were seats. He could give these votes for one candidate, or distribute them in any proportion he wished.

[2] *Nottingham Journal*, 16 November 1870.

previously sat as a Liberal, tried for election as a 'socialist', and from this date various independent working-class candidates came forward under different titles. The first member of the Board to be definitely affiliated to the Independent Labour Party was Thomas Moore, who was elected in 1895, but even he stood as 'independent'. In the compromise election of 1898 a seat was put aside for the Independent Labour Party, which was expressly named for the first time, and it was taken by George Christie, who held the seat until the dissolution of the Board.

Although the intensity of political and sectarian controversy fluctuated, it never reached, in Nottingham, the pitch typical of some other large towns. Both the main parties took a moderate line, and extremists on either flank exerted little influence. The Liberals lacked the secularizing zeal which was found elsewhere. An Anglican clergyman remarked at an election meeting in 1883 that:[1] 'he was glad that secularism in its worst phase had not been connected with the Nottingham School Board, and that the people of the town had reason to thank God that the educational scheme of this town was not like that of Huddersfield or other towns'. On the other hand the Denominational party took an equally moderate line. In London and elsewhere the high Anglican party showed itself opposed on principle to the existence of school boards, but this fundamental opposition did not appear in Nottingham. The two parties seemed to find no difficulty in cooperating once the excitement of the elections was over. For example, the scheme of Religious Education drawn up by the first Board, with a Denominational majority, was accepted without dispute, and the practice was adopted of having the religious work of the schools inspected in alternate years by Anglican and Dissenting clergymen.

It is a little difficult to find an altogether satisfactory reason why controversy in Nottingham should be relatively mild. No doubt it was largely a matter of personalities. On the Dissenting side Dr Paton exercised a powerful and moderating influence, which was matched by that of Canon Morse, vicar of Nottingham, among the Churchmen. These two men worked well together and nearly avoided the necessity of an election in 1870. Nottingham may also have been fortunate in that none of the members of the Board were engaged at national level in the religious question which so bedevilled education at this time. There is evidence to suggest that this

[1] *Nottingham Journal*, 23 November 1883.

was largely a politician's controversy[1] which did not greatly worry the parent or teacher so long as it was not stirred up artificially. Certainly there is a significant difference between the experience of Nottingham and that of Birmingham, where the dispute was kept at boiling point by eminent controversialists like Joseph Chamberlain, George Dixon and the Rev. E. F. M. McCarthy.

In the first election corruption and intimidation, although widespread, were more or less casual in nature, and there were no signs of large-scale management. The party alignment was not yet clear cut and no party was fully organized. In later elections, however, there was no lack of management, some of it within at least the letter of the law, some of it plainly fraudulent. The Liberal success of 1873 was gained as a result of a number of highly suspicious circumstances including the nomination of two fictitious candidates bearing the same name as prominent members of the Denominational party. The intention was that the vote for these members would be split with the imaginary candidates, since few of the voters would know which name on the polling sheet was the genuine one. It is not certain that the Liberal candidates were officially aware of these machinations, but they worked very much in their favour. In the 1880s both parties became aware that by issuing detailed voting instructions to their supporters it was possible to increase their representation. There was a strong tendency for one or two very popular candidates to gain far more votes than was necessary for election, and the aim was to instruct a proportion of these men's supporters to transfer their votes to less popular candidates. By this means, and by restricting the number of candidates to the minimum number necessary for a majority, it was possible to gain control of the Board on a minority vote. For some reason the Denominationalists were much more successful than the Liberals in party management, and their success in the elections of 1889 and 1892 was at least partly due to the confusing instructions issued by their rivals, which led many puzzled voters to spoil their cards.

The Denominationalists were also much assisted in their campaigning by the cost of the Board's operations. The extensive building of the 1880s forced up the education rate, and the Denominationalists were able to establish themselves as the party of economy,

[1] See R. D. Roberts (ed.), *Education in the Nineteenth Century*, Cambridge, 1901, pp. 54–5; and H. B. Philpott, *London at School*, Fisher Unwin, 1904, p. 102.

with such success that, in 1886, the Liberals were forced to issue a lengthy apologia for the expense of the Board. In the long run the Denominational criticism rebounded, since it was their failure, when in office, to keep down the rate that lost them the election of 1895. From the 1880s onwards the Liberals also suffered from the growing strength of independent working-class political interests, which drew votes from their left wing. Their failure in 1892 was certainly attributed to this cause.[1]

The first duty of the Board was to ascertain the extent of its responsibilities, and to this end it appointed a statistical committee to examine the existing provision of schools and the need for further building. Using the census returns the committee found that there were 17,988 children aged three to thirteen years in the town. One seventh of this number was deducted to allow for middle-class children who were not expected to attend Board schools, and a further 15 per cent for those unavoidably absent. This left 13,112 places to find. All schools, public or private, which charged less than 9d. per week were considered to be potentially sources of accommodation, and were inspected, doubtful cases being referred to Her Majesty's Inspectors. Of 105 schools inspected, 65 were considered efficient, and they provided places for 12,000 children at the current reckoning of 8 square feet per child. Three-quarters of the places were in Church of England schools, one-sixth in British schools and the remainder in Catholic schools.

The deficiency of 1,200 places could be reduced to 307 if certain slightly sub-standard schools were improved, and there was no urgency to build new accommodation, especially since most of the existing schools were only three-quarters filled. The Board did not, therefore, adopt an ambitious policy. Even the Liberal party, which was normally inclined to favour a more extensive provision of Board schools than the Denominationalists, adopted the view that their duty was merely to fill the gaps in voluntary provision. Up to 1877 only three Board schools were planned, and only two, Bath Street and Huntingdon Street were actually built.

After 1877 the Board had to revise its policy drastically. The Borough Extension Act of that year nearly doubled the population of the town, and several of the newly acquired areas were seriously deficient in schools. Furthermore, when the situation was examined it was discovered that the original statistical committee had left out

[1] *Nottingham Daily Express*, 26 November 1892.

of account an important factor. Between 1871 and 1881 the population of the town increased by some 10,000, when the additions of 1877 were left out of account, and this meant an increase of about 2,300 to the number of children requiring accommodation, so that, although two Board schools and some further voluntary accommodation had been added, the deficiency of accommodation was significantly greater than in 1871. A complicating factor was that some of the new areas which were being developed for housing were some distance from existing schools.

In December 1877 an enquiry showed that there were 19,421 school places in the enlarged borough, and that, after all deductions had been made, a deficiency of 4,600 places remained. The next fifteen years were occupied in almost continuous building, and it was only after 1892 that the building programme slowed down, when there were school places for every child on the school visitors' schedules. In the last ten years of the Board's life only two new schools, Sycamore Road and Mundella, were built and the second was specially planned as a higher grade school. Much enlargement and alteration of existing schools was carried out, however, partly because the Board favoured large schools, and partly because of the rapid developments in school design which took place at this period.

Some of the voluntary agencies continued to be very active. The British schools showed themselves willing to be taken over by the Board, and after 1892, when High Pavement was absorbed, there were no Dissenting schools left in Nottingham. The Anglican and Catholic interests, on the other hand, regarded the establishment of compulsory education as a challenge to further efforts and increased their accommodation accordingly. The maximum extent of voluntary provision was reached in 1882, when there were 19,721 places in Voluntary schools, compared with rather fewer than 10,000 in Board schools. Even in 1903 16,002 places were found in Voluntary schools, about one-third of the school accommodation of the borough.

When the School Board handed over to the Local Education Authority in 1903, there were 94 Board departments with places for 28,546 children, 64 Church of England departments with places for 13,079, and 14 Roman Catholic departments with 2,473 children; there were, therefore, about four times as many places as in 1870. In addition there were 39 special centres for cookery, laundry work, woodwork, practical science, gymnastics, swimming, pupil-teacher instruction, etc.

In spite of this huge increase in the number of school places, the Board was continually struggling against overcrowding. Eighteen departments were warned at the 1886 examination that further overcrowding would mean loss of grant, and one or two schools did, in fact, suffer a loss of grant for this reason. Overcrowding first became a serious problem in the 1880s and at first it chiefly affected infant schools. To some extent the Board made things difficult for itself by allowing, and even encouraging parents to send children to school when well under age. This was done with the best intentions, but it did mean that the work of the infant schools was made unnecessarily difficult. In addition, the 1880s were a time of serious industrial depression, and it has been observed previously that school attendance always took an upturn at such times.

After about 1887 the worst of the overcrowding began to move upwards to the senior schools, and this indicates one of the most interesting developments of the school board period, which was the tendency of an increasing number of children to remain after the minimum legal leaving age. This phenomenon is clearly related to the rising standards of work done in the schools which will receive separate attention, but one statistic will indicate the magnitude of the development. In 1870 about 12 per cent of all pupils in elementary schools in Nottingham were in Standard IV or above; in the 1890s the figure was rather over 40 per cent. There were, in later years of the Board about 1,600 children in the higher grade schools and a large number in ordinary elementary schools, who were above the minimum leaving age. This development, which was, of course, entirely unforeseen in 1870 and for some years afterwards, goes far to explain the overcrowded conditions of senior schools in the 1890s.

Bye-laws requiring attendance were introduced as soon as the Board took office. Children were to attend school between the ages of five and thirteen unless (a) they were ill; (b) they were educated efficiently elsewhere; (c) 'there is no public school open which the child can attend, within one mile, measured by the nearest road, from the residence of such child'. Children were to attend for 25 hours weekly, but a child of ten might attend half-time if he had passed Standard II and was 'beneficially employed'. A child of ten was totally exempt if he had passed Standard V.

In February 1872 two 'visitors' were appointed to enforce the bye-laws concerning attendance, and by October of the same year the magnitude of their task was seen to be so great that two more were added. The number steadily increased until by 1903 there were twelve under a superintendent. It is an interesting reflection of the importance attached to the visitors' work in the early days of the Board that their pay, at £100 per year was substantially better than that of an assistant teacher at £80–90. Evidently the Board took the view that its primary duty was to get the children into school; academic achievement was of less moment. Perhaps the best illustration of the success of the visitors' work is that by 1903 the emphasis had changed. The visitors' salary remained constant at £100, while an assistant teacher in the senior grade was paid £150 per year.

In March 1872 a house to house survey was made of two sample areas which illustrate the size and nature of the attendance problem inherited from the voluntary system. In all, some 4,000 children of school age were found. Half the children were in attendance at some public elementary school and there were 514 children who were not even on the books of a school. 1,232 children were found who were on the register of a school but who were not in attendance on the day of the survey. An interesting fact is that poverty was only given as the reason for absence in about twenty cases. Illness was frequently offered as an excuse, but it is very apparent that sheer indifference was the most common reason.

In order to enforce the bye-laws the town was divided into areas so that each visitor had between 3,000 and 4,000 children on his schedule. Warning notices were issued to the parents of absentees, who could appear before a sub-committee of the Board if they so wished. Recalcitrant parents were prosecuted, but, then as now, the bench showed little interest in enforcing attendence. The usual fine for a first conviction was 2s. 6d., which was quite inadequate in view of the earnings open to a truant. Since a child's income went into the parent's pocket it was well worth while for a parent to keep his children at work and risk the occasional fine, and it is quite clear that many did this. There were cases of parents being fined seventy or eighty times, and the Board several times found it necessary to prosecute firms for employing children who ought to have been at school. Small employers such as milkmen, shopkeepers and barbers were the worst offenders, and also the most difficult to deal with

4

since they did not come within the terms of different factory and workshop acts. It was possible for persistent truants to be sent to industrial schools,[1] but this was only done in extreme cases since it meant sending the child away from home. With the establishment of the day industrial school on George Street in 1886 it became rather easier to deal with persistent truants since there was a member of staff with the particular duty of following up absentees.

The Board did not rely solely upon negative means for enforcing attendance; it also instituted an elaborate system of rewards. A child who attended 400 times in a year, passed in the elementary subjects in his standard and gained a satisfactory conduct report was awarded a card embossed in bronze for the first year, silver for the second and gold for the third. A child who passed the same conditions in Standard IV received a parchment certificate and his name was displayed in the schoolroom. From 1881 onwards managers were allotted a sum of money to be spent on 'books and other useful articles' as prizes.

Attendance rose slowly in the early days of the Board; more slowly than the number of children on the registers, probably because the children who were driven into the schools by the visitors came from the families which were least interested in education. In 1873 the average was 68·7 per cent, and it rose to about 75 per cent, which was the average in the late 1870s. Eighty per cent was reached by 1885 and the rate continued to improve slowly until 90 per cent was achieved in the late 1890s. There were always great differences between schools; in May 1880 for instance, Bath Street returned 90·7 per cent while St Peter's and St Ann's could not reach 60 per cent. There was also a constant difference of about 5 per cent between Board and Voluntary schools, the Voluntary schools being apparently more tolerant in this respect.

The School Board was not at first able to make much progress in the direction of raising the standard of work done in elementary schools. The first 'Regulations for the Management of Board Schools', issued in March 1872, laid down a fairly comprehensive curriculum, but this was an ideal to be aimed at rather than a description of the existing situation. In practice the work in most schools was confined, as it had always been, to Religious Knowledge and the rudiments. Grant could be earned for 'specific subjects' which were subjects taken by more advanced pupils and examined separately,

---

[1] Industrial schools are discussed below, pp. 110 ff.

but in 1873, from an average attendance of 7,000 pupils only 610 were entered for examination in a specific subject, and 420 passed. Even this figure gives an unduly optimistic view of the state of affairs, since at two schools, People's College and High Pavement, pupils took more than one specific subject and so were counted twice in the returns.

By 1880 there had been some improvement but there was still far to go before the syllabus could be said to be anything but narrow. The schools were then fairly generally offering 'class subjects' which were subjects taken by whole classes of senior pupils. Two such 'class subjects' could be offered and 3,570 children earned grant for these, grammar, geography and English literature being the most usual. Another innovation of the 1870s was drawing under the regulations of the Science and Art Department, and in 1880 802 scholars were passed as 'satisfactorily taught'.

It appears, therefore, that the curriculum of at least the more adventurous elementary schools widened a little in the 1870s, and it is probably fair to give some of the credit for this to a slight liberalizing of the Code which allowed grant to be paid for subjects beyond the rudiments. But if the work was a little wider in scope, it showed few signs of improving in standard. The total number of passes in 'specific subjects' was still only 708, of which three-quarters were obtained by three schools. The insignificant amount of advanced work attempted is illustrated by the fact that from a gross grant of £5,244 4s. 9d., £141 6s. od. came from 'specific subjects'.

Commenting on the results in specific subjects, the report of the Schools Management Committee observed: 'The limited number of children who have been receiving advanced instruction in the above subjects does not indicate a very ambitious effort to realize secondary education in Nottingham Board schools'. Now this was an interesting comment. It appears to assume that the School Board had a duty to offer secondary education where a demand existed. At no time, either within the Board or in election campaigns, does any voice appear to have been raised to point out that secondary education was beyond the Board's powers, although this was clearly the case. Whatever interpretation was placed upon the 1870 Act it was evident that it referred to elementary education, but the Board was able to proceed with an ambitious policy of higher grade education, with, so far as can be ascertained, absolutely no local opposition, even during the economy campaigns of the late 1880s.

The efforts of the School Board in strictly secondary education are treated separately, but the same situation which led it to experiment with higher grade schools also led it to encourage ordinary schools both to widen the scope of their work and to raise its standard. A glance at the number of specific subjects passes will give an idea of the remarkable advance that was effected. From 420 in 1873 the number increased to 708 in 1880, 2,822 in 1887 and 7,821 in 1895. By the latter date the curriculum of the schools was more or less stabilized; few further developments occurred, partly because of the block put upon progress by the events centering round the Cockerton Judgment,[1] so this is a good point at which to survey the achievement of the Board schools. All girls in Standard IV and above received instruction in practical cookery and laundry work at fifteen cookery and four laundry centres, while boys in Standard V and above attended special centres for wood and metalwork. Forty-eight departments were examined by the Science and Art Department in drawing and all senior departments offered two class subjects. Substantial science and art grants were being earned by ordinary board schools, which were outside the higher grade system.[2] Every department earned the 'excellent' merit grant for its basic work, regularly throughout the 1890s.

Three of the School Board's schemes for broadening the curriculum deserve particular attention, and these are related to science, practical cookery, and wood and metalwork. The Board Inspector, W. J. Abel, who took a leading part in all these ventures, several times expressed his concern about the quality of science teaching, which was done by means of the object lesson. His conclusion was that the ignorance of the teacher was the main stumbling block. Various attempts were made to improve the quality of the object lessons, but in 1884 a new approach was tried when a demonstrator was appointed to tour certain schools, giving lessons with practical demonstrations, his apparatus being carried on a handcart. The

[1] A decision by an official auditor in 1899, which had the effect of preventing school boards from spending public money on projects which were not strictly elementary in nature. It was upheld in a subsequent appeal to the courts.

[2] The Science and Art Department offered grants on a 'payment by results' basis to teachers who entered pupils for examinations in scientific and technical subjects.

schoolteachers, who attended the lesson, followed it up with notes supplied by the demonstrator, and administered tests, the results of which were shown to the demonstrator on his next visit. The course for boys was directed at the specific subject of mechanics, 'which would be more correctly called elementary natural philosophy', while girls studied domestic economy, 'or so much of animal physiology and chemistry as is necessary to explain the facts and operations of home life'. After an experimental period in 16 schools the scheme was made general and eventually there were five demonstrators working from a headquarters at Clarendon Street, where a preparation room, laboratory and lecture theatre were provided. In each year's course there were 18 or 20 fortnightly demonstrations; a synopsis of some of the lectures given to the girls in the 1890–1 session is as follows:

(1) Meaning of the word 'matter': elements and compounds; the three states of matter: the three kingdoms of nature.

(2) General structure of the body.

(3) Composition and weight of the body; work done by and in the body; all work implies waste; how the waste of the body is repaired.

(16) Various kind of fuel; their origin and use; how coal gas is prepared.

(18) How to warm the house; grates and stoves; warming by hot air, hot water, etc.

Experiments with practical cookery lessons were initiated a few years before the science demonstrations began. Lessons in household management were not new, and domestic economy was recognized for grant as a specific subject, but these were class-room subjects. Practical cookery lessons began in January 1878 after a teacher had been sent to a short course at Leeds College of Domestic Science. The first kitchen was built in the Board room of Radford School. There is reason to suppose that the Sheffield School Board instituted practical cookery lessons a few months earlier than this,[1] but the Nottingham course attracted the attention of the Education Department, which asked the district H.M.I. for a report. He was enthusiastic and wrote a special letter to the chairman to the School Board on the subject:

[1] J. H. Bingham, *The Period of the Sheffield School Board*, Sheffield, 1949, p. 124.

I saw on Thursday and Friday last upwards of 100 girls engaged on the actual duties of the kitchen – scouring and cleaning, preparation and cooking of simple dishes. I directed my attention to the quickness and general handiness with which the utensils and materials were found and used and cleaned, or laid away when done with; to the girls' ability to tell me the reasons for the rules given them, not in scholastic phrase but in the idiom of the kitchen. I watched the results of the instruction diligently for two days, and as exhibited from four of the Board schools, and the general result of what I saw gave me the impression that an unusual branch of education was being conducted in an unusual, because unscholastic, manner, and with unusual success.

Until 1883 no grant could be earned by the girls who did practical cookery; they sat for domestic economy as a specific subject. It was, therefore, impossible to give the scheme as wide a scope as the Board would have liked, and in that year only five schools were covered, 151 girls passing the tests at the end of the course. The main criticism of the work at this period was that too many of the dishes prepared were expensive and likely to be beyond the budget of a working class family. One H.M.I. appears to have been speaking from bitter experience when he recommended that 'instruction should be given to the girls in the proper preparation of tea and coffee'. The code for 1883 allowed a grant of 4s. 'on account of any girl over 12 years of age who has attended not less than 40 hours at a cookery class and is presented for examination in the elementary subjects in any standard'. This led to a rapid development. By 1886 the number of passes had risen to 754, and extensions built in that year raised the accommodation of the classes to 2,000. There were then eleven kitchens of which three were centres to which children from other schools were sent. By 1889, after further building, all girls in Standard IV and above were covered by the scheme. In 1885 the Board issued a 'Penny Cookery Book' of recipes used at the centres, which sold well to schools and school boards up and down the country. The editor had taken the advice to concentrate on cheap dishes, and many recipes using no meat or cheaper cuts were included. There were also sections on invalid cookery, complete meals for four or six people and 'dinners suitable for carrying to places of work'.

In June 1900 the Board attempted an interesting experiment which proved to be altogether too bold for its time. It rented six cottages in New Basford to be used as a housecraft centre at which a number of children at a time could practise their work under natural conditions. This plan ran into intense criticism both inside and outside the Board, chiefly over the matter of expense, and was eventually shelved after several revisions. It is possible that the Board might have persisted at another time but the Cockerton Judgment and the impending take-over by the local Education Authority left the members disinclined to bold policies.

After the institution of cookery classes the Board was much exercised to find some equivalent practical activity for boys. In 1885 an arrangement was made by which certain boys were to attend woodwork and metalwork classes at University College. The selected boys had passed solid geometry under the Science and Art directory and attended for an afternoon per week at a cost of £2 per boy for the course. Unfortunately the Education Department refused to recognize the classes which prevented the Board from spending any public money on them. They were kept going on a small scale partly by the cooperation of the College which reduced the fees to 1s. 6d. per quarter and partly by private subscriptions to cover the fees of boys unable to pay, but there could be no question of a large-scale expansion. The Board drew up a memorial to the Department which received the support of the school boards of London, Norwich, Ipswich, Derby, Huddersfield, Gateshead, Birmingham, Bristol, Salford, and Swansea among others. It pointed out that the Department's attitude was inconsistent since it already encouraged practical work for girls and referred the Department 'to the opinion of the Royal Commissioners on Technical Education that such manual work is very beneficial as a part of the preliminary education of boys in the country who are subsequently to be engaged in industrial pursuits'.

Nevertheless it was not until 1891 that manual classes were recognized for grant, and the Board was only able to provide classes, out of private funds, for about 140 boys as opposed to the 2,000 odd girls who took practical cookery. Once the classes were recognized progress was rapid; by 1892 1,500 pupils were attending two centres, and 40 teachers were following City and Guilds classes. Ultimately there were four centres and seven instructors, who between them covered all boys of Standard V and over.

By modern standards the provision for science, cookery and practical work was exiguous. No practical work was done by the pupils in science, and there was only one demonstration every fortnight, confined to the senior grades. Cookery and manual work were done for half a day every fortnight, and most children had to travel some distance to the centres, which were ill-equipped and under-staffed. But these efforts have to be set against the situation which prevailed before the Board was established. Looked at in this light the widening of the curriculum was dramatic. By the end of the School Board period the skeleton at least of the modern curriculum was in operation.

In the School Board period important developments occurred in the training and status of teachers. Like other Boards, Nottingham soon discovered that the pupil-teacher system was not working efficiently. At the government inspection of 1881, for example, 20 pupil-teachers out of 81 failed to gain any grant at all, while only 14 gained the higher £3 grant for passing 'well'. The system was failing for two reasons. The pupil-teacher was employed more or less full time in teaching or assisting other teachers and he had no opportunity during school hours for the study required to pass the annual examination. He was, therefore, compelled to spend an excessive amount of his spare time in study, and was consequently liable to overstrain, while, on the other hand his lesson preparation was limited by academic preparation, with serious effects on his teaching efficiency. Furthermore a pupil-teacher received very little assistance with his studies. The Board regulations required teachers to spend six hours per week with their pupil-teachers outside school hours, but six hours per week is not a great deal, and even supposing that the regulations were strictly observed, the bulk of the student's work must have been unsupervised. Since a pupil-teacher began his apprenticeship at fourteen years it is hardly surprising that the results of four years virtually independent study were disappointing. The quality of assistance which pupil-teachers received varied from case to case. In the 1870s very few teachers had acquired any further qualification than the government certificate, and a high proportion of qualified teachers had received no college training. Very often the teacher must have had great difficulty in giving intelligent assistance to his apprentices.

The real answer to the problem lay in the extension of secondary education, but at that period there were no secondary schools turning out pupils who would be likely to take up their career in elementary schools. For the school boards, therefore, there was really no alternative to the pupil-teacher system, and the problem was to make it as efficient as possible. The method very generally adopted by the large boards was to establish a centre to which all pupil-teachers went for their academic work, the head teacher usually remaining responsible for the school management and practical training. At first pupil-teacher centres were evening schools, but as time passed, in Nottingham at any rate it increasingly approximated to a secondary school, even to the extent that pupils took the Oxford and Cambridge Local examination or London Matriculation as well as the Queen's Scholarship which gave admission to training colleges.

In October 1882 new regulations were introduced by the Board. Candidates[1] were to sit a qualifying examination after passing Standard VI. The subjects were reading, dictation, composition, grammar, geography, history and arithmetic, while extra marks could be earned for passes in one or two Science and Arts Directory subjects. Pupil-teachers attended the newly established centre at People's College for three nights per week, instruction being given by experienced teachers who were paid 3s. per hour, with substantial bonuses for success. Practical teaching was left to the head teachers, and the criticism lesson was introduced apparently against some opposition from the schools.

From this time onwards there was a progressive reduction in the amount of time spent by pupil-teachers in their schools, and a corresponding increase in the time spent at the centre, which received a full time instructor in 1885. Until 1895 the pupil-teachers attended the centre on a day release basis for the first two years of their engagement and then went on to evening classes, but in that year senior pupil-teachers were also put on to day release. Finally in 1899 no pupil-teachers were recruited until they were fifteen, when they spent a year full time at the centre, followed by two years part-time study. The centre steadily expanded with the system until it had five full-time instructors, two of them graduates.

It was some time before the centre system produced much improvement, and the Board's reports frequently expressed disappointment at the pupil-teachers' performance. The reason for this state of affairs was almost certainly that the pupil-teachers were still required to do most of their work in their own time, and it was not until the day release system was introduced that any significant

[1] Candidates were junior pupil-teachers in their first year of training.

TABLE 17

	Presented	1st class	2nd class	3rd class	Failed	
Whole country	2,087	345	828	276	638	Men
	7,542	1,242	2,220	1,664	2,416	Women
Nottingham	6	6	—	—	—	Men
	28	24	3	1	—	Women

progress was reported. After 1895, however, improvement was very rapid. There were several contributing factors; the pupil-teachers had more time for their work, the staff of the centre was reinforced, and a new chief instructor, Mr J. B. Hughes, was appointed. The results of the Queen's Scholarship held in December 1895 indicate how far the Nottingham results were in advance of those for the country at large, and suggest how much of an advantage it was to be a pupil-teacher in a large town where there was a centre to give assistance (Table 17).

The results continued to improve, and after 1899 they became quite remarkable, the H.M.I. observing in 1901 that 'this is a pre-eminently successful pupil-teacher centre'. His comment was justified. In general about 3,000 boys and 9,000 girls sat the examination in any year, and the great ambition was to achieve a place in the first 100 of either list. In 1899 Nottingham had three boys and two girls in the first twelve, including a girl from People's College who took first place. A Nottingham girl headed her list again in 1900 when five girls and three boys appeared in the first hundred, but this record was eclipsed in the following year, when 14 girls appeared in the first 100 including numbers 2, 8, 11, while the boys' results, in view of their small number were at least equally good – five in the first 100 including numbers 2 and 5. Nottingham and London each had five students in the first twelve of either list and Sheffield provided two, no other town being so successful. The achievement of the Nottingham centre is emphasized by the fact that London had several centres.

In 1902 and 1903 results were less remarkable since the best pupils were now creamed off to sit the London matriculation. Seven pupils matriculated in 1902 and eight in 1903. By this time the pupil-teacher system had been carried as far as it would go, and, in fact, it already resembled the bursar scheme which replaced it. In particular much progress was made in raising the academic level of the pupil-teachers, and every development was in the direction of emphasizing the general education of the potential teacher, and postponing his technical training.

This policy involved the assumption that the ex-pupil-teacher would go on to college, but in fact this was by no means always the case. Nonconformist teachers often found difficulty in finding a place, since most colleges were connected to the established Church. Some improvement was effected in this direction when the day training centres attached to the universities were opened, University College, Nottingham, having one of the first centres. But other pupil-teachers did not proceed to college because there was no great financial advantage in doing so. The Board attempted to encourage teachers to take college training by using the pay scale to benefit trained teachers, and also used negative measures. In 1898 it issued a circular which warned 'junior assistants', a term which covered all teachers who did not hold certificates, that their engagements would terminate at 25 years, when applications for re-engagement would be considered 'in connection with applications for the Board's former pupil teachers who have left to enter college.'

Untrained teachers were able to qualify themselves by private study for the certificate examinations, and the Board did its best to assist those who wished to do so, in order to raise the general level of teaching. In 1885 arrangements were made with University College, Nottingham, for evening classes to be supplied, the instruction being given by college staff assisted by experienced teachers. A joint college and board certificate was awarded to those who completed the three year course and were successful in the government certificate examination.

The magnitude of the problem presented by the untrained teacher is demonstrated by the fact that 170 teachers came under this scheme from Board schools alone, the number from Voluntary schools being unknown, but certainly higher. It was very difficult to persuade teachers to follow the course, although it was nominally compulsory and in 1886 the average attendance was only 60. By 1889 attendance had doubled and the scheme was said to be 'in good working order' although regret was expressed at the small number of teachers from Voluntary schools who had enrolled. A significant number of teachers were able to qualify themselves by these means; at least 38 certificates were awarded to successful students, and there may have been more. But the Board never looked upon the classes as more than a stopgap. It strongly favoured college training, and as early as 1886 it sent a memorial to the Education Department advocating, with a detailed argument, the establishment of day training colleges.

For the first twenty years of its existence the Board was not much concerned with qualifications beyond the government certificate, and in this period the only Board teacher who is known to have been a graduate was a Mr Tallantyre, headmaster of two Board schools, and later inspector under the Local Education Authority. About 1890, however, a fair number of teachers began to acquire further qualifications. London matriculation was popular, some went as far as the intermediate, and one or two graduated. Specialist qualifications, mainly in drawing and science were taken under the Science and Art Department. Many of the teachers concerned were in the higher grade schools where they were already on a special salary scale, but enough were in ordinary elementary schools to attract the attention of the Board. In 1893 a revision was made to the salary scale. Teachers with certain additional qualifications were placed on a special scale as first grade senior assistants which put them on a par with senior assistants in higher grade schools. Promotion to this grade carried a rise of £25 per year in pay, an increase of nearly 30 per cent, a substantial inducement. For a degree or the equivalent a grade of first-grade principal assistant was created, equivalent to principal assistant in a higher grade school. Smaller increments of £5 were offered for such successes as a first division pass in the Queen's Scholarship, or matriculation.

With these inducements offered it is not surprising to find a number of teachers working for additional qualifications. The triennial report of the Board for 1895 noted that five teachers had graduated and nine had reached the intermediate stage; all these students were external, of course. There were also several lesser successes. The majority of these teachers were in higher grade schools, but successes were noted from Berridge Road, Southwark, Bosworth Road and Ilkeston Road. By 1901 there were 14 graduates in Board schools, and it was reported that 69 teachers had passed university examinations, matriculation, intermediate or degrees, since 1895.

Apart from encouraging teachers to take advanced qualifications the Board arranged courses in professional subjects. The Board inspector, W. J. Abel, took a keen interest in infant methods, and was a supporter of kindergarten methods. In his first annual report, of 1882, he included a lengthy discussion of infant teaching which, in its emphasis upon the importance of play and curiosity, came strangely from an administrator in the depths of 'payment by results'. He described existing infant schools as resembling 'forcing houses rather than children's gardens'.

Kindergarten classes for teachers were opened in 1883 with 11 teachers in attendance, and at the same time Bluebell Hill infants' department was organized as a model kindergarten, the headmistress being a Mrs Roadknight who later became an inspector for the Board. These classes continued until the end of the School Board period, and were frequently attended by teachers from voluntary schools, private schools and surrounding school boards. Woodwork classes for men teachers were started a few years later, leading to City and Guilds examinations in which upwards of 80 teachers were successful.

An interesting innovation was the teachers' conference of which two or three were held in the last few years of the Board. The most ambitious conference was held in November 1901, when papers were read by H.M.I., a local inspector and several teachers; one or two of the subjects have a contemporary ring.

(1) Co-ordination of school work – Mr Hugh, High Pavement.

(2) Nature teaching – Mrs Gothorpe, Clarendon Junior School.

(3) The present position of reading in our school curriculum – J. B. Hall, H.M.I.

(4) The practical training of teachers – Mr Fewkes, Bosworth Road.

(5) Kindergarten in relation to our senior schools – Mrs Roadknight, Board Inspector.

(6) The function of drawing in a primary school – J. G. Saltmarshe, H.M.I.

(7) Old code subjects from today's standpoint – Mrs Baguley, Carrington Girls' School.

(8) Transfer of children – Mr Francis, People's College.

Nothing perhaps, illustrates better the rising status of the elementary school teacher than that it should be thought worth while to hold a conference at which aspects of the work could be discussed, and that most of the experts called in to deliver papers should themselves be teachers.

The Board drew up its first pay scale in 1875; it was a fairly simple document, the main interesting feature being that certificated assistants were mentioned. Such teachers were a new feature of the

TABLE 18

	Men	Women	Infant schools
Heads	£110 + £5–130 p.a. ⅓ gross grant + code payment for pupil teachers	£75 + £5–90 p.a. ¼ gross grant + pupil teacher grant	£70 + £5–80 p.a. ¼ gross grant + pupil teacher grant
Cert. Assts.	£80 + 5–£90 p.a.	£65 + 5–£75 p.a.	
Uncert.	£52–£70 according to special arrangements	£40–£60 according to special arrangements	

educational scene, and still rare. The scale is shown in Table 18. The system of paying head teachers partly by a share of the grant continued in Nottingham until 1895, when their pay was commuted to the average of the past three years. The evidence suggests that Nottingham was a year or two behind most of the larger boards in this change. Increments were not automatic; teachers applied for them and they were awarded, or not, as a result of a report by the headmaster and Board inspectors. About two thirds of the applications were granted.

In the next ten years the Board school system became more extensive and complicated. Schools were numerous and varied greatly in size; it also became necessary to offer promotion within the grade of assistant teacher, since, with the increasing size of schools, this was becoming, for the first time, a career grade. The Board therefore instituted a steeply graded pay scale for heads, related to the size of school, and four grades of assistant teacher. A first assistant with college training and a First or Second Class certificate could now earn £120 per year, which was an encouragement to acquire full qualifications. For head teachers promotion to a larger school was well worth while. The head of Bath Street boys' department in 1885–6 would receive a gross salary, including his share of the grant, of £240; his colleague at Alfreton Road received £317. A good report, or lack of it, made an enormous difference to the head's salary. The head of Alfreton Road drew £137 of his salary from his share of the grant. Even in a small infant school the difference between an 'excellent' and a 'fair' merit grant was £20, which meant a decrease in gross pay from £105 to £85.

The scale became progressively more complicated, partly because of the introduction of higher grade schools whose assistants had a special scale, which eventually reached £150 for a senior assistant and £160 for a principal assistant, and partly to give encouragement to teachers to improve their qualifications. Throughout the school board era, however, the pay of assistant teachers remained too low, particularly in relation to the pay of head teachers. The head of a higher grade school, who could earn £350 per year was paid over twice as much as his principal assistant and three times as much as most of his senior assistants, and the same proportions obtained in ordinary elementary schools. The head of a moderate sized school with an income of £240 per year was very comfortably placed by comparison with his qualified assistants whose scale ran from £75 to £135. A result of this was that there was a serious shortage of male recruits to the profession. This was a general phenomenon remarked upon by the historians of the London and Birmingham Boards.[1] In Birmingham, indeed, it was found to be impossible to recruit male pupil-teachers after 1893.

Certain interesting aspects of the Board's work require particular notice. One of these, the encouragement of secondary and technical education is treated in a separate chapter, but it will be convenient to deal here with evening schools, the education of handicapped children, welfare, and industrial schools.

For the first 13 years of the school board era evening schools in Nottingham as elsewhere were in decline. The attendance at evening schools throughout the country fell from 83,000 in 1871 to 24,000 in 1884;[2] in some areas, Birmingham and Bradford for example, evening schools ceased to exist altogether, and in Nottingham only 206 attendances were registered in the session 1882–3. The reason for this was simply that evening schools were looked upon as places where lessons in the rudiments were offered to young people who had failed to secure an adequate day school education. As compulsory education was established and enforced the need for such institutions inevitably declined.

In 1883 an entirely new start was made. Instead of being regarded as an alternative to day schools, the new evening schools were thought of as continuation schools, and they were aimed at young people who had recently left day schools, in particular the

[1] Philpott, *London at School*, pp. 185–6; A. F. Taylor, 'A History of the Birmingham School Board 1870–1903', M.A., Birmingham, 1955.

[2] E. Eaglesham, *From School Board to Local Authority*, Routledge and Kegan Paul, 1956, p. 55.

large majority who had not taken up an apprenticeship or other educational course. Pressure in support of the new development came both from the Nottingham Trades Council which favoured technical and commercial courses, and from the Recreative Evening Schools Association which asked for non-vocational classes.

The Board entered with enthusiasm into a campaign to bring the school leaver into the orbit of further education. In a report of 1889 the motives of the movement were expressed as follows. 'If we can win our young people from the corners of the streets and from the byways and alleyways into our schools and they can there learn *not to forget* what the country has paid so much for them to learn, we shall have accomplished a great and good work.' The report went on to make: 'a most confident appeal to all who desire less crime and poverty, quieter streets, more self-respect and more respect for others, to give us their sympathy and support'. Great efforts were made to interest young people in the schools. Public meetings were held, employers and trade and friendly societies were approached, as were clergymen and Sunday school organizers, and there was a liberal distribution of hand-bills.

The programme included all the subjects of the ordinary day school, which were necessary to earn grant if for no other reason, but as various voluntary agencies were brought into the work the recreative side was emphasized. By 1888 the Recreative Evening School Association had courses in wood-carving, brass-work, musical drill and needlework. Swimming classes had just begun and the Association provided the magic lantern operators who gave a regular service in history and geography lessons as well as assisting at the monthly entertainments which each school arranged. In 1890 another voluntary group, the Bowman Hart Musical Guild, began to run classes in vocal and instrumental music which ran with much support until the end of the period. It also arranged musical entertainments from time to time.

The social side of the school's work received much emphasis and determined efforts were made to build up the corporate spirit of the schools. During the 1880s each school had a tea evening every session and monthly entertainments with songs, recitations and musical drill. These were used as a means of advertisement and free tickets were issued to school leavers. In the 1890s the efforts became increasingly ambitious. The Leen Side School, selected as being in one of the poorest parts of the town, was opened one night per week as an institute where games were played, papers and magazines read and refreshments purchased. Other schools used the same plan in a modified form as a means of holding the interest of their pupils during the summer when no classes were held. Students were allowed to use the schools as meeting places on one or two evenings each week and rambles, outings and paper chases organized. From the reports of superintendents it is evident that in some schools at least these activities were organized by students' committees. One superintendent reported that 23 students had spent a day in London.

By 1898 the list of subjects offered had been greatly expanded. Since 1891 evening schools had beeen divided into two grades, elementary and advanced. Twenty-one centres were open for elementary work and they offered English reading and literature, composition, arithmetic, geography, experimental science, cookery, laundry work, needlework (including dressmaking and millinery), ambulance work (boys), sick nursing (girls), singing and musical drill. Woodworking and gymnastics were offered at special centres. Advanced evening schools ran courses in conversational French, music and various kinds of handicraft.

The popularity of the evening schools increased as their scope expanded. In 1882 206 students enrolled; in 1891, 1,298 students entered elementary centres and 718 enrolled at advanced centres. This was in addition to a substantial attendance at advanced technical and commercial classes, which receive separate treatment. In 1900 the total enrolment at all classes was 7,105.[1] An interesting feature of the later enrolment was that the majority of the students were over 16; in 1900 4,082 out of 7,105 were in this class. This suggests that the efforts of the schools to attract older pupils were enjoying some success. On the other hand it was apparent that a large number of school leavers were not being drawn into the schools.

The Board was very conscious of this last point. In its report for 1891–2 the Evening Schools Committee calculated that there were 6,000 potential pupils of between 13 and 16, and it drew the inevitable conclusion: 'whence it appears that, in spite of all the efforts which have been made, the majority of the children most needing assistance are still untouched by the evening school system.' The problem, of course, was the same one which had plagued the voluntary elementary schools before 1870. It was one thing to provide

---

[1] Excluded from this figure are students at University College and the School of Art.

schools, and quite another to persuade pupils to use them; and, as the Board realized, if their campaign against ignorance and crime was to enjoy any hope of real success, it must draw into the schools those very pupils who were being left out. The only solution, as the day schools had proved, was compulsory attendance, and, as early as 1892 a memorial was sent to the Education Department suggesting compulsory evening attendance for all children under 16 years who were exempt from day school. The same plan was proposed in 1900 to a meeting of the Association of School Boards, but on neither occasion did the suggestion arouse much interest.

The School Board's experiments in evening continuation schools were carried out in the face of apathy, or even active hostility from the Education Department. Until 1893 the Department was absolutely wedded to the conception of evening schools as merely alternatives to day schools. It reflects considerable credit on the Board that it continually supported the innovations of its superintendents even when they meant a loss in government grant. Indeed the Board adopted a most unapologetic attitude in this matter.

The results as measured by the Government examinations alone do not indicate nearly the value of the work done in the evening schools inasmuch as the multiplication and more popular treatment of subjects introduced into the syllabus of work for 1884/5, while adding considerably to the usefulness and attractiveness of the teaching, necessarily somewhat diminished the time devoted to bare code work ... The still broader and more attractive course suggested for the coming session may tend still further to lower the government assessment of the classes, unless the code for evening schools is made much more elastic in the interim.

After 1893 there was some relaxation in the Department's attitude, but the Board's evening schools remained well in advance of what the Department was prepared to sanction.

Evening continuation schools were not the only aspect of the Nottingham School Board's work which was in advance of what the Education Department was prepared to sanction. The education of handicapped children also occupied its attention from an early date. Deaf-mute children were the first group for whom special provision was made. A centre for teaching these children was opened in 1883, with Mr C. W. Green as headmaster. He had been trained at a college in Ealing which specialized in this work, and was assisted by two pupil-teachers who remained as assistant teachers when their articles expired; Green remained as head for upwards of 40 years. There were generally about 35 children in attendance, which gave a pupil/teacher ratio quite unusual in elementary schools. There were three groups of children who all learned lip-reading language, spelling, reading, arithmetic and drawing. In about 1890 geography, grammar, needlework, drill and woodwork were added. From 1888 onwards an annual seaside trip, usually to Skegness, was paid for by private subscriptions.

The Board's great problem was financial. It was only in 1893 that the Elementary Education, Blind and Deaf Children, Act made possible any special provision for such children, and a grant of £5 5s. 0d. per year was then payable for each pupil. For the first ten years of the school's life it could only earn grant by being reckoned as an infants' class of the nearby Clarendon School. By this means a grant of about 17s. per head could be earned. This was quite inadequate in view of the staff/pupil ratio necessary in such institutions, and the Nottingham Board joined with various others in requests to the Education Department that special consideration be given to schools for handicapped children. The Department, as ever, remained quite unmoved by these representations.

Until 1901 it was not necessary for the Board to provide for blind and partially sighted children, who were looked after by the Midland Institute for the Blind. After the act of 1893 it was possible to make a contribution out of public funds to support these children, and the Board paid £7 per year for day pupils and £21 per year for boarders. In June 1901 the Institute ceased its teaching activities and the Board established a centre for blind and partially sighted pupils, which had 13 pupils in 1903.

In January 1893 two classes were established for children who 'although not actually imbecile, require a special course of teaching based on kindergarten principles'. Eventually six centres were set up; two for defective and four for dull children. Classes were restricted to 15 for defective and 30 for dull classes. The work was described in the triennial report for 1895.

The mistresses are selected from among the brightest kindergarten teachers under the Board . . . The results so far as they can be estimated appear to be most gratifying, several of the scholars having sufficiently developed under the special instruction to permit of their being transferred to the ordinary Board schools. Both parents and scholars, moreover, appear to greatly appreciate the classes.

In 1901 classes were opened for physically handicapped children, who were sent to the centres after examination by the Board's medical officers: 75 were in attendance in 1903.

The impossibility of using public funds severely restricted extra-curricular activities in Board schools; they did not appear in the Code, and therefore, not only was no grant payable, but any expenditure upon them from the rates was liable to be charged to individual members of the Board at the annual audit. Under these circumstances not much could be done in the way of organized games, and the only athletic activity which was at all general was swimming, perhaps due to the fact that Nottingham was rather unusually well provided with swimming baths. In 1882 the Board accepted an offer from the Nottingham Swimming Club to teach a number of boys to swim free of charge, but nothing more active was done for ten years, when an agreement was reached with the Corporation to allow school-children into the Sneinton Baths at a reduced charge, which was remitted if the teacher certified that a child was unable to pay. Nearly 20,000 tickets for boys were issued in a year, and 750 for girls. At the same time a bonus was offered to teachers for giving swimming instruction. One shilling was given for every boy who was taught to swim a length and every girl who was taught to swim a width of the Sneinton large bath. From 1892 there was an annual swimming gala and in 1895 a swimming association was formed which arranged competitions and classes for awards of the Life Saving Society. In the Society's examinations for 1900 234 Nottingham children took awards, which, according to the School Board minutes, was 129 more than any other board. Some of the later Board schools were built with their own pool, Leen Side, High Pavement, Mundella, Sycamore Road and the Albert Street Technical Centre being equipped in this way.

Association Football made some headway. A cup for competition among evening schools was presented by the Mayor in 1894, and within a year or two day schools had their own competition which included Voluntary as well as Board schools. Representative matches were played against nearby Boards, Derby, Leicester, Sheffield, etc. Athletic sports were held from 1895 with a substantial entry, but fewer than half the departments in the town took part in either athletics or football, even when infant departments are discounted.

It is mildly surprising that almost nothing is heard of cricket, since this was the classical period of the Nottinghamshire County side. The Nottingham High School and the local private schools were playing regular matches at least as early as the 1830s, but it must be supposed that the Board schools found that the cost of equipment and lack of space were insuperable obstacles.

Apart from official action by the Board, unofficial ventures in the field of welfare were made by Board members, officials and teachers, the Board giving what assistance it could by way of accommodation, heating and so on. An interesting example of this kind of work was the 'Children's Guild of Play' or 'happy evening'. This was started by Mrs Roadknight, the Board inspector, in 1896, in the Leen Side school in Narrow Marsh, one of the poorest parts of the town. The aim was to provide an evening of harmless enjoyment, particularly for young children. The triennial report of the Board for 1898 commented at some length on the experiment:

The evening is divided between songs, games and fairy-tales and the behaviour of the children in the school is very encouraging ... The girls and boys who come with babes in arms are told off into a large classroom set apart for the purpose and directed by sympathetic workers. It is a pleasant yet pathetic sight to see hundreds of neglected children, all ages up to fourteen – many only a few weeks old, being carried in arms – hurrying to the 'Happy Evening' which is certainly one of the brightest hours of their lives.

The average attendance was 300, and frequently rose to 500, and Mrs Roadknight wished to extend the scheme to other poor neighbourhoods, but, as the report observed, 'the work is so trying and uncongenial to any but the most zealous, that it has not at present been found possible to obtain a sufficient band of efficient volunteers'. In Jubilee week the children were taken for a picnic on the river, and there were other visits and a Christmas party. It is a comment on the failure of Sunday schools to reach this stratum of the population that these treats were particularly welcome to children who were excluded from Sunday school outings on account of their ragged appearance.

A similar unofficial measure was the provision of 'penny dinners' which was started in 1884 by Mr Peacock, a radical member of the Board. At least two centres were set up, using the Board schools' kitchens, and the cooking was done by girls as part of their practical cookery course. Children received two courses, usually soup and a pudding for a penny. No record has survived of the extent of the scheme, but it was still operating in 1903. Other members of the Board formed a boot fund which provided boots for needy children, parents being expected to repay half the cost by instalments. Some 2,000 pairs of boots were provided by the end of the Board period.

An aspect of the School Board's work which calls for separate treatment relates to children who, for one reason or another, found themselves in trouble with the law, and were sent away to 'industrial schools'. Children were sent to industrial schools under the provisions of three acts, the Industrial Schools Act of 1866, the Prevention of Crimes Act of 1871, and the Elementary Education Act of 1876, generally known as Lord Sandon's Act. Under these acts the schools received a heterogeneous collection of children guilty of crimes which would have carried a prison sentence for adults, truants, children found begging or not having proper guardianship, uncontrollable children, refractory workhouse children, and the children of criminal parents.

Industrial School children, of whom there were nearly 10,000 in 1877, were, in theory, taught a trade, and the proceeds of their work was used to defray the cost of their upkeep. In practice, however, the industrial training was usually valueless. The most popular trades were tailoring, shoe-making, brush-making, firewood-cutting and box-making. The first two were genuine trades, but they had been condemned by the inspector of workhouse schools 30 years earlier,[1] on the grounds that they were sedentary and unhealthy for children, and that the trades were over-manned already. The other trades offered neither educational advantages nor the possibility of future employment; they were hardly more than a means of keeping the children occupied. A rather more hopeful course was that offered by a few training ships, but by no means all the alumni of these went to sea, so it may be supposed that much of their training was wasted from a vocational point of view.

When the School Board took up its duties it found that Nottingham children were at four schools, and grants were made to these to help to pay for the maintenance of the children. But as time went

[1] *Minutes of Committee of Privy Council on Education*, 1848–50, Schools of Parochial Unions, p. 8.

on it became increasingly difficult to place children, since the schools were generally in or near large towns which monopolized the available places. Nottingham had to spread its net wider, and, by 1878, 99 children were placed in 14 schools. Four schools took the majority of the children; the training ship *Southampton*, at Hull, had 31, Bradford Industrial School 16, York Industrial School 14 and the *Clio* training ship at Bangor 8; the other schools had three Nottingham pupils or fewer.

The schools varied greatly in their efficiency and the Board members took considerable trouble to inspect them personally. The Bradford School was a bad one. It was visited in October 1878 by two Board members who reported in a very critical manner.

this instruction compares unfavourably with those previously visited (*Clio*, *Southampton*, and York). The premises are ill adapted for an industrial school – inconvenient, airless and not particularly clean. There is no playground, the narrow yard which bears that name being quite unsuitable for the purpose . . . The industrial training is most defective . . . 16 boys are sent out to work in a brickyard, an occupation which cannot be considered desirable for boys of this class. It is apparently resorted to in this case because of the wages the boys can earn, a large part of the income of the school being derived from the earnings of the boys . . . The education given cannot be considered satisfactory . . . The managers of the school do not have enough personal interest in it.

No further boys were sent to Bradford from Nottingham, and it closed a few years later.

The *Southampton*, at Hull, on the other hand, received consistently good reports:

The arrangements are admirable and the appearance of the boys everything which could be desired. The discipline, though strict, is maintained without undue severity. The Captain's wife is at present living on board, takes an interest in the boys and knows them individually, and the committee have reason to believe that her presence helps to infuse the home element into the life of the ship . . . There is a brass band of 25 instruments on board . . . The food is as follows: Cocoa or coffee with bread or biscuits for breakfast with tea with bread or biscuits for supper. The dinner varies every day and it consists alternately of roast beef and vegetables, salt pork, suet dumplings, puddings, Australian meat, fish, etc.

The York school was also a particularly good one with an unusually varied industrial training. It was notable for the amount of voluntary help it received and its after-care of pupils. Positions were found for boys who were not provided for by their parents, and small financial rewards were made to boys whose conduct was satisfactory for three years after leaving.

The Board was not long in contemplating the idea of establishing an industrial school of its own. The number of children detained rose from 23 in 1871 to 69 in 1876 and 141 in 1883, and the cost rose accordingly. The difficulty of placing the children has already been referred to, and as more schools were used it became increasingly difficult to exercise personal supervision of the children in them, a task which the Board took very seriously. It was further hoped that opening a local industrial school would make it possible to tackle recalcitrant children earlier in their career, since to commit children to a local school did not entail removing them entirely from their family, a step which the Board was always unwilling to take until all other courses had failed. The problem of expense prevented the scheme from coming to action for 15 years, but in 1885 a subcommittee of the Board reported favourably on the idea of a day industrial school. There were, at that time, 12 such schools in the country, and the members of the committee had visited several, noticing particularly that the children were released from the schools on licence after a relatively short stay, on condition of regular attendance at an ordinary elementary school.

A day industrial school was opened on George Street in January 1886 with accommodation for 100 children. The staff consisted of a qualified mistress as superintendent, an assistant mistress, a man to act as caretaker and to supervise the industrial work, and a cook. Children arrived at the school at 8 a.m. and remained until 6 p.m., receiving three meals during the day. Half the working time was spent on industrial work and half in the classroom. The industrial work was limited to wood-chopping and mat-making, anything more ambitious being precluded by the short-term detention system which operated in the school. Twice a week the children were bathed, an experience they were said to enjoy. The menu for the school is interesting as representing current ideas of a suitable institutional diet. The cost was 1s. 5½d. per child per week, and sometimes one of the cheaper dishes prepared at the school cookery centre was substituted for the usual dinner (Table 19).

For a number of years the government reports on the school were very good. In 1889 the Inspector remarked:

I am glad to be able to report favourably on the condition and general management of the school . . . What I have observed today proves to me that the school exercises a powerful influence for the welfare and training of the children who attend . . . The premises satisfy the usual conditions very well . . . My visit has satisfied and pleased me.

In 1893 the report was considered good enough by the Board to justify the paying of a special bonus to the staff, and in the following year particular praise was given to the assistant, who was leaving:

'Could her services be retained without difficulty, I think it would be of the greatest advantage to the school. The teacher in question has much influence and performs her duties with much energy, tact and temper'.

TABLE 19. *Menu for Nottingham Day Industrial School*

Ingredients for every 10 children

Tea 1¾ oz. Coffee 2 oz. Milk 1½ gills, Sugar 6 oz. Treacle 6 oz. Dripping 5 oz.
Currant dumpling. Currants 4 oz., flour 2¼lb., suet 6 oz.
Rice pudding. Raw rice 2 lb., milk 2½ pts., sugar 10 oz.
Soup (to every 10 pints). Peas 1¼ pts., bones 3 lb., meat 10 oz., barley 4 oz., vegetables.

	Breakfast	Dinner	Tea
Mon.	¾ pt. tea, coffee, cocoa, with milk, sweetened. ⅝ oz. bread with treacle dripping	4 oz. cooked meat without bone. 8 oz. potato 2 oz. bread	¾ pt. tea, coffee, cocoa with milk, sweetened. 6 oz. bread with treacle or dripping
Tue.	do.	1 pt. soup with veg., peas, barley, meat 4 oz. bread Currant dumpling	¾ pt. hot milk and water sweetened 6 oz. bread
Wed.	do.	8 oz. bread 2 oz. cheese	As Monday
Thur.	do.	1 lb. rice pudding 2 oz. bread	do.
Fri.	¾ pt. hot milk and water, sweetened 6–8 oz. bread	½ lb. fish with sauce 2 oz. bread 8 oz. potato	do.
Sat.	do.	4 oz. tinned meat 6 oz. bread	Half holiday

After 1896 the reports changed in tone. To a large extent this was due to the appointment of a new inspector who was bitterly opposed to the short detention system, and could see no virtue in it. For some reason he appeared to think that the system was peculiar to Nottingham, a curious error for a government official to make, since it was used extensively elsewhere, notably in Sheffield,[1] and London,[2] where the historian of the Board, a contemporary authority, speaks of it with approval. An interesting feature of the inspector's remarks was his wholesale condemnation of the buildings; it is a reflection of the rise in educational standards which occurred at this time that the buildings which 'satisfy the usual requirements very well' in 1889, were 'inadequate' in 1896, and 'unsuitable for the purpose' in 1903.

When due allowance is made for the fact that the inspector could not be troubled to ascertain the facts before making his report, it still remains true that the school appears to have declined in the last years of the Board. The necessity for such a school was disappearing as the problem of chronic truancy was conquered, and in 1898 the Board expressed the view that the school had done its job and would soon be closed. The Local Education Authority did close the school shortly after taking over. As the truant became less common the school encountered, in an acute form, a fundamental problem which continually plagued the industrial school – the heterogeneous nature of its pupils. When the government inspector fulminated against the short-term detention system he was on the edge of an important criticism, although he never succeeded in articulating it. The short term system was quite effective in reforming children who were mischievous rather than vicious or seriously disturbed, particularly where their home background was respectable. In these cases the shock of a month or two in a day industrial school was sufficient, and it was good policy to return them as soon as possible to a normal environment. The more hardened offender, on the other hand, frequently needed to be removed completely and for a substantial period from his old influences, and in such cases the short-term school was inevitably unsuccessful. This was not a problem peculiar to the Nottingham school, or even to day industrial schools, but, as the day schools ceased to be largely filled with children whose chief offence was truancy, and whom they were well suited to handle, they

---

[1] Bingham, *Sheffield School Board*, p. 217.
[2] Philpott, *London at School*, p. 192.

came to be used more by hard core juvenile delinquents, who needed the more concentrated and continuous attention which a residential institution could offer.

Between 1870 and 1903 elementary education in Nottingham was transformed. The primary problem, that of getting all children into school, was solved, and compulsory attendance was enforced between five and eleven years, and for most children between five and thirteen. Average attendance improved from 60 to 90 per cent, and it may be said that, from 1890 onwards or thereabouts, all children in Nottingham attended elementary school regularly for at least six years, unless they were educated elsewhere. The Board was far from satisfied, and wished to lengthen school life by making education fully compulsory to thirteen or even older, and it left uncured some grave abuses concerning the part-time employment of school-children, but its achievement by 1903 has to be set against the position in 1870, and when this is done the improvement is seen to be dramatic.

Equally creditable was the success of the School Board in widening the scope of elementary education. No-one had seen fit in 1870 to define the limits of elementary education. The question simply did not arise; a school which taught its pupils to read and write and do some simple calculations was doing very well. If the girls did a little plain needlework in addition, and a few senior pupils acquired some historical or geographical facts, it was a good school. Its main function was far less academic than social; it tried, in Kay-Shuttleworth's words, 'to get rid of the wild, untamed barbarism of such children', and to civilize them to some degree. During the school board period the curriculum of the elementary schools was expanded to include, science, practical cookery, manual work, and a fairly wide range of academic subjects. Some of these subjects were taught badly. This was inevitable. They were new subjects so far as schools were concerned, and nobody was very sure how they ought to be taught; it was at this very period that many associations of teachers were formed with the specific aim of improving teaching technique. Furthermore Board schools were desperately hampered by the restrictions of the Code. Nevertheless the curricula of Nottingham Board schools revealed a very liberal interpretation of the concept of elementary education, and a very serious attempt to make the work of senior pupils approximate to that done in secondary schools.

The outlook was, indeed, so liberal that the Education Authority, on assuming power immediately issued instructions that the curriculum was to be narrowed and advanced work cut out.[1] It was not until the 1920s that another period of expansion and experiment began.

[1] D. Wardle, 'The History of Education in Nottingham', Ph.D., Nottingham, 1965, pp. 976 ff.

6

SECONDARY, TECHNICAL AND HIGHER EDUCATION

At the beginning of the nineteenth century secondary education in Nottingham was in a relatively flourishing condition. Three public institutions offered secondary education, the Free Grammar School (now the Nottingham High School), the Bluecoat School and the High Pavement School. In addition a number of private schools offered their services. A parent who was prepared to lay out money could have his son or daughter given a good secondary education.

But such an education was expensive. A classical course leading to university almost certainly involved attendance at a private boarding school, and if one of the small select academies was chosen the fee would certainly be £50–£80 per year. Even the larger and cheaper schools charged about 30 guineas. At the other end of the social scale a boy could be prepared for the office or warehouse at a writing school for three or four guineas per year. Men of quite moderate means paid substantial fees for their children's schooling; one well known Nottingham academy had among its boarders the sons of framework-knitters, gardeners, book-keepers and game-keepers. But, as a rule, even a day education at a good private school would be beyond the reach of most working men.

Technical training hardly existed. Writing schools prepared pupils for commerce but otherwise there was no vocational training. Nor, in spite of the decline of apprenticeship, was there any demand for it. The curriculum of the academies was deliberately 'liberal' except when a rather furtive commercial bias was allowed to creep in. Similarly, facilities for higher education were lacking. Oxford and Cambridge were expensive and socially and religiously exclusive. Businessmen and industrialists considered their courses to be archaic and irrelevant, and careful parents were dubious about their moral tone. Here was an obvious gap in the existing educational provision.

Another gap was in the field of education of women. Schools for girls did not, as a rule, give as good an education as boys' schools. There were exceptions, but most schools concentrated upon a 'genteel' curriculum. This gave much emphasis to conduct in society with some attention to the 'accomplishments' – water-colour painting, dancing, a little music. The programme was intended to turn out young ladies who would be an ornament to homes which kept sufficient servants, but the teaching failed on every count. It gave no serious training in household management at a time when the home was the centre of every woman's life, while intelligent women received no preparation for any intellectual pursuit. Even the accomplishments were treated at a most superficial level; any real ability or profound interest was discouraged as being unbecoming in a young lady.

In 1800 there were three quite clearly understood grades of secondary education which were essentially distinguished by the age at which the pupils left school. The three classes anticipated very closely those distinguished by the Taunton Commission. First there was the 'classical' curriculum which, in theory at least, was a preparation for a course at one of the universities. For Nottingham boys an education of this type was provided by a number of small 'classical' academies,[1] generally run by a clergymen as an addition to his stipend, and there was one larger school, the Nottingham Academy on Parliament Street, which gave a similar education to a large number of boys.

A step lower in social estimation – and cost – was the 'English' education which included Latin, but which emphasized English, mathematics and modern languages. This course was invented at the end of the eighteenth century as schoolmasters realized that the classical curriculum was losing its attraction and that the children of the commercial and industrial middle class would not stay at school beyond the age of 14–16 years. Several private schools in and around Nottingham provided an education of this type and the Free Grammar School competed in this class, with varying success according to the energy and competence of the headmaster of the day.

The third class of secondary school was the 'writing school', which had a strictly vocational course aimed at preparing boys for work as clerks, book-keepers and warehousemen. These schools assumed that their pupils would leave at 12 or 14 years. Most of them were privately run, and there were many such schools in the town, but the Bluecoat and High Pavement schools both turned out boys who were being trained for the same kind of post.

[1] Private schools are treated in greater detail in chapter 7.

In discussing the development of secondary education in Nottingham in the nineteenth century it will be convenient to deal first with
the three old-established schools, then to look at one or two foundations of the early nineteenth century, and finally to examine the
higher grade schools. Technical and higher education will then be
treated separately, although it will be appreciated that these divisions are made purely for convenience of treatment, and that it is
often very doubtful whether a particular institution should fall into
one class rather than another.

The Free Grammar School[1] was founded, or perhaps refounded,
in 1513 and enjoyed a period of eminence in the seventeenth century
under a succession of good masters. It shared the decline of grammar
schools in general in the eighteenth century, and until about 1830 it
served as a superior elementary school, or low-grade secondary
school, with a purely English curriculum. Its reputation for scholarship, very high in the seventeenth century, died, but at least the
school was efficient at a modest level and did not completely close
down, like the grammar school at Mansfield, fifteen miles to the
North. After 1833 the school was reorganized under a new headmaster, but no real recovery occurred until 1869 when the school
moved from the centre of the town to a new site on Forest Road.
Under Dr Robert Dixon the school then grew in size and some good
work was done especially in science, geology being Dixon's particular interest. But as Dixon lost his grip under the stress of family
troubles and ill-health there was another decline, and at no time was
it possible to raise the average age of leavers above 14 years.

The problem which the school was unable to solve at this time
was expressed by the Town Clerk in 1835[2] when he remarked that
the school would recover if 'they could make it an object of ambition
to the more opulent classes'. Unfortunately the 'more opulent
classes' sent their children to classical academies or, as they were
improved by Arnold and his followers, to the Public schools or the
new proprietorial schools. The boys who attended the Free Grammar School, or High School as it was called after 1868, were mainly
designed for commerce or industry and the school was, in fact, a
superior writing school. In the 1880s the school suffered from competition by the Board's higher grade schools, which offered a com-

[1] A. W. Thomas, 'The History of Nottingham High School', Ph.D., Nottingham, 1956.
[2] *Ibid.* pp. 191–2.

parable course at less than half the price, a big inducement to a parent who did not object to the stigma attaching to Board school education.

In 1884 Dr James Gow became head, and remained until 1901, when he left to become headmaster of Westminster School. In his headmastership the school revived and reached a higher level of academic achievement than at any time since the seventeenth century. Gow cooperated with the School Board in a scheme which allowed Board school pupils to go on to the High School on a scholarship, several proceeding from the High School to University in the 1890s. The recovery of the High School in his time was undoubtedly due in part to the surge of interest in secondary and higher education which occurred at that period, leading to the establishment of University College, Nottingham, the Nottingham Girls' High School and the higher grade schools. Certainly Gow was fortunate in being headmaster at a time when even the Corporation was infected by the current enthusiasm for education, but he took full advantage of his fortune and the school was in a most flourishing condition at the end of the nineteenth century.

The Bluecoat School[1] was founded in 1711 as a Church of England charity school and pursued a useful but uneventful course throughout the eighteenth and nineteenth centuries. At the beginning of the nineteenth century it was an elementary school with the curriculum confined to the three 'Rs' and Religious Instruction, with needlework for the girls. The school was raised in standard by Thomas Cockayne, who was headmaster from 1825 to 1850, and who introduced history and geography to the curriculum and turned it into a low grade secondary school. He was the father of one of the proprietors of Standard Hill Academy, a noted local private school, and, in addition to rebuffing an attempt to introduce the monitorial system – in a school with two teachers and 60 pupils – he adopted enlightened disciplinary methods similar to those used in some of the better private schools. His efforts were not unappreciated by his pupils, and when he was seriously ill in 1850, a number gathered to hold a reunion and present an address to their old headmaster.[2] His son was head for some years and then was succeeded by J. W. Curtin who was head for 46 years. The school never increased significantly

---

[1] F. W. V. Taylor, *History of the Nottingham Bluecoat School*, Nottingham, 1956.
[2] *Nottingham Journal*, 15 February 1850.

in size, remaining at 40–60 boys and half as many girls, and as the curriculum did not change significantly either, the school tended to be overtaken by its more adventurous contemporaries and remain in a backwater. At the end of the nineteenth century it stood somewhere between an elementary and a secondary school. An old boy recorded that the work was given a pronounced commercial slant.[1]

The High Pavement School is interesting as an early higher grade school, and also because it has been claimed that it is the oldest unsectarian school in the country.[2] This claim has no foundation in fact. The minute book of the High Pavement Society is in existence and the relevant minute[3] clearly states that the institution was 'a charity school for the children of poor persons belonging to this society'.

The school was founded in 1788 as a charity school for the children of High Pavement Unitarian Chapel, and in its early years it worked on very much the same lines as the Bluecoat School, providing schooling, clothing and apprenticeship for a limited number of pupils. As the minute of the vestry meeting makes clear, there was no question of the school being undenominational; entry was restricted to children of the congregation. Within a few years the school did become more or less undenominational, but this was not due to a liberal policy on the part of the Vestry but to force of circumstances. The High Pavement congregation was not a poor one, and there was probably not much call for a free school; a secondary school providing a commercial training like that of a writing school was more to the purpose, and the members of the congregation were ready and able to pay a fee for such a school, especially since attendance at a charity school carried a certain stigma. At any rate, within a few years the congregation had virtually ceased to support the school; subscriptions were frequently less than £30 per year and never significantly above £50, a very small sum from so wealthy a Chapel and less than half the subscriptions of the Bluecoat School, which also had substantial endowments. About 1820 the supply of clothes to children was stopped, the clothing fund being heavily in debt, and fees were instituted, and at this time, if not earlier, the

[1] Taylor, *Bluecoat School.* p. 35.

[2] See, e.g. R. V. Holt, *The Unitarian Contribution to Social Progress in England*, 2nd ed., London, 1952, pp. 22, 225.

[3] High Pavement Collection, Nottingham University Department of Manuscripts, No. Hi Mi. Vestry Meeting, 20 October 1787.

5

religious restrictions on entry were lifted. The school had thus become undenominational at the cost of ceasing to be a charity. By 1859 the total income of the school was £261 16s. 8½d. of which £145 19s. 9d. came from fees and only £50 16s. 6d. from subscriptions.

The claim that the school had been founded as an undenominational institution arose from this situation. As the school increasingly became a secondary school drawing its pupils from any families which would pay the fees, a party arose among the congregation which argued that the school no longer served any useful purpose to the Chapel and that support for it should be stopped. By this time the connection between the school and the Chapel was certainly tenuous as was demonstrated by the balance sheet for 1888.[1]

	£	s.	d.
Grant from Education Department	507	12	10
Grant from Science and Art Department	22	0	0
Stationery sold	235	16	4
Fees	700	4	6
Subscriptions	50	5	10
Endowment	16	4	0

A committee of enquiry which was set up found that the only way to combat the argument that the school was not fulfilling the intentions of the founders was to argue that the school had never been intended solely for the congregation, and in its report it stated that 'it was never any part of the scheme that these schools should act as a feeder to the congregation; they have been established and supported by friends of unsectarian education both within and without the High Pavement body'. The immediate effect of this statement was admirable since it decided the Chapel not to close down the school as was proposed. Nevertheless as a statement of the motives of the founders of the school it was clearly false and was probably intended merely as ammunition in the current controversy. It was elaborated by William Hugh, one of the headmasters, into a claim that the school was the first unsectarian school in England.[2]

For the first half of the nineteenth century the school followed a course very similar to that of the Bluecoat School. For most of this

[1] *High Pavement Collection*, No. Hi S 30.
[2] W. Hugh, *Some Notes ... Relative to the High Pavement Higher Elementary School*, 2nd ed. Nottingham, 1905, p. 3.

time the headmaster was John Taylor, who came to the school after serving as an assistant at a well known local private school. His work was justly summed up by a contributor to the *High Pavement Chronicle* in 1914, who said that 'he gave them a sound, if simple, elementary education, turning out many good scholars who were keenly sought after by local business houses'. It is only necessary to add that Taylor's work, elementary from the point of view of 1914, was obviously on a level with that of a writing school.

With the introduction of fees numbers in the school rose, and by 1859 there were 100 boys and 135 girls. In the 1840s the question arose of applying for government grants, and since by this time the school was largely independent of the Chapel, there was no objection to government inspection. The girls' school accepted grant in 1849, and the boys' school was only prevented from doing so by the objections of Taylor, who was over 60 and did not wish to change. When he was succeeded by William Hugh in 1861[1] the boys' school also accepted government inspection and grant.

Hugh was head from 1861 to 1905 and in his time the school rose rapidly in standard and increased in size. As early as 1862 it was decided to form a senior class of boys who had passed the Sixth Standard 'and who are willing to pay an extra fee for having their education carried beyond the government requirements'. This was followed by turning the school into an 'Organized Science School' to undertake work for the examinations of the Science and Art Department. The curriculum was relatively wide. All boys studied the three R's, mathematics, geography and singing, and senior boys added two specific subjects which varied from time to time.

By the 1880s the school's future was very much in question. The attempt to close the school, or at least to sever its connection entirely with the Chapel, was thwarted by the efforts of Hugh and his allies on the Committee of Management, but there was obviously no chance of any large investment and the buildings were in a poor state. In 1883 the government inspector remarked that 'it is unfortunate that this important school should be conducted in such antiquated and inconvenient buildings'. Since the school had an overdraft of nearly £500 and subscriptions were only £50 per year there was little prospect of improvement and in 1891 the school

[1] Taylor's son was head for a few months after his father's retirement, but resigned to run a private school.

passed to the School Board as a higher grade school. Its career in that capacity will be considered later in this chapter.

It was only in the second half of the century that it began to be generally realized that efficient technical training must be built upon a sound general education, and it was at the same time that working-class leaders began to agitate seriously for secondary education for at least selected members of their following. Except by a few advanced thinkers it was generally agreed that the working class had neither the time nor the inclination for secondary education, and, until elementary education had been made general, this was probably a fair assessment of the situation. On the other hand there was some realization, both among manufacturers and working-class spokesmen, that talent was being wasted because of the absence of schools giving a basic technical training comparable to that given in the commercial field by writing schools.

In Nottingham it was in the field of design that the first efforts were made in technical education. From early in the century the more critical manufacturers were aware that the continental lace firms, especially the French, had a distinct lead in design. Several of the Nottingham witnesses before the Children's Employment Commission of 1842 spoke of the need for a School of Design, and one mentioned that an attempt had been made to establish such a school in connection with the Mechanics' Institute, but that it had failed through lack of funds.

In October 1842 a very strong and representative committee was elected to float the idea of a School of Design, and after a certain amount of negotiation the government decided to subsidize a school in the town. A guarantee of local subscriptions to the value of £150 and a local management committee was required, the master being appointed by the Government School of Design. The Government made a grant of £500, which, it was calculated, would leave about £200 over when the cost of equipment was met, and also gave a maintenance grant of £150 per year. Books worth £100 were presented along with a number of casts.

The school opened in April 1843 in a building in Heathcote Street which was later converted into the People's Hall, a centre for adult education. Classes were held in the mornings and evenings and the fees were 2s. per month in the morning and 4s. per month in the evening. For ten years it had to struggle for existence, and it was not until 1850 that it was at all financially secure. The reason for this, curiously enough, was the lack of support by local manufacturers, who neither contributed to its funds nor encouraged their work-people to take courses. The local subscription rarely reached the stipulated £150, and was frequently only half as much, and a meeting to launch an appeal for funds 'was remarkable for the extreme tenuity of attendance'. The evidence suggests that aware-ness of the need for technical training was restricted at that time to an enlightened minority and that the majority, while willing to give lip service to the idea needed the excitement stirred up by the 1851 Exhibition, or the panic caused by the results of the 1867 Exhibition before they were willing to take any positive action. This apathy was not restricted to Nottingham; the Manchester School of Design had a similar troubled history in the 1840s,[1] while the jurors for the Exhibition of 1851 remarked in their report that most of the 21 existing schools of design had degenerated into 'mere drawing schools'.[2]

In spite of the discouraging attitude of local industry and constant financial worry the school was firmly established by 1850. The first master left after a short stay, and was succeeded in July 1845 by J. A. Hammersley. He, too, only stayed for three years but his work was of major importance in setting the school on its feet. His method was to widen the scope of the courses making them much less specifically vocational in nature. The government inspector noted with approval that the whole school studied the figure, and that plant drawing was done from nature. An evening class was started for women, and Hammersley's success is shown by the fact that he more than doubled the enrolment, which reached 120 in 1846.

When Hammersley was transferred to the Manchester school in 1848 his policy of emphasizing general art education rather than strictly vocational work was continued by his successor Thomas Cotchett. The school was slowly acquiring a more stable financial basis as local industry became interested, spurred on, no doubt, by the publicity given to technical education by the 1851 Exhibition. In 1850 Mr Heymann, a prominent lace manufacturer instituted a campaign which allowed the school to purchase its premises, while

[1] R. B. Hope, 'Education and Social Change in Manchester, 1780–1851', M.Ed., Manchester, 1955, p. 79.
[2] H. K. Briscoe, 'The History of Technical Education in Nottinghamshire, 1851–1902', M.A., Sheffield, 1952, p. 65.

subscriptions were nearly doubled. Determined efforts were made to excite local interest by holding exhibitions and soirées in the school, while the field of work was further widened. Special courses were offered for:

(*a*) schoolmasters, pupil-teachers, etc.,
(*b*) machinists and engineers,
(*c*) carpenters, builders, etc.,
(*d*) lace designers,
(*e*) general art education,
(*f*) decorators, industrial artists, etc.

From 1850 onwards the school began to attract favourable notice from outside observers. The jurors at the 1851 Exhibition commented enthusiastically on the improvement which they had observed in the quality of textile design, concluding that: 'We think it right to state here that the Government School of Design has materially assisted the enterprising manufacturer and artizan'.[1] The inspector of elementary schools for the area also made favourable mention of the classes for pupil-teachers.

In June 1865 the school moved to a new building in Waverley Street and the work continued to expand. In the session 1864–5 teaching was started in elementary schools for the examinations of the Science and Art Department, nearly 15,000 children coming into the scheme in the first year. Advanced students at the school were beginning to win prizes regularly at the examinations of the Science and Arts Department, and in 1869, according to the man who distributed the prizes at the annual speech day, the school was the most successful in the country.[2] One hundred and twelve art colleges in the country competed for 80 medals, and Nottingham had secured eight. Only Manchester equalled this record, and Nottingham had the advantage of two Queen's Prizes. In addition Nottingham was one of only two provincial schools to gain gold medals for design.

One other development in the field of art education deserves notice. Nottingham Castle, which had been derelict since its destruction by rioters in 1831 was restored by the Corporation at a cost of nearly £30,000 and opened in July 1878 by the Prince of Wales as an art gallery and museum. From its earliest days the museum

---

[1] Briscoe, *Technical Education*, pp. 64, 65.
[2] *Nottingham Journal*, 16 January 1869.

was regularly used by parties from the local Board schools. Infant schools appear to have been first in the field with school visits, but senior departments soon followed.

In the 1840s two quite separate lines of reasoning led men to consider the possibility of widening the scope and availability of secondary education. On the one hand it began to be realized that modern industrial conditions required a higher level of education among artisans than had hitherto been thought necessary. On the other hand it was the opinion of the 'moral force' wing of Chartism that the demands of the working class for political enfranchisement could be made irresistible by raising the educational level of the working man. Nottingham was a notable centre of Chartism; Fergus O'Connor was Member of Parliament for the town, and his statue is still to be found in a rather obscure corner of the Arboretum. The views of the moral force wing of the movement produced some interesting educational experiments, especially in adult education, and these did not perish with the collapse of Chartism as a political force after 1848.

Enlightened members of the middle and upper classes were not opposed to these examples of self-help. Some, no doubt, saw only a choice between moral force and physical force, and found moral force the less frightening alternative; others hoped to use the radical alliance for their own political purposes. Others, again, were positively benevolent, considering the improvement of the lot of the working class a good thing in itself. For one motive or another men like J. E. Denison, Speaker of the House of Commons, and J. S. Wright, a prominent local banker, much interested in educational ventures, assisted the local operative libraries with gifts of money and books. The Mechanics' Institute made a serious attempt to cooperate with the operative libraries. This attempt foundered as relations between manufacturers and workmen were too strained in the 1840s for continued cooperation, but it suggested that there was the possibility of progress when the peculiar bitterness of the Chartist period had faded.

It was at this time that the Nottingham People's College was founded, chiefly due to the efforts of George Gill, who a few years later founded the People's Hall as an adult education centre. The aim of the People's College was to provide for the working-class child an education comparable to that obtainable in a good writing school or English academy. The school was not free, although provision was made for a limited number of pupils to be admitted at half price, and the fee was 1s. per week or 10s. per quarter, so that it may be assumed that the founders of the school had in mind the upper reaches of the working class, and in their statement of the aims of the institution they gave a wide interpretation to the term which they defined as 'the labouring population, clerks, warehousemen and others receiving wages or salaries for their services'.[1] The management of the school fell half-way between that of the People's College, Sheffield, on one hand, where the students were powerful, and the London Working Men's College on the other, where they had no say in the administration whatever. At the Nottingham College there were 24 managers, of whom 16 were elected by subscribers and eight by the parents of pupils. The subscription list was such that an immediate start could be made on a building which included a lecture room and six class-rooms, and the new school opened in August 1847.

The institution was warmly greeted in radical circles. The *Nottingham Review*, a radical paper, printed a leader in which it harped upon its favourite theme that ignorance was the prop of tyranny and that the spread of education was the necessary prerequisite of political reform:

the real power of democracy – the power of thought, virtue and brotherhood against whose pressure no tyranny, however antiquated, can stand, will grow up in vigor [sic] and glory neath the fostering sunshine of knowledge . . . We are assured that our People's College will be Nottingham's best agitator and lecturer, doing more towards the ultimate enfranchisement of the masses than more political combinations can possibly accomplish . . . .[2]

The Journal of the Sheffield People's College added its congratulations, making particular note of the Nottingham College's success in raising funds for its own building, and concluding,

George Gill is Nottingham's William of Wykeham and by his opportune gift he has at one laid the foundation of a great institution and as fairly purchased a cheap and honourable celebrity as Raikes or Howard or Catherine [Elizabeth?] Fry.[3]

---

[1] *A Digest of the General Objects, Rules and Regulations of the People's College, Nottingham*, Nottingham, 1846.
[2] *Nottingham Review*, 13 November 1846.
[3] *Ibid.* 11 December 1846.

The People's College did not quite achieve the fame which the *Nottingham Review* had predicted, but it was a success from the start and proved to be a thoroughly useful institution, exactly fulfilling its founder's intentions that it should provide a sound education of the kind offered by the lower grade secondary schools at a moderate price. Originally it was planned as a boys' school, but a girls' section was added in 1850 and the full complement was about 170 boys and 75 girls. The programme for the boys was stated to be the three R's, and singing, with object lessons, natural history, physiology, social economy, history, natural philosophy, mathematics, Latin and French. Presumably boys took a selection of the advanced subjects, but, unlike many schools of the day, the People's College does seem to have taught all the subjects on the prospectus. The emphasis was on the sort of work done in a writing school for most pupils; the annual report for 1865 noted that 'the pupils have been proceeding through the usual English and Commercial course'. The girls' curriculum was rather less ambitious, being restricted to 'the usual branches of a sound English education, and plain needlework'.[1] There was an extensive range of evening classes. In 1855 these covered the three R's, grammar, algebra and book-keeping. French, German and singing were taken at two levels and a class in conversational French had just begun.[2] In order to allow students to follow a coherent course the first headmaster, Hugo Reid, drew up a series of courses of directed study after the manner of modern correspondence courses. A library and reading room were a further assistance to part-time students, and regular lectures were held.

The College had only three headmasters in the nineteenth century. Hugo Reid only stayed until 1851 or 1852, but he gave the institution an excellent start. He enjoyed some reputation as a writer on scientific education and at least one of his books was bought by the Mechanics' Institution of which he was an active member. He was succeeded by T. Buckley Smith who was head for 30 years. In 1860 he was presented with a 'handsome purse containing 60 guineas' by the directors, so it may be assumed that they were satisfied with his work. The third headmaster was Edward Francis, who saw the school through the extensive developments of the school board period. In his time the school enjoyed a high musical reputation as well as achieving academic success.

[1] *Nottingham Journal*, 4 January 1850.
[2] *Nottingham Review*, 5 January 1855.

The school was almost unique in the voluntary period in its staffing ratio. In 1855 the boys' department had two qualified assistant masters, two pupil-teachers and two monitors or probationary pupil-teachers; the girls' department had a mistress and two pupil-teachers. Part-time visiting teachers were employed for particular classes. It was considered a distinct professional recommendation to have been a member of staff. At least three assistants, Oliver Wainwright, Joseph Bright and Elizabeth Sunter, opened private schools which flourished for many years. In 1865 the second master and the assistant mistress both left to take up headships, one in Norfolk, the other in Dublin. A particular feature was made of training teachers and governesses, and advertisements were put in the papers that 'suitable youths are received as normal pupils and trained for teaching'.[1] Owing to the school's reputation such pupils found no difficulty in securing posts. In view of the interest taken by the College in teacher training it was fitting that the first normal master, later Professor of Education at University College, Nottingham, should be Amos Henderson, who was assistant master at the College under Francis.[2]

In 1880 the College was handed over to the School Board to serve as the first higher grade school. The directors felt that the opening of University College removed the need for the further education side of their work, and since the Board was showing interest in post-elementary schooling it was a logical step for the College to come under the Board's control, and it was handed over as a going concern.

Towards the end of the 1870s the Nottingham School Board began to interest itself in education beyond the elementary stage. The struggle to get reluctant children into schools was being won and the Board and its teachers had energy to spare from its basic duties to plan for an expansion of the scope of its work. The Borough Extension Act of 1877 seems to have encouraged it to take a large view of its responsibilities. The directors of the People's College showed themselves willing to entertain the idea of a take-over by the Board. But much the most important cause of the Board's ventures into secondary education was internal pressure by pupils and parents who wanted more than a merely basic education. The School Management Committee remarked in 1882 that the main reason for

---

[1] *Nottingham Review*, 5 January 1855.
[2] Mellors, *Men of Nottingham*, p. 283.

maintaining the People's College as a higher grade school was: 'The considerable and increasing number of scholars in the elementary schools of the town who have passed the sixth standard and are still under the limit of school age laid down by the Code, and whose parents desire to keep them longer at school.'

In 1880 the People's College was taken over as the Nottingham Board's first higher grade school. Only children of Standard IV and above were admitted, and there was an entrance examination, the ancestor of the 11+, which was taken by pupils of Board schools or any other pupils who wished to be admitted. The fee was 9d. per week and pupils paid for books and stationery, but:

for the encouragement of merit and in order to connect the People's College, as a higher grade school, with the other elementary schools in the Borough, all scholars passing Standard V before Her Majesty's Inspector in any other elementary school in the Borough may be admitted at 6d per week, or at such lower fee as the Board may in exceptional cases decide.

The ordinary code subjects were taken, together with music, geography, history, grammar, needlework, domestic economy, mathematics, French, German, drawing and subjects from the Science and Art Directory selected according to local requirements. A Standard VIII was provided for children who had passed other standards. The curriculum of this class was aimed at the Oxford and Cambridge Local Examinations, and pupils took at least two Science and Arts subjects, the grants from which helped to pay for the instruction. By 1886 there were 104 boys and 65 girls in Standard VII and beyond, so the school was obviously performing the task for which it was intended.

The higher grade system expanded rapidly. By 1889 two new schools had been opened at Queen's Walk and Huntingdon Street, and High Pavement was taken over in 1891. The report of the People's College for 1888 shows how the school's work had developed. A commercial side had been opened and pupils took elementary and commercial French, commercial forms, précis writing, commercial geography, arithmetic and mensuration. Boys in Standard VII and VIII attended woodwork classes at University College. Girls took botany, domestic economy, algebra and French, with electricity and magnetism and physiography from the Science and Arts Directory. From the start an attempt was made to give a reasonably balanced curriculum which was not too heavily biased on the vocational side. In this the Nottingham schools were different from higher grade schools elsewhere, where there was often an excessive emphasis on technical work. For example, the income of the Birmingham seventh Standard school in 1886 was made up of £963 from the Science and Art Department and only £105 from the Education Department.[1] In contrast the People's College in 1888 received £482 18s. 0d. from South Kensington and £360 6s. 3d. from Whitehall, which suggests a less exclusive pre-occupation with technical subjects.

In 1892 the expansion of the higher grade system led to a re-organization, in which the schools were divided into science and commercial departments. People's College boys', Queen's Walk boys' and both departments of Huntingdon Street were made into science schools, while both departments of High Pavement and the girl's departments at People's College and Queen's Walk were commercial schools. In the commercial schools prominence was given to shorthand and typing, French or German, commercial correspondence and arithmetic; science schools offered a formidable array of Science and Art subjects. In both types of school the specialist subjects were taken in addition to the ordinary subjects of the Board school curriculum.

By 1900 the School Board had built up a system of education which allowed children of ability to climb from elementary school to university, and a number had already done so. Some did so by passing through the higher grade schools to the Nottingham High School and then to University. Cyril Shelbourne, the first student of University College to obtain a higher degree, was an example; he proceeded to M.A. in 1897. Others went directly from higher grade schools to university or other institutions of higher education. The triennial report of the Board for 1898 gave a list of five former higher grade school pupils who had graduated in the previous three years, and six who had obtained scholarships to different universities.

These were the outstanding scholars. At least equally interesting were the results obtained by less pre-eminent pupils who nevertheless clearly benefited from a secondary education. In the three 'organized science schools' 284 students earned grant in 1898 at the rate of £5 12s. 6d. per head. In the literary and commercial depart-

---

[1] Eaglesham, *From School Board to Local Authority*, p. 38.

ments the first year above the standards was spent in working for the College of Preceptors examination, the second for the Oxford or Cambridge Locals and the third and fourth for London Matriculation. This scheme had not long been in operation when the Board reported in 1898 and no full class had yet taken the matriculation examination, but in the previous three years 237 pupils had passed the College of Preceptors examination and 51 the Oxford or Cambridge Local examinations; 48 were in the second year of the matriculation course.

The higher grade schools encountered little local criticism. This is rather surprising since the cost of the Board's activities were a constant cause of complaint, especially by the Corporation, which in the Board's early days had to be forced to pay the precept on the rates by the threat of legal action. Popular clamour occasionally forced the Board to give up its more adventurous schemes.[1] The higher grade schools were expensive. They had large staffs which were paid on a higher scale than normal, and laboratories and scientific equipment increased the cost of building and maintenance. And yet there were no complaints in the press, and the business community contributed with some generosity to an appeal to form a scholarship fund. The Corporation, apparently spontaneously, offered to pay the examination fees of successful candidates in examinations of the standard of College of Preceptors and above; by 1903 it had paid out £450 on this scheme. In short, the cost of the higher grade schools was cheerfully borne because they appeared to be performing a useful function.

Testimony to the work of the schools comes from a most unexpected source. In 1897 the headmistress of the girls' department of People's College received a letter from Robert Morant at the Education Department. He had seen a copy of the timetable and curriculum of the school, and wrote to congratulate Miss Beard 'upon its excellent curriculum, and stating that the school appears to be superior to any similar one in the South of England'.[2] This letter has an ironical ring, in view of the fact that Morant played the leading part, not only in destroying the higher grade system, but in rejecting its basic principle that elementary and secondary education should be closely related.

The School Board's schemes for secondary education ended in

---

[1] See the case of the housecraft centre, above, pp. 94–5.
[2] *Minutes of the Nottingham School Board*, 12 November 1897.

frustration and disappointment. After the Cockerton Judgment had clearly declared such work to be illegal there was bound to be a delay in further development, although enabling acts permitted the work in hand to be carried on. The hostility of both the Government and the Corporation to school boards was a further discouraging factor. When the Higher Elementary Schools minute of April 1900 finally gave legal sanction to higher grade work it proved to be a bitter disappointment because of the restrictions it placed upon the curriculum and the age of pupils.

Higher grade schools provided the first organized system by which poor children could rise from elementary schools to high positions in industry, commerce and scholarship, and by which less gifted children could acquire the qualifications necessary for entry to 'white collar' jobs. The lists of successes published in the triennial reports of the Board show that these opportunities did not exist only on paper. The curricula of the schools did not exhibit that rigid division between 'vocational' and 'liberal' subjects which has remained a problem in both secondary and technical education until the present day. In the higher grade schools even those pupils who specialized in science or commerce studied the normal code subjects, and the 'organized science schools' had matriculation classes. Finally there was a close relationship between the higher grade schools and the elementary schools. Teachers moved from one to another; the schools competed against one another at swimming, athletics and football.

It was on the last two counts that the Higher Elementary Schools minute and later regulations relating to secondary schools were so disastrous. A sharp distinction was drawn between the elementary system, in which schooling finished at 15 with no prospect of promotion to higher education, and the secondary schools which led to the universities and professions. The higher elementary schools were restricted to younger children and their curriculum given a strong technical bias. The secondary schools, in contrast, were pressed to emphasize literary subjects, and technical and vocational work was downgraded, thus sharpening the distinction between the two systems. The higher grade schools, as they developed in Nottingham, offered a genuine secondary education which allowed the academically able child to pass on to the universities and professions, while they did not deny the less gifted child a preparation for technical or commercial training or for white collar jobs. Unfortunately the system was swept away, and a narrower conception of secondary education took its place.

As early as 1883 the School Board came under pressure, particularly from the Nottingham Trades Council, to introduce commercial work into its evening classes. The Board was very willing to do this, but was prevented from making the progress it would have liked by the completely negative attitude of the Education Department, which persisted until the 1890s in regarding evening schools as an alternative to day schools, and in refusing to countenance any work beyond the rudiments. Nevertheless the Board persevered with the provision of technical and commercial classes in an inevitably small way, and in 1891 set aside two evening schools, Queen's Walk and Huntingdon Street for higher grade work with a bias towards commercial subjects. Courses were offered in commercial geography, history, commercial arithmetic, book-keeping and shorthand, together with cookery, laundry work, dressmaking and musical drill for girls. Characteristically the Education Department refused to recognize typewriting, singing, dressmaking, gymnastics, musical drill and ambulance work as grant-earning subjects, but they were continued by the Board, partly with the support of fees, and partly by the use of voluntary teachers. Prolonged negotiations between the Board and the Department about the status of typewriting, produced from the Department a final refusal to pay grant:[1] 'My Lords cannot accept typewriting under Article 2 or Article 3 of the Continuation School Code as they do not consider that, however practically useful, it has a substantial educational value. It is a mechanical exercise.' The logic of this reply is hard to grasp, since the Department already paid grant for book-keeping and shorthand, subjects hardly distinguishable from typewriting from an educational point of view.

As the attitude of the Education Department became a little more benevolent throughout the 1890s the evening technical classes increased rapidly in number and scope. By 1895 nearly 8,000 students enrolled in six higher grade schools, by then known as 'Commercial and Technical Centres'. All classes were free, and admission was by a ticket which cost 4d., the payment, which went to the prize fund, being chiefly intended to discourage frivolous enrolments. All students had to attend two classes which were eligible for grant, and

[1] *Minutes of the Nottingham School Board*, February 1896.

no-one was admitted until they had passed Standard VI unless the classes bore directly upon their daily work. Students in commercial classes were prepared for the examinations of the Society of Arts. The more advanced students were referred to University College or the School of Art. The Evening School managers claimed that the subjects offered 'include almost the whole of those required to fit our young people for any branch of work in which they may be engaged'. At that time the following courses were taken at the Board's Commercial and Technical Centres:

ambulance work
arithmetic
book-keeping
carving
cookery
dressmaking
gymnastics
home reading
hygiene
languages
laundry work
clay modelling
shorthand
cardboard modelling
mensuration

social economy
typewriting
vocal music
wood-work
musical drill
writing
machine construction
commercial correspondence
sick nursing
history
geography
life saving
solid geometry
building construction

Students who wished to undertake more advanced studies could pass on to University College where an equally extensive list of courses was available:

practical, plain and solid
   geometry
mathematics
machine construction
building construction
applied mechanics
steam and the steam-engine
theoretical mechanics
magnetism and electricity
heat, light and sound
theoretical chemistry
physiology
mineralogy

botany
metallurgy
physiography
hygiene
English correspondence
shorthand
commercial arithmetic
book-keeping
French
German
Spanish
political economy
geology

In addition the Municipal College of Art offered a number of courses in art and design. Elementary work was done at several branch classes which had been opened in Board evening schools, while more advanced classes were taken at the College itself.

The last significant development in technical evening classes in the Board period was the introduction, in the 1900–1 session of a number of grouped courses designed for different kinds of student. There were five grouped courses, each of which offered a selection of subjects from which a student might choose three. The courses were as follows:

(*a*) for clerks, shopkeepers and warehousemen,
(*b*) engineers and electrical works employees,
(*c*) builders and allied trades,
(*d*) railway employees, policemen, etc. (a general course including English, arithmetic, etc.),
(*e*) a domestic course for women students.

The Board's aim in introducing these courses was to counteract the increasing tendency towards over-specialization and fragmentation of subject matter. It was a very modern-sounding attempt to broaden the base of technical training, but like many modern schemes with the same intention it was unpopular with the students, who were exceedingly reluctant to study any subject whose relevance was not immediate and obvious, the criterion of relevance generally being an increase in earning power.

The first institution of higher education of which any record has survived was the short-lived Nottingham Medical School. In May and June 1833 a series of meetings was held by the medical men of the town, and it was decided to open a medical school. For some reason there was opposition to the proposal from the staff of the General Hospital,[1] but a stiff letter from the Duke of Newcastle, patron of the hospital, put an end to this. By September 1833 lecturers had been elected by ballot from among the local practitioners and, assisted by a donation of £500 from the Duke of Newcastle, the committee took premises on St James's Street which were later to be used by the Mechanics' Institute. Lecturers were chosen for anatomical demonstrations, materia medica, theory and practice of medicines, anatomy and physiology, chemistry, mid-

1 *Nottingham Journal*, 7 June 1833.

wifery and diseases of women and children, medical jurisprudence, botany, surgery and clinical medicine and surgery. Evening classes and demonstrations began in October.

Unfortunately evidence about the work of the medical school is almost completely lacking. It did not last for many years. In 1838 when the Mechanics' Institute took over the building a clause in the agreement allowed members of the Institute to attend demonstrations in the school, so some work was presumably still being done at that time. Glover's history of Nottingham of 1844 makes no reference to the school, however, and, since it gives an unusually full and accurate account of contemporary institutions, this strongly suggests that the school was defunct by that date.

It is not difficult to account for the rapid failure of the medical school. The hospital staff were hostile from the start and the election of the lecturers gave rise to a series of bitter wrangles, so that at least two meetings had to be repeated in order to consider complaints of irregular procedure. It is very likely that those doctors who failed to secure election as lecturers refused to support the school.

Until the establishment of University College in 1881 the bulk of the technical instruction done in Nottingham was given at the Mechanics' Institute. Classes in various subjects were carried on by the Institute from its foundation in 1838, the usual arrangement being for a teacher to have the use of a room in the Institute, paying himself from the fees he received from students. Most of these classes were elementary or recreational in nature, and little or no advanced work was done. In 1846 the following classes were running:[1]

French	30 students
drawing	23 students
writing, arithmetic and grammar	38 students
music	
ladies' French	
discussion of literary and scientific subjects	

Although the classes were so few they were not well attended and frequently fell through from lack of support.

Until the late 1850s the Institute continued to provide classes but on the same very inadequate scale, and it cannot be said that there was any very serious attempt at technical education. About 1857,

[1] *Nottingham Review*, 13 February 1846.

however, a change occurred which was undoubtedly connected with the contemporary national wave of interest in technical instruction. In that year Dr W. T. Robertson gave a course of 30 lectures in chemistry which were well attended and there was a proposal to establish a chemical laboratory which fell through owing to the Institute's financial difficulties. In 1859 the sum allotted for the payment of professional lecturers was increased and the Institute cooperated with the People's Hall and the Artizans' Library to run combined lectures. In the following year the Nottingham board of examiners for the Society of Arts examinations was established and the Mechanics' Institute had two representatives on the board.

The most important step taken at this time in the provision of technical instruction was the founding of Science and Art classes at the Mechanics' Institute. The first class was opened in October 1862 when 61 students enrolled for a course in inorganic chemistry. For two years this was the only Science and Art class; then a course in physiology was added. After this rather hesitant beginning a rapid development took place, and Science and Art classes remained an important part of the work of the Mechanics' Institute until they were transferred to the newly founded University College in 1881. In 1880 City and Guilds classes were added and in that year classes were running in the following subjects:

geometry	botany
machine construction	steam
building construction	blowpipe analysis
mathematics	mechanical engineering
organic and inorganic chemistry	steel manufacture
heat, light and sound	carriage building
magnetism and electricity	French
animal physiology	German
physiography	biology

Altogether 358 names were on the rolls of the various classes, although the number of individual students is impossible to estimate since many must have taken more than one course.

By 1880 there was a clear need for an institution designed and equipped for professional and technical education at an advanced level. The climate of national opinion was favourable to the development of higher education, and the extensive enrolment for classes at the Mechanics' Institute revealed a demand for vocational training. The lack of elementary education which had undermined earlier attempts at technical training was rapidly being corrected by the spread of universal education under the School Board, and already the Board was being pressed to enter the field of secondary education.

The proposal to establish a University College in Nottingham arose in the first place from the advocates of university extension,[1] but the Corporation, in supporting the proposal, was far more interested in using the opportunity to provide a technical college for the town, 'for without such a school Nottingham is not likely to hold its own in the severe demands made upon us by competition with other countries'.[2] The committee appointed to consider the project referred to the possibility of affiliation to Oxford or Cambridge but recommended that the teaching of the college should 'very largely, if not chiefly' be directed to assisting elementary school leavers to pass the examinations of the Science and Art Department.[3] No doubt in the conditions of 1880 the committee had some justification for stressing the importance of relatively low grade technical instruction. In the long run, however, the limited outlook of the Corporation was severely to cramp the development of the college.

For some years, however, the new College made good progress. Four professors were appointed to cover the following fields:

(a) Languages (ancient and modern);
   literature,
   history,
   political philosophy and economy,
   logic and philosophy.

(b) Mathematics,
   mechanics,
   physics.

(c) Chemistry – organic and inorganic; pure and applied.

(d) Biological science; to include botany, zoology and physiology: also geology and the allied subjects.

Three demonstrators were also appointed and a number of part-time teachers engaged. The enormous fields which the professors were expected to cover emphasized the fact that little instruction of genuine university level was anticipated.

[1] See below, chapter 8, p. 191.
[2] Report of University College and Free Library Committee, 7 February 1881, p. 12.
[3] *Ibid.*

The College's work fell into three divisions of which the third was, from the outset, much the most extensive. The first division included university extension work, which continued, but rapidly declined in relative importance. It also tended to lose its non-vocational character since the courses were used by students, particularly private school teachers, who wished to obtain Cambridge University certificates as professional qualifications. The second class of work was the preparation of advanced students for university examinations, and this branch developed rapidly. Finally came the technical college work which included Science and Art classes and an increasing number of more advanced courses provided independently by the College. The university extension movement is treated separately in chapter 8; the other branches of the College work will be considered here.

The original intention of the founders of the University College was that the College should be affiliated to Cambridge University, and a scheme was approved so that a three year course at Nottingham exempted a student from one year's residence at Cambridge. Within a very few years, however, students were looking towards London University rather than towards Cambridge because they were able to take London external degrees and by the middle of the 1880s the most advanced academic courses were those directed at students for London matriculation and external degree examinations. The first student from the College to obtain a degree was Henry T. Saville, who passed the London B.A. in 1885. In the same year three students passed the London intermediate examination in arts and one in science while seven passed the matriculation. By contrast only four students passed the Cambridge higher local examination and these were all women, at least two of them private school teachers.[1] From this time there was generally at least one student in each year who obtained a degree and by 1890 three or four was normal. In 1891, for example, the College obtained eleven successes in matriculation, six in the London intermediate, one B.A. and two B.Sc.[2] The College obtained its first M.A. in 1897 when Cyril Shelbourne passed in Classics.[3] This was a particularly interesting success since Shelbourne had started his school life in a Board school from which he had obtained a scholarship to the Nottingham High School.

---

[1] *University College, Nottingham, Calendar*, 1885–6.
[2] *Ibid.* 1891–2.   [3] *Ibid.* 1896–7.

A feature of the College's work was the large number of women who attended the courses and frequently passed the examinations. The university extension classes, especially those on the arts side were chiefly supported by women who generally took most of the Cambridge certificates.[1] As one might expect, courses in English literature, history and foreign languages attracted most support from women students, but a fair number took scientific subjects. In 1886 two women gained certificates in experimental mechanics, five in hydrostatics and five in light. Women also took a substantial share in the more advanced work. The second College student to gain a degree was Louise Appel who took a B.Sc. in 1886, and two more women graduated in 1889. Five of the eleven students who matriculated in 1891 were women and it appears that there were almost as many women as men on the degree courses at that time.

An extensive programme of technical instruction was undertaken as soon as the College was opened. Most of this work was done in evening classes and by part-time instructors. Many of the instructors were certificated teachers, but others were recruited from outside the profession. One of the original instructors was C. L. Rothera, a vice-chairman of the Nottingham School Board.

This branch of the College's work developed rapidly. Commercial classes started in 1884 and were so popular that it was found necessary to add lecturers in book-keeping and shorthand for the next session. In 1885 classes were begun for the Government teacher's certificate, the expenses being met by the School Board. Engineering made a slow start. A professor of engineering was appointed as early as 1883, but he left almost immediately and was not replaced. Classes in lace, hosiery and mining as well as general engineering were started but there was an acute shortage of accommodation and equipment and progress was disappointing. By 1893, however, new buildings had been provided, the cost being covered partly by the use of the Corporation's share of 'whisky money'[2] and partly by grants from the Draper's Company and the trustees of Mr F. C. Cooper, a Nottingham man who left money 'to promote technical education in arts and sciences among the working class in Nottingham and the county of Nottingham'. In 1890 a professor of engineer-

---

1 See below, chapter 8, pp. 193 ff.

2 Under the terms of an act of 1889 government money was made available to county councils for the encouragement of technical instruction. The money had originally been intended as compensation for publicans who lost their licences in temperance legislation, and it was referred to as 'whisky money'.

ing was appointed, although by a return to a vicious system which was being abolished elsewhere in the educational world, he was paid partly by a share of the fees he took.

Until the turn of the century the development of University College was rapid and the outlook bright. By 1903 there was a staff of 55, the engineering department, with 15 teachers being the largest. In that year a charter of incorporation was taken out and the achievement of university status appeared to lie in the immediate future. The College's work attracted official approval; it first received a government grant of £1,200 in 1889, and by 1902 the grant, at £1,700 was higher than that received by any other similar college. The inspectors were much impressed by the College's success in attracting students of every social class. In 1902 they remarked:[1]

the college stands, so far as we are able to judge, at the head of all English colleges in the number of students who enter it from public elementary schools . . . The opportunities afforded to young working men of ability and promise are very considerable, and from this point of view we think that the college exhibits the nearest approach of all the colleges we have visited to a People's university.

No doubt the democratic nature of the College's enrolment was due, in part at least, to the existence in Nottingham of an extensive higher grade system which made it possible for members of the 'industrious classes' to prepare themselves for, and benefit from, higher education. Where no such system existed a college would have no pool of duly qualified working-class students upon which to draw. However this may be, the inspectors' comments are supported by an analysis of the occupations of students contained in the report of the University College Committee for 1887–8. There were 1,097 students, classified as follows:

teachers in elementary schools	181
teachers in private schools	50
clerks and warehousemen	256
artisans	237
regular students and persons of no specified occupation	194
shop assistants, etc.	179
	1,097

[1] Quoted by A. C. Wood, *A History of the University College, Nottingham*, Blackwell, 1953, p. 42.

And yet from this excellent start the College failed to move forward, and, while other provincial colleges followed the example of Mason's College, Birmingham, in developing into universities, Nottingham remained a university college until after the Second World War. It is hard to explain this curious and disappointing failure with confidence. An important factor in the situation was that no large single benefactor came forward until the days of Jesse Boot in the 1920s. Where other colleges raised £100,000 or more in the early years of the century, an appeal for £50,000 to mark the 25th anniversary of the Nottingham College was a failure. Perhaps this was due in part to the small-scale organization of local industry so that there was no one to start the fund with a large donation. But this can only be a very partial explanation; when all is said and done a local business man started the College in 1880 with a donation of £10,000, and the scale of local industry had not decreased in the intervening years. That there was a measure of public apathy is obvious. Why this was so is less clear.

One fact is certain, however. The College suffered severely from the attitude of the Corporation towards education. The Corporation had succeeded in gaining complete control of the College in its earliest days and its grip tightened with time since the governors appointed by Oxford and Cambridge universities were rarely able to attend meetings and were sometimes not even nominally appointed.[1] The Corporation, at this period, showed itself very determined to gain control of all local educational institutions. It made great efforts to take over the duties of the School Board, even going to the lengths of proposing a private parliamentary bill to anticipate, in this respect, the 1902 Act. Unfortunately the effect of Corporation control upon education was stultifying. Elementary and secondary education, which had been brought to a high degree of efficiency by the School Board were allowed to stagnate or even decline.[2] By 1914 the Board of Education was being forced to bring heavy pressure to bear on the Education Committee to secure a modest rate of progress, and by the 1920s a smaller proportion of Nottingham children were attending secondary schools than in any other similar authority. This was a sad decline from the 1880s and 1890s when the experiments of the School Board in secondary and technical educa-

---

[1] Wood, *University College*, pp. 32 ff.
[2] D. Wardle, 'The History of Education in Nottingham', Ph.D., Nottingham, 1965, chapter XII *passim*.

tion were carried on in spite of the apathy or opposition of the Education Department. It is not really surprising that the University College, under the same management, should suffer a period of stagnation, and it is worth while remembering at this point that even in the first enthusiasm of the 1880s the Corporation had shown little interest in the College as an institute of higher education, and had emphasized its value as a centre for low-grade technical training. It was only in 1912, under pressure from the Board of Education, that the enrolment of students under 16 years of age was discontinued and many elementary courses transferred. Until this reform was effected the elevation of the College to university status was out of the question.

One other institution must be mentioned, the Girls' High School, founded in September 1875 by the Girls' Public Day School Trust. The school received enthusiastic support from the leading local educationalists. Canon Morse and Dr Paton sent their children there, and Dr Gow, headmaster of the Boys' High School was 'a constant friend to the school'.[1] Morse, in a letter to Paton described the school as 'a priceless boon to the town'.[2] Unfortunately, while the school undoubtedly provided efficient teaching for those parents who could afford the fees, its service to the town as a whole was negligible. The school insisted upon fee payment and, in contrast to the Boys' High School, which regularly took boys on scholarships from elementary schools, it refused to entertain any suggestion for a scholarship scheme. This attitude came out very strongly in 1905 when the governors applied for a grant from the Board of Education. The Local Education Authority suggested that in return the school should make ten places per year available to scholarship holders, but the governors bluntly refused saying that there were 'no funds available for scholarships'. The most that they would offer, under intense pressure, was to allow the Education Authority to recommend, on payment of fees, pupils up to 2 per cent of the intake. The Authority's comment was:[3] 'This generous concession would provide secondary education for three scholars every two years. It is impossible to see how, under such conditions, this school can form any

---

[1] L. Magnus, *The Jubilee Book of the Girls' Public Day School Trust*, Cambridge, 1923, p. 84.
[2] *Ibid*. p. 80.
[3] *Minutes of the Nottingham Education Committee*, 21 December 1905.

material part in a general scheme for secondary education in the City.'

The Education Committee attributed the school's attitude to an excessive preoccupation with profit, and it must be said that they had a prima facie case. The Girls' Public Day School Company made substantial profits, which were distributed to shareholders, while individual schools which failed to show a profit were closed – the Education Committee was able to refer to the recent closure of Clapham Modern School for purely financial reasons. The Nottingham school was eminently vulnerable to attack on this point. In the same year that the governors declared that they had 'no funds available for scholarships', the balance sheet showed a profit of £781 1s. 9d. It is hard to avoid the conclusion that these schools were simply unusually well organized private schools.

On the other hand it is an interesting fact that girls' private schools retained their popularity, in Nottingham at least, long after boys' private schools had gone into decline in the 1880s.[1] The main reason for this appears to be that parents continued to look for a 'genteel' education for their daughters and preferred them to attend a school in which there was no risk of them mixing with children of a lower social class. The reluctance of the governors of the Girls' High School to allow a significant scholarship entry was probably inspired, at least in part, by a fear that this would lower the social status of the school. For whatever reason, the Girls' High School, in the period covered by this study, functioned as a fairly exclusive private school, and, unlike the Boys' High School, showed no interest whatever in contributing to the developing system of education which grew up in the School Board period.

[1] See below, chapter 7, p. 162.

7

PRIVATE SCHOOLS

It is a curiosity of educational history that very little attention has been given to the work of schools which were run for profit. In the field of secondary education interest has been almost exclusively concentrated upon the public and grammar schools, and private schools are mentioned in passing if they are mentioned at all. But the most cursory glance at readily available statistics will demonstrate that in dismissing private schools in this manner one is writing off the schools which provided, at the most conservative estimate, three-quarters of all the education which could be reasonably called secondary, at any time before 1890, at the very earliest. For example, Mann, who compiled the educational section of the 1851 census, calculated that there were 600,000 children receiving some form of secondary education; 50,000 of these he estimated to be in public and grammar schools, 50,000 were educated at home by tutors or parents, and 500,000 were in private schools.[1]

Local evidence bears out Mann's estimate. The only local public school providing recognizably secondary education in the town in 1851 was the Free Grammar School which provided places for some 200 boys; there was no public secondary school for girls at all. At the same time there were about twenty private academies and seminaries in the town providing secondary education for girls and boys. None of these was as large as the Free Grammar School but several of the larger boys' schools had 40–100 pupils; girls' schools were rather smaller. But at the most conservative estimate these schools provided accommodation for 600–700 children.[2] It is true that some of these children were younger than secondary school age, but the same was true at the Free Grammar School. It remains the case that at least three-quarters of children undergoing secondary education in the town were at private schools, and this estimate does not take into account either those children who were attending private schools in the suburbs or nearby towns and villages, or those

[1] Mann, *1851 Census*, p. xliv.
[2] The census recorded 100 private schools of all types in the town with 2,563 children in attendance.

children who were educated at home – and at a rather earlier date one teacher alone visited 76 private pupils over a seven-year period. In addition to the 600 or 700 children mentioned above a similar number attended some 25 private writing schools doing work exactly comparable with the Bluecoat School and High Pavement.

Secondary education at the present day is dominated by non-profit making institutions, whether independent schools or schools within the state system. It is natural, but mistaken for historians to read this state of affairs backwards into the nineteenth century and to ignore the notorious decline of grammar schools in this period and their inadequacy to cope with a rapidly rising population. Private schools, by their nature, do not tend to keep or transmit comprehensive records, while public and grammar schools are generally well documented. The tendency is, therefore, for historians to ignore private schools or to follow the dangerous policy of using works of fiction – Dickens and Brontë are generally quoted – as sources.

In elementary education the practice of historians is not so much to ignore private schools as to dismiss them all as rather comically inefficient and educationally insignificant. Thus S. D. Chapman, in compiling a list of Nottingham day schools, omits 'the infamous dame schools which, in Nottingham as elsewhere, were merely convenient arrangements for childminding'.[1] But not all private elementary schools were 'dame' schools; some were quite respectable institutions, limited in achievement and equipment certainly, but hardly more so than contemporary public elementary schools. And, good or bad, they provided places for half the elementary school children in the town, even in 1851 when public provision was expanding rapidly. One cannot simply dismiss the education of a large section of the population – there were 14,000 such schools in England in 1851 – without a serious attempt to discover its quality.

With these thoughts in mind it is proposed to examine Nottingham private schools in some detail. For this purpose it will be convenient to adopt the classification used by Mann in 1851.[2] He divided the schools under three headings:

(1) Superior (Classical, Boarding, Proprietory, Ladies) . . . 4,956 schools.

[1] Chapman, *Evangelical Revival*, p. 47.
[2] Mann, *1851 Census*, p. xxxiii.

(2) Middling (commercial, etc.: teaching arithmetic, English grammar and geography) . . . 7,095 schools.

(3) Inferior (principally dame schools; only reading and writing taught; the latter not always) . . . 13,879 schools.

The first category of school may be definitely described as secondary. Boys' schools in this class may be subdivided into 'Classical' and 'English' academies; girls' schools were generally described as seminaries, but there were variations in nomenclature. The 'middling' schools, as the word suggests, came in between elementary and secondary. They took elementary pupils, but carried their work up to the age of 12–14 years, most of their older pupils being intended for jobs as clerks, cashiers, warehousemen, etc. In the seventeenth and eighteenth century they were generally known as 'writing schools' and this usage will be continued here, although the name became obsolete in the first half of the nineteenth century. High Pavement and the Bluecoat School competed in this field, as did People's College at a later date. Mann's description of the third class of schools expresses their function admirably and there is no need to elaborate on it at this stage. The only point to make is that schools regularly moved from one class to another according to their success or their proprietor's ambition.

The period from 1780 to 1880 was one of great prosperity for 'superior' private schools, as indeed for private schools of all kinds. Such schools catered for the children of the prosperous and expanding middle class, whose parents wished for a fairly substantial education for their sons, and a training in the 'accomplishments' for their daughters, and until well into the second half of the nineteenth century the private schools, in Nottingham at least, had the field virtually to themselves. Until the 1830s the Free Grammar School was in an inefficient state, and even as late as the 1870s most boys were leaving at 13 or 14 years. The public schools, until the age of the railway, were difficult of access. Until well into the century their reputation, intellectually and morally, was low, and they had no attraction for families with no public school tradition. Even when Arnold and others had removed the worst abuses there remained their expense and their insistence upon an exclusively classical curriculum.

To meet the demand for secondary education three types of private school flourished in and around Nottingham. First, the small select boarding academy with a classical curriculum aimed avowedly at university entrance, and almost always run by clergy-men in their own house, without regular assistance. Second, the much larger 'English' academy, which concentrated on a com-mercial, and sometimes a technical course. The distinction between the first and second was as much social as academic, a fact which was reflected in their fees. The third class of school was the 'Young Ladies' Seminary'.

Purely classical schools were not numerous and were nearly always small. They catered for a class which could afford fees of 50–80 guineas per year plus extras, and wished for the classical curriculum of the public school but with close personal supervision and a measure of comfort. Parents who sent their boys to these schools objected to the moral and physical conditions of the public school, and yet wished for their children to have some contact with other – selected – boys. Advertisements for these schools laid signi-ficant stress upon personal supervision, the limited number of pupils, good living conditions and the absence of an institutional atmosphere. The headmaster of the Castle Gate Academy, which flourished in the first quarter of the nineteenth century strikes exactly this note: 'Pupils regularly breakfast, dine and drink tea with himself – they constituting a family establishment, which it is his endeavour to regulate with paternal attention, rather than to govern with the authority of a master'.[1] The evidence suggests that the classical academies were the first private schools to die out. They flourished exceedingly until about 1830 and a few continued into the 1850s, but shortly after this they disappeared. It is reasonable to assume that the improvement of the old public schools, and the appearance of new, or revived, independent schools drew off their clientele. No doubt declining interest in the classics contributed to their decay.

Two advertisements for local schools will serve as illustrations. In October 1784 the Rev. Gilbert Wakefield, of Bramcote, an-nounced that he proposed to: 'educate young Gentlemen in the Greek, Latin and English languages. Terms: For Boarders, con-fined to 10, 50 guineas per annum and 3 guineas entry . . . Those of proper age will be instructed in the principles of Mathematics and Philosophy. One vacation per year i.e. five weeks beginning at Midsummer'.[2] A few years later the Rev. W. Beetham, vicar of Bunny, 'purposes to take six young gentlemen into his house to

[1] *Nottingham Journal*, 1 January 1820.   [2] *Ibid.* 9 October 1784.

prepare them for the university. The treatment will be liberal and particular attention will be paid to their morals'.[1] Beetham's fees were the same as Wakefield's, and there was little difference between the fees of different institutions; schools of all classes kept to a well understood, if unwritten, scale of charges. Six to ten boarders was the customary number and several masters, like Wakefield, offered to include mathematics and science. Many of the men who ran these small classical academies were highly educated, even eminent in their field and there is no doubt that they provided a good education, perhaps as good as was obtainable at the time. These schools were, of course, the direct descendants of the 'dissenting academies', which have attracted much attention from educational historians. In the Nottingham area, there is no evidence that these academies were a specifically dissenting venture; there were at least as many Anglican clergymen as Dissenters offering their services. The newspaper in which Beetham advertised also contained notices about schools kept by four other local Anglican clergymen.

One or two schools made a particular point of offering advanced work to older pupils. In 1808 Mr Catlow, of Mansfield, offered[2] 'private tuition for foreign gentlemen and others who, having finished their school education, may wish to pursue their literary and commercial studies with the advantages of access to a select library, philosophical apparatus, etc.'. Many years later the Rev. B. Carpenter, minister at High Pavement Unitarian Chapel observed of his school, which enjoyed much esteem in the mid-nineteenth century: 'the plan is principally adapted to those young persons who wish to continue their improvement after their school education is finished'.[3] It is not clear, at this distance in time, whether these two clergymen, both Unitarians, were offering a university education for Dissenters who did not wish or could not afford to travel to Scotland or the Continent, or whether the advertisements were merely politely disguised offers of cramming for university entrance. Both schools enjoyed a high reputation for scholarship and were patronized by pupils of all denominations; one former pupil of Carpenter's became Dean of St Paul's.

The small classical academies were not quite without competition. One or two of the headmasters of the Free Grammar School advertised for private pupils on exactly the same terms, and offering

---

[1] *Nottingham Journal*, 15 June 1793.   [2] *Ibid.* 23 January 1808.
[3] *Nottingham Review*, 14 January 1842.

the same advantages – small numbers, comfortable quarters and personal supervision.[1] The larger 'English' academies also generally had classical wings, and it was customary to employ a clergyman as classical master. The work of the classical students always loomed large in advertisements because of its prestige value, but it seems likely that the only important academy in Nottingham which genuinely concentrated on classical rather than commercial work was Nottingham Academy. This school was established in 1776 on Parliament Street, then rather unhappily known as 'Back Side'. For some years it functioned as an ordinary English and Commercial Academy, taking boys up to about 14 years of age and charging fees of 14 guineas per year. At this stage Latin and Greek appeared on the list of extra subjects for which an additional fee was charged. After 1814, however, it was bought by a Dr Nicholson who raised it in social and academic status. Its fees rose to £35, and vacancies were advertised for older pupils who were 'finishing their education' at 50 guineas. The school was a very flourishing concern at this time, employing six assistants. Nicholson sold out about 1830 and moved to Twickenham where he had another successful school.

Far larger and more numerous than the classical academies were the 'Literary and Commercial' or 'English' academies. These were substantial institutions with a good many pupils – 60–120 appears to have been usual – and as many as four or six assistants, of whom one was almost invariably a clergyman, responsible for the classical side, and another a foreigner who taught modern languages. 'English' academies often outlived the original proprietor, because there was good-will, equipment and often a building to transfer. At least one Nottingham school lasted for over 90 years and others exceeded 50.

Proprietors of academies were very conscious of the changing educational demands of the period. They found that, although there was a growing demand for secondary education, the traditional curriculum did not meet the need. The particular problem was to strike a balance between general education and technical instruction in a course finishing, for the great majority of pupils, between 14 and 16 years of age. In their attempted solution they found themselves forced back upon a rather desperate trust in formal training. It has been assumed that the doctrine of the transfer of training was merely a rationalization justifying adherence to the classics. In fact

[1] See, e.g. *Nottingham Journal*, 11 April 1794.

nineteenth-century teachers were rather prolific in inventing new subjects, but they were very aware of the impossibility of providing pupils with specific training in every skill – social, political, technical – which they would require in later life. The alternative was to produce a 'core' curriculum and hope for transfer to take place.

Something very like the curriculum of a modern secondary school emerged from these experiments – the Classics, English, mathematics, science, modern languages, history and geography – accompanied very often by a speciality of the school, commercial work perhaps, or drawing. But these subjects were rarely taught well. With the exception of classics and mathematics they did not exist as school subjects and few teachers had given much thought to why or how they should be taught. Very frequently a teacher who attempted one of the new subjects found it necessary to write his own textbook, and it was not until the last quarter of the century that the external examinations began to bring about a measure of standardization in method and content.

Parents, too, were inclined to overset schemes of conscientious headmasters. It was virtually impossible to persuade them to allow their children to follow complete and balanced courses. Boys were entered for narrow, strictly vocational courses and subjects with no immediate utilitarian value were condemned as irrelevant frills. Girls' schools, in contrast, were forced to follow a completely fragmented curriculum with nothing pursued in any depth. If advertisements of private schools are examined the result is always the same. The basic fee covers the three R's only; everything else is extra. Only in the 1830s and 1840s were a few of the better established schools able to widen their basic course. In 1836 Standard Hill Academy offered 'Board and reading, English grammar, penmanship, arithmetic, book-keeping and the rudiments of geography', and this was typical of contemporary advertisements. The best private school masters, Catlow from Mansfield or Goodacre at Standard Hill, struggled hard to persuade parents to accept a consolidated fee, but with little success.

Even when pupils were persuaded to follow a rational course of study they rarely stayed at school long enough for it to be carried to completion. Catlow proposed a course which lasted for six or seven years. Goodacre was more modest and aimed at four years, but the records of his school show that even this period was rarely achieved, at least by his boarders. Of the 28 boarders who entered the school in 1809:[1]

> 5 stayed less than 1 year
> 12 stayed 1 year and less than 2
> 5 stayed 2 years and less than 3
> 1 stayed 3 years and less than 4
> 4 stayed 4 years and less than 5
> 1 stayed 5 years

Thus most pupils must have taken an incomplete course, and the curricula designed by Goodacre, Catlow and others need to be seen as ideals at which to aim rather than descriptions of an existing situation.

Private schools frequently specialized in some branch of study. Standard Hill, for example, appears to have provided some sort of training in pharmacy. Certainly the pupils who stayed longest were very often the sons of apothecaries, and the school possessed a 'lecture room for applied science'. It is known that parents and old boys were invited to attend lectures in the evenings. Another speciality of Standard Hill was astronomy. The founder, Robert Goodacre, achieved some prominence as a lecturer in the subject and there was an observatory in the roof, and apparatus. George Packer, who was one of the best known local schoolmasters in the middle of the century, advertised that 'pupils intended for the Practical Arts or Agriculture are taught chemical analysis in a Laboratory provided for the purpose', and Chestnut House Academy at Arnold and Sherwood House Academy on Mansfield Road were two other schools which made a point of their facilities for practical work in science. At least two schools are recorded which claimed to prepare pupils for civil engineering, among other pursuits.

All schools offered commercial work, but one or two made a particular point of it. Scott's Academy on Parliament Street, considered one of the five most prominent schools in the town by the historian Blackner in 1815, emphasized office training, and book-keeping was part of the basic course rather than an extra as was more usual. Scott claimed to have made a special study of the office methods of local firms.

Modern languages and drawing were taught in most schools by

[1] Standard Hill Manuscripts, Nottingham Public Library.

peripatetic teachers. The Revolutionary wars and the periodic political disturbances on the Continent meant that there was usually a supply of educated foreigners willing to make a living by teaching. French was universally offered and German was common. The George Street Academy added Italian to the list and one academy at Wetherby, which advertised in Nottingham around 1800 offered Persian. Curiously, no school has come to light which offered instruction in any of the Indian languages, especially surprising since old boys of the schools regularly went to India. The Standard Hill manuscripts record one boy who distinguished himself in the Burmese War and another who died in India, 'devoured, as is supposed, by a tiger'. Drawing was a special interest in some schools. The artist R. P. Bonington assisted his mother in running a school in Arnold which later moved to Nottingham, and at about the same period Brockmer's Academy at Mansfield advertised that 'any pupil with a genius for drawing or engraving is especially encouraged'.[1]

In the second half of the nineteenth century there was a marked tendency for courses to become more uniform. This was undoubtedly much to do with the spread of external examinations. The grants of the Science and Art Department were avowedly designed to stimulate private enterprise in science teaching, and, as well as providing revenue, success in these examinations was useful for advertising purposes. The same was true of the examinations of the College of Preceptors and the Society of Arts and the prizes offered by bodies such as the Royal Geographical Society. The Oxford and Cambridge Middle Class examinations appeared in the 1850s and ten years later University Extension certificates became popular as targets for private schools. No doubt the increasing uniformity of courses in private schools meant the loss of interesting experiments, but there was a reverse side. The increasing demand for universally acceptable proof of educational achievement made it easier for schoolmasters to insist upon the pupils following a rational course.

Private schoolmasters reacted strongly against the traditions of public and grammar schools. The public schools, in particular, were grossly understaffed and many of their moral and disciplinary problems derived from this. In the more prosperous academies a ratio of 15–20 pupils per teacher was usual. Nottingham Academy had seven teachers for rather over 100 boys in the 1820s, and a few years later Standard Hill had five full-time teachers to 80 boys.

1 *Nottingham Journal*, 27 November 1802.

With this staff/pupil ratio headmasters had a fair chance of preventing misconduct and of detecting it when it had been committed. They thus enjoyed a distinct advantage over public school masters who were compelled to rely upon the deterrent effects of draconic punishment, and many teachers appear to have conscientiously attempted to avoid corporal punishment except as a last resort. Instead they adopted a policy of very close supervision and constant competition. Every effort was made in class to excite emulation, with frequent promotion and relegation and complicated systems of rewards. The aim, as it was expressed by Goodacre of Standard Hill, was to 'remove temptation to wrong (and) to interest the community of pupils in correcting or exposing the follies and vices of individuals'.

In marked contrast to the public schools of the day some private schools at least did attempt to secure the cooperation of their pupils by avoiding harsh and authoritarian teaching methods, and giving the curriculum breadth and relevance. University House School, for example, had a workshop about which it would be interesting to know more. Mathematics was frequently given a practical slant by relating it to engineering and surveying, and foreign languages were taught colloquially. When the railways made travelling easier educational visits were not uncommon, sometimes undertaken by two or more schools together. In 1846 a party from Standard Hill, University House and Packer's Academy visited Lincoln. Several schools went to the Mechanics' Exhibition in Derby in 1843.

Much use was made by local schools of the university extension classes, especially after the opening of University College. A number of schools used the facilities of the College to supplement their own, a process made easy by the fact that the fashionable area for private schools in the 1880s was around the Arboretum, a very short walk from the College. Schools frequently advertised in the College Calendar, and a typical advertisement was for University House School,[1]

Arrangements have been made by which the course at this old-established school will be preparatory to the course at University College, and the elder boys who have arrived at a certain standard may receive instruction at the College from the Professors, and thus avail themselves of the affiliation of the College to the University of Cambridge.

[1] *University College, Nottingham, Calendar,* 1883-4.

Girls' schools also used the classes at University College; in fact women, and particularly private school teachers, provided the principal support for university extension classes. Derby House School, run by Mrs and Miss Lacy, appears to have enjoyed much success in the College examinations. In its advertisement in the College Calendar it pointed out that its course was planned to include attendance at College classes, and went on:

During the last two years 56 certificates have been obtained by pupils in the examinations, and in 6 cases the candidates passed with distinction. 6 Vice-Chancellor's certificates have been obtained during the same time. Last year the Mayor's, the Sheriff's and two other prizes were taken by pupils of this school.

It was extremely easy to set up as a school teacher. Masters of public and grammar schools, like the proprietors of classical academies were generally graduates, and often clergymen; they of course had no training for the profession of teaching. It was notorious that the proprietors of cheap private schools frequently had neither training nor education. An examination of the careers of the masters of the substantial academies which are discussed in this section, shows that they generally spent some time learning the trade in an established school before setting up on their own, and that they began in a small way, rising in the social scale as they prospered. It was not unusual for an intending teacher to serve a formal apprenticeship. Advertisements for articled pupils were frequent, and at least one well known Nottingham teacher, Henry Shipley, who was tutor to the poet Henry Kirke-White, served an apprenticeship to Wilkinson, the original proprietor of Nottingham Academy. A typical advertisement for an apprentice appeared in August 1810; unfortunately the academy was not named;

To Schoolmasters

Wanted in a respectable academy where there are three assistants, a young man about 17 years of age to be engaged for four years. He must understand common arithmetic, write a promising hand, and be in some degree acquainted with English grammar. He will possess ample means of improvement in all the various branches of education, and be allowed a proper salary. A schoolmaster's son who has assisted his father will be preferred.

The qualifications stipulated in this advertisement were repeated in others, and where a formal apprenticeship was not taken up, it was quite usual for young men to be employed as junior assistants, and be allowed 'ample means for improvement' a phrase which occurs quite frequently. Young women also served apprenticeships, either formal or informal, and once again the accomplishments expected of a trainee were fairly constant;

The friends of a young lady, seventeen years of age, are desirous of placing her in a respectable Ladies' Establishment, where her services may be made a sufficient remuneration for the completion of her studies. She is competent to take the classes in English, to give instruction in wax flowers and fruit, and to assist in drawing, French and music . . .[1]

The apprenticeship system meant that there was much inter-connection between local academies. Goodacre learned the trade with Cursham of Mansfield, and at least three of his assistants later ran successful schools. Men who were setting up schools frequently used as a recommendation the fact that they were former pupils or assistants of notable teachers. Thus in 1860 a Mr Theker, then opening Angelo House School which flourished for many years, drew attention to his long engagement as principal tutor to Sampson Biddulph, who ran a school for over fifty years, his pupils including W. G. Ward, Mayor of Nottingham and original vice-chairman of the Nottingham School Board, and William Booth, founder of the Salvation Army. The network of relationships extended into the public schools of the town. Two headmasters of High Pavement claimed to be pupils of local teachers. John Malbon was an assistant of Shipley, and John Taylor had worked for J. D. Rogers of St James's Academy. Taylor's son, after succeeding his father at High Pavement for a few months, resigned and ran a school on Forest Road for many years.

The amenities offered by the academies varied very widely. Some country schools were well provided by any standards. Catlow's school had 12 acres of ground and a swimming bath 20 yards by 12 yards. Chestnut House at Arnold was specially built as a school and had 'a private and spacious playground, a gymnasium with all requisite equipment and a new and capacious lecture and recreation hall, 36 feet by 17 feet. Hot and cold water baths have also been constructed'.[2]

[1] *Nottingham Journal*, 20 December 1850.
[2] Wright's *Nottingham Directory*, 1877.

Schools in the town itself suffered from the prevailing shortage of space. Nottingham Academy and Standard Hill both stood in their own ground, but a picture of Standard Hill shows that the grounds were no more than a moderate sized garden, although it was equipped with a maypole, climbing frame and other apparatus. The many schools which were situated round St Mary's Church and High Pavement must have been very cramped for in that area even a small yard was a prized possession. Biddulph's well known school in Halifax Place, for example, can have had virtually no room for recreation, although he improved the situation by moving to Willoughby House, which even today possesses an unexpected and attractive garden on the rock overlooking Broad Marsh. After about 1850 most of the more fashionable schools were to be found in the district around Waverley Street, Forest Road and Mansfield Road. Many of the houses in that area have substantial gardens and the nearby Forest and Arboretum provided ample space for exercise and recreation.

Classrooms and domestic accommodation were seriously over-crowded by modern standards. Many schools took 'parlour boarders' who paid extra for having a room and bed to themselves, and this suggests that the other boarders were packed in very tightly. An advertisement for the Nottingham Academy, a well known and expensive school, made a special mention of the fact that there were only two beds to a room and not more than two boys to a bed.[1]

On the whole schools of this class drew their pupils from a small radius round Nottingham. A few particularly well-known schools had a wider sphere. At the height of its fame Standard Hill drew pupils from Manchester, Knighton, Waltham and London, apart from a few French boys, who presumably had connections with Nottingham through the lace trade. Newton at Chestnut House offered testimonials from the Isle of Man, Lincoln and Scarborough. A schoolmaster from Wetherby found it worthwhile to advertise in Nottingham. But the great majority of the country schools which advertised in Nottingham newspapers fell within a radius of 25 miles of the town. Between them the local schools educated an impressive list of important citizens:

Between 1797 and 1825 eleven of the Nottingham hosiers of the 1840s attended Standard Hill Academy. These hosiers came from the leading Whig families of the city. More than a dozen other future hosiers whose

[1] *Nottingham Journal*, 9 January 1802.

careers were shorter, and who did not fall within the sample dates of this study, attended the Academy during these years, as well as other students who became drapers, dyers, bleachers and lace merchants.[1]

Other schools did not leave records, but enough is known of their alumni to show that the private academy was the normal route by which middle class boys acquired a secondary education in the nineteenth century. Among local poets and authors, Byron attended Roger's St James' Academy, Henry Kirke-White went to Nottingham Academy and later to Shipley's school. Philip James Bailey, author of the immensely popular poem 'Festus' attended a small but select school kept by the Rev. B. Carpenter, minister of High Pavement. James Prior Kirk another prolific but almost forgotten writer, was educated at the Misses Goodall's preparatory school, followed by Cleveland House Academy, kept by Gregory Porter. Bailey's contemporaries at Carpenter's school included Richard Enfield, prominent in the foundation of University College, Nottingham; Dr Gregory, Dean of St Paul's; E. J. Lowe, a noted meteorologist and Francis Hart, a local banker. Sir Arthur Liberty attended University House School, where another pupil was L. P. Jacks, principal of Manchester College, Oxford. Among distinguished local men who were educated at private schools outside the town were William Felkin, Gilbert Wakefield and the artists Paul Sandby and R. P. Bonington.

As a school achieved a reputation its clientele rose in the social scale, but the evidence suggests that Nottingham schools drew their pupils from a wider social range than might be expected. Among the boarders at Standard Hill in its most prosperous days were the sons of several framework knitters, a book-keeper and a gamekeeper. Attendance as a day pupil was not expensive and it is likely that day boys were even more mixed than boarders.

It may be useful to give a very brief summary of the history of two individual schools, as this will illustrate certain aspects of the rise and decline of such institutions.

Robert Goodacre was the son of a village schoolmaster and learned the trade as an assistant to Cursham at Sutton-in-Ashfield, opening a small school in Nottingham about 1798. This was purely a day school and probably classed as a 'writing school', and Goodacre

[1] C. Erikson, *British Industrialists, Steel and Hosiery, 1850–1950*, Cambridge, 1959, p. 40.

added to his income, like many other teachers, by taking evening classes, attending private pupils at home, and acting as visiting teacher at girls' schools. As he prospered he gave up first the evening work, then the private pupils and finally, but not until 1817, attendance at girls' schools; this appears to have been thought consonant with the dignity of the proprietor of an academy as both Scott and Biddulph are known to have continued in the practice. In 1801 Goodacre took over the school of a Mr Kell on Parliament Street. He started taking boarders and engaged a clergyman as classical assistant, thus raising the school to the status of an academy. In 1807 he moved again, to Standard Hill where the academy remained for 50 years. On his father's death in 1836 William Goodacre, who had assisted in the school and also taught art in America, took over, being joined as partner shortly afterwards by Thomas Cockayne, son of the master of the Bluecoat School, who had been an assistant for eleven years. A move to Chilwell in 1859 proved to be a mistake and the school settled on Forest Road where it remained until it closed in 1891, Goodacre having retired 17 years earlier. There are grounds for believing that it had been in a run-down condition for some years before closing; possibly the competition of higher grade schools and the revived High School was too much for Cockayne who must have been well into his seventies.

The St James's Academy differed from Standard Hill in remaining in the same building, but passing several times under different management. J. D. Rogers, the founder, started, like Goodacre, in quite a small way with a day school offering instruction to 'ladies' as well as 'gentlemen'; no doubt, as in Biddulph's school, there was a 'separate apartment for young ladies'. It was at this period that he was engaged as classical tutor to Lord Byron. By 1810 he was established at St James's Street where he continued until 1824, his school being recognized as one of the principal academies in the town.

On his retirement in 1824 he sold out to two of his assistants, who in turn sold the school to two men, Oliver and Wells who had previously run an academy on George Street. In 1834 a Mr Noyes bought the school, and in the next few years, the school, which retained its reputation through its changes of management, played several cricket matches against Standard Hill and the Free Grammar School, the earliest inter-school sporting events of which any local record has survived. In January 1850 a Mr Danford took control and the school continued to flourish until 1860 when it disappears from the records.

Girls' private schools were extremely numerous and continued to flourish after the decline of the boys' schools had set in. In 1879, out of 82 schools mentioned in a local directory, 69 were run by women, and allowing for a few mixed kindergarten it is safe to say that three-quarters of all private schools were for girls. By 1899 the situation was still more clearly marked for only 5 out of 46 schools were run by men. On the other hand many of the girls' schools were small and few, if any, were of the size and permanence of Standard Hill or St James's Academy. Much of what has been said of boys' schools applies to girls' schools as well, but certain features of the girls' schools merit special attention.

The girls' schools generally offered a less substantial curriculum than boys' schools. A typical school at the beginning of the nineteenth century offered 'English grammar, French, music, needlework and writing'. Other schools offered a large variety of extras – dancing, painting on silk, embroidery – but it is significant that writing frequently appeared among the extras for which additional payment was required. It may be said as a generalization that the education offered in a girls' school was neither useful nor intellectually stimulating. There is no trace whatever of a training suitable for a future housewife, and little encouragement to study any subject in depth. Of vocational training there is, as was to be expected, almost no sign. One school in 1810 did offer a course which included arithmetic and book-keeping but this was very much the exception, and this school was run by a man; it was not particularly unusual for men to run girls' schools at the period.

At least one school in Nottingham offered to girls a curriculum very similar to that found in boys' academies. This was founded about 1823 by Mrs Catherine Turner, widow of a minister of High Pavement Chapel, and one of the visiting masters was the father of Herbert Spencer, who visited weekly to teach natural philosophy. Writing and arithmetic were taught by John Taylor, headmaster of High Pavement school. A letter from a girl who boarded at the school in 1842[1] shows that the course included English grammar, French, Latin, arithmetic, geography, dancing, drawing and singing.

In the second half of the century the curricula of girls' schools

1 Preserved in the Nottingham University Department of Manuscripts.

became more substantial under the influence of external examinations and the university extension movement. The extension classes at University College were dominated by women, many of them teachers or pupils of private schools. Women tended to concentrate on the arts side, but some ventured to take courses in geology, botany and mechanics. In 1886 two women took Cambridge certificates in experimental mechanics, five in hydrostatics and five in light.

Teachers were prominent in these examinations, and, once again, some of them took courses in science, and presumably passed on their knowledge to their pupils. Louisa Billings, who ran Hailebury House School on Park Row, took a College certificate in chemistry and qualitative analysis and a Cambridge Higher Local certificate in chemistry, geology and physical geography. At about the same time Miss Annable of Laureate Villa, Forest Road, advertised that she was certificated by the Science and Art Department and that pupils were prepared for the Department's examination, and the Oxford and Cambridge Locals. The case of the Derby House school has already been mentioned.[1]

No very clear line may be drawn between writing schools and academies; indeed many academies began as writing schools and moved up the scale as they prospered. Certain fairly definite points of difference do emerge, however. Writing schools very seldom offered languages; their curriculum was more confined than that of the academies, with fewer extras and usually with a marked bias towards commercial subjects. They were generally smaller than academies, often one-man concerns and frequently only occupying one or two rooms. It was not usual for them to take boarders; their clientele was local and when they did take boarders they were few in number, perhaps four or six. Finally there were very few writing schools for girls. Charles Watson ran a girls' school which offered book-keeping and accounts about 1810, and T. W. Turner, who had a large establishment on Parliament Street about 20 years later, had an evening class for girls. Generally, however, the assumption was that commercial training was for boys.

The curriculum of the writing school was fairly limited. Reading, writing and arithmetic – generally described as 'accounts', book-keeping and mathematics were the staple subjects, while 'geography and the use of globes', shorthand and surveying appeared quite

[1] Above, p. 157.

commonly. Drawing was offered by a few schools, a logical extra since penmanship was still considered as something of an art. A characteristic advertisement is that of Paul Bull and son who announced in 1793 that they had 'fitted up a commodious schoolroom in the Swan Yard, Beastmarket Hill as a day school. English, writing and arithmetic (vulgar and decimal). They will instruct their pupils in mensuration and surveying (theoretical and practical) as often as opportunity will permit'. A later advertisement gave further details;

English . . . 4s. per quarter.
writing and arithmetic . . . 7s. 6d. per quarter
    (including pens and ink)
mensuration . . . 10s. 6d. per quarter.
Plain trigonometry, land surveying, algebra, merchants' accounts . . .
    5s. per quarter extra.
Evening schools (1) 6–8 p.m.
               (2) 8–9 p.m.[1]

Few of the masters of writing schools relied solely upon their day school for their income. Many had evening classes which were presumably intended for older pupils who were at work during the day; several had two evening classes each night, like the Bulls, which meant a long working day. Others worked as visiting teachers, and there was a brisk demand for their services both from schools and from private individuals. The Free Grammar School, after its reorganization in 1834, employed two writing masters, both of whom also had their own school; Nottingham Academy employed two more, and other schools had one or more. Much of the private teaching they did was not specifically commercial in nature. They competed with other teachers for the private coaching posts in the neighbourhood, and this was a large and profitable market; Goodacre, in his early days, had 76 private pupils between 1798 and 1806, which represented a considerable addition to his income.

A few teachers combined teaching with entirely different jobs. The earliest teacher whose advertisements have survived was a Thomas Peat who announced in the Leicester and Nottingham Journal in 1758 that he was a 'writing master, accountant and surveyor'. Turner of Parliament Street was another who offered his services as an accountant, a fairly common and logical alternative profession for a commercial teacher. It is rather more surprising to find a man described in a directory of 1844 as 'schoolmaster and corn

[1] *Nottingham Journal*, 19 September 1793.

inspector', and yet this man's school flourished for at least 15 years.

On the whole the writing schools were small institutions and their life was confined to the career of one proprietor; there is little evidence of the transfer of schools from one man to another, as with the larger secondary schools. Nevertheless, they were not ephemeral institutions. Many can be traced for 25 to 30 years and some for longer still, and the absence of record does not necessarily mean that the school was defunct. Most of the evidence about them comes from advertisements and if a school did not advertise it might be simply because the master had as much work as he could manage, and many schools were one-man affairs.

But, although they were not in a big way of business it would be a mistake to think of writing masters as the disreputable and ignorant failures who appear as private school teachers in fiction. There was a substantial difference between an established writing school and a common day school, although, of course, some schools spanned the gap. Writing schools catered generally for the skilled artisan and clerk class of family, which could afford to lay out two or three guineas per year at the least on the education of its children, and the masters were men with a definite and recognizable skill to offer. Several of them rose to take charge of an academy, and were men of education, and others who did not aspire to this, or who could not afford the necessary capital, were employed by the Free Grammar School, or by the major academies of the town. These establishments which between them educated the children of all the leading families in the town, were in the highest degree unlikely to employ men who were either incompetent or disreputable. The profession of writing master stood rather below that of the proprietor of an academy intellectually and socially. It corresponded exactly with that of master of a charity school like Bluecoat or High Pavement, or of a master at the People's College and there was, in fact, a continuous inter-relationship between these groups. John Malbon, master of High Pavement, advertised his services in 1811 as a visiting teacher of writing and arithmetic. Another High Pavement master, J. Barradell, opened his own writing school which prospered for over 30 years, while at least one assistant from People's College ran a successful school.

Writing schools were among the earlier private schools to die out, and did so shortly after the classical academies. There was a marked reduction in their numbers after 1870, and after 1880 they disappeared completely. They were peculiarly vulnerable to the competition of Board schools since their basic work was the provision of a type of higher elementary education which Board schools could provide at a far lower fee. The appearance of higher grade schools with commercial departments in the 1880s must have been a severe blow to the writing schools which had survived as long as that, and it may be said with a fair degree of accuracy that this event marked the end of the writing school in Nottingham.

The 'common day' and 'dame' schools formed much the largest class of private school. These were the schools which fell into Mann's 'inferior' class, and may be distinguished from the less prosperous writing schools by the narrowness of their curriculum, which Mann described as 'reading and writing only . . . the latter not always'. An alternative method of classification, used by the School Board in its enquiries, was that schools which charged a fee of less than 9d. per week were put in this class. These schools are very difficult to trace since they rarely advertised in the press, and could function for many years without attracting the slightest attention; no single school can be studied throughout its career as can most academies and many writing schools. However there were so many schools that it is possible to collect enough information to give some account of their conditions and of the lives of their teachers.

In 1851 there were about 75 common day and dame schools in the town and the surrounding poor law districts, and in 1871 the Statistical Committee of the School Board found 33 such schools in the borough alone. In the first half of the century these schools were much the most numerous form of educational agency. But, although numerous, the schools were generally very small. When the statistical committee conducted its enquiry in 1871 it found six schools markedly larger than the rest, with enrolments of 110, 94, 80, 60, 45, and 39 pupils respectively. These were quite substantial schools which probably occupied two or three rooms, a converted chapel or some similar accommodation. By the standards of the day they were respectable establishments and the School Board was prepared to accept five of them as efficient with only minor amendments. They, however, were exceptional and 20–30 pupils would constitute a sizeable school. Many were much smaller than this and in 1871 ten schools had fewer than 12 pupils; Mrs Gamble, on Alfred Street had four.

These figures serve to point out a distinction between two classes of school. The dame school catered almost entirely for very young children and was usually no more than a baby-minding establishment, while the common day school took some rather older pupils and perhaps added writing and even a little arithmetic to its curriculum. The distinction was not a clear one, but it is obvious that the man whose school in the People's Hall had 110 children, and was considered as acceptable with only minor alterations by the School Board, was in a very different way of business from Mrs Gamble with four babies in a tiny room on Alfred Street.

The amenities offered by the worst schools were very bad. One school in 1871 had 27 children packed into a room of 130 square feet and another had 36 children in a room 14 feet long by 10 feet wide. Equipment sometimes amounted to no more than a couple of forms and a few damaged reading cards. However, these were extreme cases. Applying the Education Department's formula only six out of the 33 schools investigated in 1871 were seriously overcrowded and 22 were not full.

In speaking of the qualifications and character of the teachers caution is necessary. It was dangerously easy to set up a school; all that was needed was a room and a notice to put in the window. Many teachers were notoriously recruited from those who had failed in other occupations and were, in the words of the Children's Employment Commission, 'entirely disqualified for their office'. On the other hand some of the private school teachers were regarded as respectable and competent. The founders of the first Sunday schools contracted with 'keepers of schools' to do the teaching, and it must be assumed that they were satisfied of the efficiency and moral status of these men.

Although information about individual teachers is lacking it is possible to make a few observations about the life of the proprietor of a cheap private school, provided that it is noted that any general description of so large a class must involve an element of over-simplification. A rough division may be made into two classes depending on whether the teacher made his living solely by teaching or used it as a sideline, the first class including the common day schools and the second the dame schools. The Hammonds state that the national average fee for dame schools was 4d., and the income £17-£20 per year.[1] In Nottingham in 1871 the average size of the

[1] J. L. and B. Hammond, *The Age of the Chartists*, Longmans, 1930, p. 169, and see *Children's Employment Commission*, 1842, 2nd Report, App. part 1, p. 37.

cheap private schools was 21 pupils, and if one allows a fee of 4*d*.–6*d*. this gives an income of rather over £20, which agrees well enough. This was hardly a living wage, and it is obvious that the proprietors of the smallest schools with fewer than 12 pupils cannot have depended entirely on their schools for support. Mrs Gamble cannot have charged her four pupils more than 8*d*. per week; any increase would have put her school beyond the scope of the School Board's enquiry. Her income therefore, was not more than 2*s*. 8*d*. per week. Teachers of these schools were so inconspicuous that only one definite case of a teacher of this class who had another job has been recorded, that of Mrs Eliza Taylor who was a 'medicine vendor' in addition to running a little school on St Ann's Well Road, but it is a safe assumption that Mrs Gamble and others had other strings to their bows.

Larger schools showed a better profit. The six larger schools which were recorded in 1871, varying from 39 to 110 children produced a weekly turnover of £1 to £2 10*s*. per week at the very least. The overheads of such a school would be very small so that the income was at least comparable with that of a skilled craftsman, with the added advantage that business was not adversely affected by depressions in trade; rather the opposite in fact since it was a universal phenomenon that schools filled when trade was bad. Some of these schools were rather surprisingly long-lived concerns. One was recorded by the School Board in 1886 which had been taught by a mother and daughter since 1821; another had been run by one teacher at the same address for 31 years. The way in which such establishments could continue to prosper without attracting attention is illustrated by the fact that neither of these schools, and only one of the six larger schools revealed by the 1871 enquiry can be traced in any other source. Presumably they found enough business in their immediate neighbourhood and did not find it necessary to advertise, while they were too inconspicuous to attract the attention of editors of directories or guide books.

For this reason it is difficult to give any very close estimate of the number of children attending these schools. In 1851 there were probably about 1,000 to 1,200 children in common day and dame schools within the borough. In 1871, when the Statistical Committee of the School Board enquired, it found 33 schools with 853 children, but it was known that some schools, probably among the more expensive, lifted their fees above the 9*d*. limit so as to fall outside the range of the investigation. According to the School Board, the first effect of the introduction of compulsion was to increase the trade of private schools; many parents were prepared to pay a fairly high fee to avoid sending their children to Board schools. The period from 1870 to 1890 was a prosperous period for the cheap private school, and in 1891 there were 43 schools in the town with about 1,000 children. The abolition of fees in Board schools in 1891 was the death blow to the private schools, which then became a very expensive luxury. By 1895 there were only 24 schools with 489 children and the number continued to decline until 1898 when there were 13 schools with 270 pupils. Stability was reached at this figure which did not materially change; there were still 13 schools at the end of the School Board period.

8

ADULT EDUCATION

Adult education in the nineteenth century presents itself in two aspects. The efforts of middle-class philanthropists to imbue the working class with their own values and virtues give one side of the picture, while on the other were attempts at self-improvement by members of the working class themselves. But both movements conceived adult education as a working-class necessity. It might often enough be provided by the middle class; it was always intended for the working class.

Whatever the class basis an important motive for adult education was political. Of course the bias was different. Much middle-class support sprang from the belief that educated men made more responsible citizens and more amenable employees. Advocates of self-help, in contrast, saw in the spread of education among the working class the way to political power. It was not mere coincidence that activity in this field increased significantly in the 1830s and 1840s when Chartism was at its height.

One feature shared by patronage and self-help was to cause repeated disappointment and failure. This was a confused and inadequate idea of the character of the class in whose interest they were working. To speak of 'the lower orders' or 'the laborious classes' was to bring under one heading a number of quite incompatible elements. At one end of the scale stood the unskilled workers and paupers whose sufferings attracted so much attention and for whom much educational activity was initiated. Speaking generally this group showed little enthusiasm for education, either because they had lost hope of improvement or because the strain of making a living was too great to leave them the energy for sustained study. Opposed to them were the clerks, artisans and small shop-keepers, articulate men with an acute political consciousness and often a surprising appetite for intellectual work. Repeated attempts at adult education foundered through failure to realize that these men were not typical of the working class as a whole.

Sir Michael Sadler suggested[1] that adult education in the nineteenth century may be considered as falling into four periods. The first ran from 1780 to 1830 and was characterized by the work of religious bodies, and the desire of working men for political enlightenment. The main features of the second period were increased efforts to provide technical training, and the political and social movements associated with Chartism; 1848 may be taken as marking the end of this period. From then until 1870 the essential feature was 'a deepened sense of personal responsibility for collective welfare', while the period from 1870 onwards was marked by the growth of the state's powers in education and the improvement of the education of girls and women. The writer obviously did not intend that the dates should be taken as absolute dividing marks, but allowing the necessary elasticity, his scheme does provide a useful framework within which the extensive and ill-defined topic of adult education may be studied. It will be used for that purpose here.

Nottingham was not entirely devoid of opportunities for adult education, allowing a wide interpretation of the term, when the first period opened. For example, it was a common occurrence for peripatetic lecturers to give series of lectures, generally on scientific subjects. These lectures were given in series of varying length, anything from 6 to 12 lectures being common, and longer series being not unusual. They attracted a good audience and remained popular throughout the century, and a successful lecturer could make a very good living; Robert Goodacre gave up a flourishing academy to follow a career as lecturer in astronomy. The usual fee at the beginning of the century was 2s. 6d. per lecture or one guinea for the course, and few if any were much cheaper; obviously the lectures were aimed at a prosperous middle-class audience. Most speakers advertised an extensive set of apparatus, and practical demonstrations formed an important part of their stock in trade. One lecturer, for instance, had apparatus which included ' and double barrelled air-pumps; an elegant air fo working models of the steam engine; wh batteries of great magnitude and powe apparatus including various single, lantern and solar microscopes; came apparatus; and a great deal more'.[2]

[1] M. E. Sadler, *Continuation Schools in Engla* 2nd edition, 1908, pp. 10 ff.   [2] *Nottin*

The subject matter of these lecture courses was diffuse and they provided more entertainment than education. One lecturer offered, in nine lectures, 'the Arts, Domestic Economy, Galvanism and the nature and effect of different poisons'.[1] The lecturer whose equipment was detailed above offered 24 lectures which covered: 'a general view of the laws of nature and the economy of the Universe; properties of matter; affinity; crystallization; magnetism; pneumatics; hydrostatics; hydraulics; optics; electricity; galvanism; mechanics; modern experimental chemistry and the philosophy of vegetation'. Courses of this nature were not calculated to have any substantial educational value, and, of course, any continuity between one course and another was purely coincidental.

An alternative source of education for the literate adult was reading. Nottingham was ill-provided with libraries at the time except for one or two commercial libraries – Wilson's Circulating Library in the Market Place had 2,400 books[2] – but these again were rather expensive and did not favour clients from the working class. Novels formed the bulk of their stock. More useful were the numerous books aimed at the man who wished to educate himself. Some of these were extremely expensive; *Every Man His Own Gardener* sold at 5s. and *The Complete Young Man's Companion – An Early Introduction to the Most Useful Parts of Learning* for 2s. 6d.[3] But many books came out in weekly parts, usually at 6d. per issue, and these were within a working man's reach. Among those offered in advertisements during 1786 were: *The Universal Magazine of Knowledge and Pleasure, Millar's New Natural History,* and *Chambers' Cyclopaedia.* Shorter books which could be bought cheaply included several on arithmetic, several on gardening, two or three history books, Gordon's *Complete Family Physician* and *The New Art of Speaking.*

Evidently, a demand for education existed, and it was strong among the class of people who preferred to buy books in instalments at 6d. per week. These were presumably artisans and clerks who had acquired, probably in private schools of the 'writing school' type, sufficient competence in the rudiments to have the ability and inclination to pursue their studies further. No doubt it was the same class which patronized the evening classes which most writing

[1] *Nottingham Review,* 1 February 1811.
[2] *Nottingham Journal,* 6 November 1784.
[3] *Ibid.* 4 March 1786.

schools found it profitable to run. That many men of this class were rather more than literate is demonstrated, if it needs demonstration, by the rather surprising number of workmen poets who were active in Nottingham at the turn of the eighteenth and nineteenth centuries, especially among framework knitters. None of these poets were of any literary importance and only one, Robert Millhouse, achieved even contemporary note. Their verse tended to be intensely derivative, Gray in particular being faithfully reproduced, but this in itself is interesting as proving beyond doubt that these men achieved a fair breadth of reading. What was very conspicuously missing was any institution of adult education. It is very likely that there were small mutual improvement societies, either literary, like a rather later club at the 'Old Ship Tavern' on Pelham Street, or political, especially about the time of the French Revolution. But if such clubs existed they were small and informal.

The revival of religious enthusiasm of the late eighteenth century made its first, and major, impression in the educational field with the establishment of Sunday schools. It was a logical development to found schools for adults, either those who had passed through the school, or those whose schooling had been entirely neglected. An adult school was opened in Nottingham in 1798 by William Singleton in a room belonging to the Methodist New Connexion, but it passed within a short time under the control of Samuel Fox, a member of the Society of Friends. This school is considered to have been the first adult school in England,[1] and when Joseph Sturge initiated an expansion of the adult school movement in the 1840s he was moved to do so by a visit to Fox's school.[2] Although the school thrived in a modest way, with a normal complement of about 80 pupils and eight teachers, it made very little impression locally, and there are no discernible traces of attempts to copy it. Carter, writing the history of the local Sunday schools in the 1860s makes no mention of the venture whatever, and it seems to have made curiously little effort in the missionary field. In general the religious bodies in Nottingham showed rather little interest in adult education at this time, perhaps because their attention was occupied by the education of children.

[1] Sadler, *Continuation Schools*, pp. 15–16; G. Currie-Martin, *The Adult School Movement*, London, 1924, p. 12.
[2] Currie-Martin, *Adult School Movement*, p. 17.

There is even less evidence of a demand among the working class for political enlightenment. One or two subscription news-rooms were established where newspapers could be consulted, but these were mainly middle-class affairs, and of autonomous working-class ventures there is hardly a trace. The difficulty, however, is to know to what extent a lack of evidence implies a lack of activity. It is always easy to under-estimate working-class activity because their institutions tended to be small, and, of course, at the time of the Revolutionary and Napoleonic Wars, working-class political associations were necessarily disinclined to advertise their existence. Working men successfully ran friendly societies which at that period had a membership of at least 2,000 in Nottingham alone, and the existence of this extensive movement, which had some kind of central organization has only been accidentally recorded. In a different field the activities of the Luddites revealed considerable organizing skill. The best that can be said at this time is that it is very likely that societies existed which were concerned with political ideas, but that no trace of them has survived.

The most notable institution to be established at this period was the Nottingham Subscription Library which was opened in 1816, later moving to Bromley House, where a 'Society for the Discussion of Literary and Scientific Subjects' was joined to it in 1824. This was very much a middle and upper-class venture, and its sponsors would have rejected the suggestion that it had anything to do with adult education. E. M. Beckett has described Bromley House as 'the main centre of intellectual life in Nottingham',[1] but this is over-generous. It is true that lectures were given and occasional papers read by members, and on a rare occasion the Society organized essay competitions, but no sustained intellectual work was done, and the lectures followed no pattern whatever.

In the middle 1820s a new wave of activity began in adult education. The usual motives were at work. Employers saw mechanics' institutions and libraries as a way of producing more amenable employees, while working men hoped to improve through education their own position or that of their class. But this was the period of the lace boom when Nottingham experienced for the first time an acute shortage of skilled labour, and the desirability of an extension of technical education was brought very forcibly before the public. Another idea much canvassed at this time was an interesting antici-

[1] E. M. Beckett, *The University College of Nottingham*, Nottingham, 1928, p. 10.

pation of that thinking which underlay university extension. It was argued that education carried with it a certain responsibility. As one speaker at a public meeting put it:[1] 'It was the plain duty of all who had quaffed from the fountain of knowledge to extend as far as possible the refreshing influence of its stream'.

Three institutions appeared in 1824, one of them of considerable importance and permanence. Their establishment and decline repay study as examples of a phenomenon which was to be repeated throughout the century, and because the causal factors can be observed with peculiar clarity.

The Artizans' Library was opened in April or May 1824, shares of £5 each being taken up by 30 men prominent in local charitable work. Ordinary members paid a deposit of 2s. 6d. and a subscription of 1s. 6d. per quarter. The library was open every evening for two hours. Up to a point it was a success. It became a large library, perhaps the largest in the town; in 1833 it had 2,658 volumes, and by 1850, 5,000. In 1854 it moved to new premises on the site of Thurland Hall where it remained until, in 1868, it was handed over to the Corporation to form the nucleus of the Nottingham Public Library.

The library's failure lay in its lack of appeal to the class for which it was intended. Within a few months of its opening a local newspaper was commenting on its unenthusiastic reception by working men. The cost of entry may have put some people off; 2s. 6d. constituted a week's rent for a working man. But it is very likely that the continued domination of the library by members of the local 'establishment' was the real cause of its failure to attract working men. All power was in the hands of the shareholders, and even 30 years after its founding the library was still run by members of the original founding group. The more politically conscious working men probably suspected, with some justice, an aura of patronage about the library, and were at the same time suspicious of the political motives of the shareholders. At all events the Artizans' Library became and remained a very respectable institution with a mainly middle-class clientele.

The establishment of the Artizans' Library was immediately followed by the founding of a 'library for females' on Hound's Gate. The fee was 1s. per quarter and members had to produce a 'reference

[1] *Nottingham Review*, 5 August 1836.

from a respectable householder'. Although this library existed for some years it never achieved anything like the size of the Artizans' Library.

The same group of men was also responsible for the 'Nottingham Scientific and Mechanical Society', which existed for at least a year, although its life was troubled. Meetings were held monthly at the 'Durham Ox' public house, when papers were read in the inconsequential manner common to such societies, successive subjects being 'The Mutability of National Glory', 'The Nature of Commerce', 'Surveying', and 'The Arctic'.[1]

The failure of this society illustrates one of the perennial difficulties in the way of adult education in the nineteenth century. Thomas Wakefield, at a later date, when discussing the proposal to form a Mechanics' Institution, attributed its collapse chiefly to 'bickerings and animosities' which arose because workmen wished to turn the society into a forum for debate.[2] The fact was that Wakefield and others of his circle were prepared to do a great deal on behalf of the working class, but on condition that they remained firmly in control of any institution which was established, and that discussion upon the dangerous subjects of politics and religion was avoided. As good Whigs these men were in favour of the working class improving its general education and assuming political responsibilities, so long as this was a theoretical proposition; but the practical application of this theory was less attractive and they saw nothing but danger in working men discussing political, social and religious matters. Thus the sponsors of the Artizans' Library kept firm control, and the Scientific and Mechanical Society failed because the sponsors rejected the very subjects for discussion which the working men felt most interest in. The working men for their part were acutely suspicious of the motives of the middle-class sponsors, and offended by their refusal to allow them a measure of control. The Society hardly had a chance from the outset, and its position was made worse by its failure to secure its own premises. The exact date of its collapse is not known but it is unlikely that it survived until 1826.

One or two other institutions were established as a result of this particular wave of enthusiasm. In 1836 an Artizans' Library was founded in Radford and an Artizans' News Room in Nottingham. Neither of these was of great significance, and far more important

---

[1] *Nottingham Review*, 1825, *passim*.   [2] *Ibid.*, 30 May 1834.

was the opening of the Nottingham Mechanics' Institute in 1837.

The Mechanics' Institute was much the largest and most prosperous affair of its kind in the town, and owed its success very largely to the powerful support of local nobility and gentry. John Smith Wright, the banker, was its most prominent benefactor, but the list of life members, who made substantial contributions included most men of local importance. The first patrons were the Duke of Newcastle, the Duke of Portland, the Earl Manvers and the Earl of Scarborough, and with backing of this calibre it was not difficult to overcome the 'strongly marked feeling of hostility to Mechanics' Institutions as having inherent in their nature something of the revolutionary spirit'.[1]

The Institution started with its own premises in St James's Street, in rooms recently occupied by the medical school. They were small, but at least they belonged solely to the Institution, and it was possible to start classes as well as lectures. In a few years it was decided to seek a new building and as one means of raising funds an exhibition of arts and sciences was held in Exchange Hall in 1842, which realized £802. Smith Wright presented the site and the new building was opened in 1845.

From many points of view the Mechanics' Institution was a success. With minor fluctuations the membership rose year by year – 427 in 1843; 579 in 1850; nearly 3,000 in 1881. The list of lecturers included men eminent in many fields; Dickens read there more than once; Sir Samuel White-Baker spoke on his explorations; Sir Robert Peel gave an address on 'The Progress of Society'. Other speakers included R. W. Emerson, Fanny Kemble, W. Cowden Clarke, and in later years, Justin McCarthy, Charles Dilke, Conan Doyle, Edward Whymper and Sir Ernest Shackleton. At a charity performance in 1852 the performers included Dickens, Dudley Costello, John Tenniel, Mark Lemon and Augustus Egg, while two Royal Academicians designed the scenery. From 1862 the Institution was the venue for Science and Art classes. The library increased in size and was well patronized.

With all this on the credit side the fact remains that the institution exemplifies the failings of adult education at this period. The two criticisms most frequently voiced at the time were that the

---

[1] J. Granger, *History of the Nottingham Mechanics' Institute*, 1837–87, Nottingham, 1887, p. 1.

membership was overwhelmingly drawn from the skilled artisans and white-collar workers and hardly touched the lower working classes at all, while for the mass of the members the Institution was a social centre and any educational work was incidental. Both criticisms are amply borne out by the evidence. The list of members for 1850 reveals very strikingly the preponderance of clerks, shopkeepers and people in similar circumstances:[1]

Professional men and manufacturers	16
Shopkeepers and tradesmen	80
Clerks, warehousemen, shopmen	236
Lace and stocking makers	38
Joiners, masons, plumbers, painters	10
Smiths, engine and bobbin and carriage makers	35
Handicraft trades not specified	20
Servants, labourers, gardeners	10
Artists, schoolmasters, excisemen	14
Youths	56
Females	64
	579

The sponsors of the Institution were inclined to attribute this position to the apathy of the working class towards education, but as Richard Enfield pointed out at the annual meeting of 1850, this explanation did not stand up to examination.[2] There were, he said, five operatives' libraries in the town with 700 members and 5,000 volumes, all established by the efforts of working men. It was nonsense, therefore, to say that the working man was apathetic; the fact was that he did not favour the particular services offered by the Mechanics' Institution;

It had been said that one man could bring a horse to water, but five could not make him drink. In their own instance they had found the water, but for some reason or other the operatives would not drink the water they had found them; while on the other hand, they found 700 of them drinking other water their own way.

It was open to question how much educational work the Institution was doing even for its middle-class members. In 1855 five classes were held with attendance as follows:

[1] *Nottingham Journal*, 1 February 1850.   [2] *Ibid.*

French	8	writing and arithmetic	12
vocal music	59	Chess	22
discussion	30		

Classes in geography and grammar failed during the year for lack of interest. This does not represent a very ambitious programme of adult education. The chess and vocal music were certainly valuable in their way, but were primarily recreational; the discussion class met 13 times during the year, and its topics followed the same aimless sequence as the public lectures. Six topics selected at random from the list will illustrate this:

(1) life and writings of Edgar Allen Poe,
(2) Russia, its history, population and government,
(3) Turkey and its population,
(4) Christmas; its customs and observances,
(5) life of Washington,
(6) hydraulics and hydrostatics.

The classes which were definitely educational had less to do with the Institution as time went on. In the first days of enthusiasm the teachers had been paid a fee by the Institution, $2\frac{1}{2}$ guineas per quarter was usual, and all arrangements had been made through its officers. The committee was quick to realize, however, that the majority of the members were interested in social rather than educational activities and the classes were increasingly neglected. From Christmas 1841 teachers received only the fees from their pupils,[1] and the classes were, to all intents and purposes, independent. By the 1850s the amount of sustained educational work done in the Institution was negligible.

A study of the library returns reinforces the impression that the interests of the members were overwhelmingly recreational. On the average half the total issue of books came under the heading of 'poetry and fiction'; no other class of books was used even a quarter as much. This fact is even more striking since the popular section was not even the largest in the library. The section on 'philosophy, science and general literature' was a little larger, but whereas each book in the latter section had been used, on the average, twice in twelve months, each book in the fiction section had been used 15 times. The figures for 1855 are given in Table 20.[2]

[1] *Minutes of Nottingham Mechanics' Institution*, 2 September 1841.
[2] *Nottingham Review*, 19 January 1855.

TABLE 20. *Library returns*

Classification	No. of volumes	No. of issues
History and biography	778	4,800
voyages, travel, geography	655	3,193
philosophy, science, general literature	1,499	3,142
miscellaneous	428	4,396
poetry and fiction	1,341	19,864
theology and moral philosophy	227	680
bound magazines	843	3,168
foreign books	58	63
reference	53	110
	5,882	39,416

Hugo Reid, headmaster of People's College, who played an important part in the affairs of the Institution at this time, took an optimistic view of the position:[1] 'They should remember that a man after a hard day's work, was not capable of sitting down and studying a scientific or philosophical work. He himself had often found a work of fiction in the evenings a great recreation . . . Light reading possessed another advantage. It led the mind on by degrees to studies of a higher and more intellectual character.'

Reid had put his finger upon a very real problem in describing the difficulties in the way of part-time study, and he showed himself more liberal than many educationalists of his time in that he did not condemn novel reading as a pernicious habit. But his suggestion that novel reading led to more serious studies was not borne out by the evidence. Twenty years later the reading of the members was still overwhelmingly confined to fiction. 18,000 novels were issued in one year, as against 125 books on domestic economy and eight on political economy.

Whatever its success as a centre for rational recreation the Mechanics' Institution failed to attract the working class in any numbers, and failed as an agency of adult education. Why was this so?

The principal difficulty lay in the impossibility of cooperation between the middle-class sponsors of the Institution, who represented as a whole the manufacturing interest, and the workmen. Relations between masters and men were embittered in Nottingham,

[1] *Nottingham Review*, 1 February 1850.

and particularly so in the 1830s and 1840s, and the workmen regarded this as an insuperable bar to any continuing scheme of association. Charles Paget, a Member of Parliament and chairman of the Institution, observed many years later, that:

he recollected the strong expressions which were used at the time [1846] as to the impossibility of the masters and men meeting together in the same association. There was one in particular which one of the men used in reply to an observation made by the speaker [Paget]. It was, if he remembered rightly, 'we are at daggers'.

To aggravate the situation, the sponsors banned from the Institution the discussion of politics and religion which, they feared, would lead to the expression of revolutionary or blasphemous opinions. They had some grounds for their fears; the contemporary operatives' libraries had close connections with Chartism. Nevertheless the ban removed most of the Institution's attraction for many intelligent working men, while insulting them with its implication that they were not to be trusted with such subjects.

The founders of the Institution had supposed that the working men would be interested mainly in technical instruction, but in the event, the classes in technical subjects which were established, especially after 1861, had only a peripheral connection with the rest of the Institution's work. Mabel Tylecote has pointed out that the pursuit of technical knowledge was an individualistic rather than a cooperative activity[1] and this may have a bearing on the isolated position of the technical classes. Certainly there was an appreciable fall in the membership of the Nottingham Institution when the Science and Art classes were transferred to the new University College[2] and this does suggest that a number of members joined merely to qualify for the classes.

Two other factors discouraged working people from making use of the Institution for other than recreational purposes. Many working men lacked an effective elementary education, and found themselves quite out of their depths when attempting to follow technical courses. Few had the determination to acquire the necessary preliminary competence in their spare time. This was one of the recurrent stumbling blocks in the way of adult education, and the classes for

[1] M. Tylecote, *The Mechanics' Institutes of Lancashire and Yorkshire before 1851*, Manchester, 1957, pp. 109 ff.
[2] Granger, *Mechanics' Institution*, p. 43.

working men sponsored by the university extension movement went into a rapid decline for precisely this reason.

This difficulty was aggravated by the long working hours and wretched living conditions of the working people which sapped their energy and undermined their health, making attendance at Sunday and evening classes an exhausting and unrewarding task. J. F. C. Harrison quotes a writer of 1858 who was speaking of Leeds.[1] His comments are equally relevant to the workpeople of Nottingham:

under the best of health which they enjoy they are subject to feelings of languor and weariness which people do not feel who live in healthy situations and breathe pure air when they are asleep. This feeling is forced off by necessity on the six days of labour; but on Sunday, when this is not the case, it is felt perhaps more than at any other time, giving them a disinclination to exert either their mental or physical powers.

Sheer weariness and exhausted lethargy was one of the most difficult obstacles for educational projects to overcome at that period. When a twelve- or fourteen-hour working day was the ordinary thing only those working men could pursue self-improvement who had an immense fund of enthusiasm. Those whose driving urge was less powerful fell away as soon as the initial burst of excitement about a particular course or association had died. The notable increase in the number of older children who attended evening schools between 1842 and 1862 was largely due to the increasing public interest in education, but it is very likely that it was also related to the fact that, according to local experts, the working day had shortened by two hours in the period.

The Artizans' Library and the Mechanics' Institute were middle-class foundations intended for the working class. The working men were also active on their own behalf. At the time of the founding of the Scientific and Mechanical Society, when disputes between middle-class sponsors and working-class members were at their head, there was talk of the artisans founding their own independent society. So far as is known nothing came of this although the extreme difficulty of discovering traces of working-class movements at that time makes it impossible to be certain upon this point. In the 1830s, however, the scheme reached fruition.

The reason for this development was avowedly political. Nottingham workmen had a reputation for radicalism in politics and the

[1] Harrison, *Learning and Living, 1790–1960*. Routledge and Kegan Paul, 1961, p. 13.

town was a centre of Chartism. The rules of Operatives' Library Number One lay down quite explicitly the aims of the whole movement.[1] 'Being deeply impressed with the importance of knowledge, we resolve to establish a book society, because that as we progress in knowledge we must advance in freedom, knowledge being the only lever that can raise the working class into a fit condition to possess electoral privileges.' A later statement in the rules makes it apparent why the members were not prepared to go to the Mechanics' Institution for their reading. 'As politics concern our welfare here, and religion affects our happiness hereafter, and as we believe that no political institution ought to stand which cannot bear examination, and no creed ought to be believed that cannot bear discussion, we therefore resolve to purchase books of every description, political and theological as well as those embracing history, science and literature.' This was an obvious reference to the ban placed by the Mechanics' Institution upon books and lectures of a controversial type, and the same attitude is shown in a remark made by a speaker at the annual meeting of the library in 1842, who claimed that the library's success showed 'that the working man properly appreciates the means of instruction when it is unconditionally put within his reach'.[2]

The establishment of the first Operatives' Library was something of an accident. A few working men clubbed together to buy a copy of Howitt's *History of Priestcraft*, and nine of them agreed to subscribe to a weekly fund to buy other books. Other men joined them and in August 1835 a regular society was formed at the 'Rancliffe Arms' on Sussex Street.[3] It was rapidly followed by several other similar institutions. The second library opened at the 'Alderman Wood' in Charlotte Street in 1836, a third at the 'Seven Stars' in the following year. In 1840 a library was opened in New Sneinton at the 'Queen Adelaide' and four years later there was one at the 'Pelican' in Radford. Meanwhile the Nottingham Temperance Operatives' Library was started in 1841, and after some wanderings, found a home in a coffee house in Hound's Gate. The activity did not stop there, because in 1842 two news rooms were opened, one in the Democratic Chapel in Riste's Place off Barker Gate, and the other

---

[1] *Catalogue and Rules of Operatives' Library No. 1*, 1843, Nottingham Public Library.
[2] *Nottingham Review*, 14 January 1842.
[3] *Ibid.* 30 December 1836.

in Swann's Yard. The political affiliations of these were manifest, since the Democratic Chapel was a Chartist headquarters, and the Swann's Yard newsroom was run by the Complete Suffrage Association.

The exact connection between the Operatives' Libraries and Chartism is difficult to determine. That they both gained strength from the same working-class unrest is perfectly certain, and the expressed aims of the first library were exactly those of the 'moral force' Chartists. The 'Rancliffe Arms' was a centre of Chartist activity, and it is hard to believe that it was purely coincidence that the first library should be established there. On the other hand the libraries were being established before Chartism got under way as a major political movement, and they flourished long after Chartism was dead.

The Operatives' Libraries were all organized in very much the same way. Their headquarters was almost always a public house, and there is no record of them paying a rent; probably the landlords thought it worthwhile to store the books because of the custom which the libraries brought to their house. The libraries were open two or three nights per week, and sometimes on Sundays. Two or three of the libraries, at least, had annual dinners, and it is very likely that there was a convivial side to their activities, as was almost inevitable since they were obliged to use public houses for lack of any alternative accommodation. There were minor variations in the scales of fees, but 6d. entrance and 1d. per week subscription were usual; working men probably found it easier to pay 1d. per week, than the 1s. 6d. per quarter of the Mechanics' Institution. Novels constituted much the largest class of books and the reading habits of the members were similar to those of the Mechanics' Institution. In 1854 when Operatives' Library Number One had 2,200 books, they were classified as follows:[1]

History	180	Biography	180
Novels	700	Arts and sciences	290
Travels	160	Periodicals	250
Poetry	150	Miscellaneous	290

Number Two and Three Libraries showed an even more marked preponderance of fiction. At Number Two 1,000 out of 1,520 books were novels and only 40 were classified as science, while Number

[1] Wylie, *Old and New Nottingham*, London, 1855, p. 350.

Three had 1,100 novels out of 2,050 volumes. The Number Three library at the 'Seven Stars' was the first recorded library in the area to have a children's section. The 1855 report mentioned that juvenile readers were well catered for; the books in that section included, among others, *Aesop's Fables, Robinson Crusoe* and works by Mayne Reid, a prolific writer of adventure stories in his day.

All the libraries appear to have been spontaneous working-class products; there is no sign of initiative by members of the upper or middle classes. This is not to say that they were necessarily hostile to the middle class, although they certainly began in a spirit of reaction against the patronizing and suspicious attitude of the sponsors of the Mechanics' Institution. A conference was held in 1846 between J. E. Denison and Charles Paget, two of the more adventurous middle-class leaders, on the one hand, and representatives of the Operatives' Libraries on the other with a view to introducing a scheme of cooperation. The scheme fell through due to the peculiar bitterness of relations between the classes at that time, but the evidence suggests that the libraries lost some of their political fervour, especially in the 1850s when relations between employer and employed became less hostile. Denison was in the habit of donating books to the libraries, and in 1855 the chairman of the Number Three Library was Samuel Gale, an architect.

The libraries had a central organization but it is not clear what powers it possessed. The very fact that the libraries numbered themselves suggests a measure of cooperation, and during the 1840s at least general gatherings of members and friends of all the libraries were held at the 'Rancliffe Arms', the centre of the movement. The libraries were substantial bodies, and three were much larger than the others, these being Number One at the 'Rancliffe Arms', the Number Two at the 'Alderman Wood' and Number Three at the 'Seven Stars'. Between them these three had 5,770 books in 1854, rather more than the Mechanics' Institution. The other libraries were small, but still by no means negligible, with 1,500 books between them. At this time each of the larger libraries was adding up to 300 new books per year to their shelves and had a weekly turnover of 250 volumes. Their income averaged £50 per year, and with no premises or wages to pay for this allowed a good rate of expansion.

It is not known when the libraries closed. At least four were still flourishing in 1862 when the 'Rancliffe Arms' and 'Alderman Wood'

7

each had over 3,000 volumes. The 'Rancliffe Arms' library reached 4,000 books by 1869, and was still in existence with 8,000 books in 1893, by which time all the other libraries had disappeared from the records, no doubt rendered unnecessary by the opening of Nottingham Public Library in 1868. On the other hand it must be remembered that, since virtually all the information about these libraries is gained from occasional newspaper accounts, it is quite possible that the libraries continued an unmarked existence for far longer than this.

The period from the middle 1820s to 1850 was one of great effort in adult education in Nottingham, and of not inconsiderable achievement. If adult education is thought of as a mass movement in search of technical knowledge and profound scholarship, and this was the aim of its most enthusiastic advocates then and later, the efforts of this period failed on two counts. Neither the Artizans' Library and the Mechanics' Institute on the one hand, nor the Operatives' Libraries on the other, made any serious impression on the mass of the working class, while their success lay in providing facilities for recreation rather than education.

All this must be said, but there are two considerations which are to be taken into account in arriving at a fair assessment of the efforts of this period. The problem of making adult education a mass movement and of giving it a substantial instructional content has never been solved. Repeatedly, new agencies – university extension, the Workers' Educational Association – have started with high hopes and large enrolments, only to see the classes dwindle to a nucleus of earnest, largely middle-class, supporters, and at the present time a depressingly high proportion of extra-mural work consists of very short and necessarily superficial courses or of longer courses in which entertainment is at least as important as instruction.

In the provision of facilities for rational recreation important progress was made. In 1820 there was no library in the town within reach of the working man. In 1850 a subscription of 1s. 6d. per quarter would secure the use of libraries of 5,000 books at either the Mechanics' Institution or the Artizans' Library, both with newsrooms attached. A similar fee admitted to one of the Operatives' Libraries where the amenities were less comprehensive, but the company perhaps more compatible for the working man. All these institutions made some efforts to guide their members towards serious reading, and, although the efforts usually failed, credit should be given for the attempt. The Mechanics' Institution, in particular, provided a valuable service in its regular lectures. These covered every conceivable topic and followed no detectable plan. They were the direct descendants of the public lectures mentioned earlier in the chapter, and suffered from the same faults of aimless variety and superficiality. But they were the only existing substitute for the type of informal education which is now picked up from radio and television.

All this represented progress of the most substantial kind. In 1850 the facilities for adult education were miserably inadequate; the combined public libraries of the town and surrounding villages possessed perhaps 20,000 books for a population of 100,000; there were a few classes, almost all elementary, and a limited number of lectures and readings. The critics, contemporary and later had grounds for complaint. But at the beginning of the period there was nothing. Criticism of the work of middle-class and working-class efforts must be viewed in the light of these facts.

Sir Michael Sadler considered that one of the chief characteristics of the period from 1850 to 1870 in adult education was 'a deepened sense of personal responsibility for collective welfare', and this was indeed very apparent in Nottingham. It was one of the factors leading to the university extension movement, and its effect can be traced in the rather numerous philanthropic educational societies of the day, of which the People's Hall and the Town and Country Social Guild were perhaps the most significant. Certain other factors, however, were at work in this period.

There was a distinct improvement in the relations between masters and men. This was a national phenomenon and in Nottingham it meant that, whereas class hostility had prevented cooperation in the 1840s, by 1870 the Mechanics' Institute under the leadership of Denison, Enfield, Canon Morse and others was negotiating successfully with representative working men with a view to promoting a series of lectures which was an immediate predecessor of university extension. An important change was taking place in the attitude of the middle class towards the political education of working people. Adult education had long been recommended as a way of reconciling the working man to his subordinate place in society. It now became apparent to the more far-seeing men that the political power of the working class had increased and was soon to increase very much more. It therefore became more than ever necessary to raise the educational level of future electors. The point was made by Richard Enfield, speaking in 1871, at the Mechanics' Institution. He referred to the 1867 Reform Act and the 1870 Education Act and continued:[1]

These two measures, working as it were together, seemed to him to cast the responsibility on institutions like theirs – whether that, while the Elementary Education Bill provided for the education of the poorer classes, Mechanics' Institutions ought to provide for a higher education for the same classes.

Enfield's mention of the provision of elementary education is a reminder that great progress was made in this direction between 1850 and 1870. By 1870 schools had been built for virtually every child in the town, and, although disappointing results were obtained in the efforts to secure attendance, there was a significant spread of literacy. It is likely that the rising number of literate adults led to a demand for further education, in the same way as the increased efficiency of elementary schools in the 1870s and 1880s led to a demand for secondary education.

The institutions founded in this period were so numerous that it is necessary to deal rather briefly with most of them. It will be convenient to consider first those which had a distinctly religious motive. Singleton's idea of the adult school had not been followed up, and it was not until Joseph Sturge revived the notion in 1842 that there was an expansion. In 1851 there were eight schools with 468 pupils, and in 1862, 13 schools with 851 pupils. The St Mary's school was typical. It was attended, on the average, by 150 women, the attendance fluctuating widely with the state of trade. The great problem facing the teachers was the extremely rapid turnover of pupils, which must have restricted the work to the barest rudiments. Between 1844 when the school was opened, and 1851, 1,857 pupils passed through,[2] which gives an average of two complete changes of pupil every year.

Adult schools were concerned chiefly with teaching adults to read. A related development, aimed at providing recreation with a

---

[1] R. Enfield, *Scrapbook, University College*, under 1871.
[2] Wylie, *Nottingham*, pp. 96–97; Mann, *1851 Census*; *Children's Employment Commission*, 1862, 1st Report, p. 270.

measure of education, was the Working Men's Association. There were several of these attached to various churches, and although the exact date of their establishment is not known, they flourished in the 1860s and 1870s. Meetings were held every week, and were partly social, with tea and discussions, and usually a lecture or reading from a popular book. Successive topics at Trinity Working Men's Association were 'The eventful reign of King John', and 'Rambles in Egypt and the Desert'; at the same time St Mary's Association heard lectures on 'The Microscope' and 'The Life and Character of John Kitto, who by his perseverance and piety, raised himself from a poor, deaf workhouse lad to the honourable position of Doctor of Divinity'.[1] The educational value of the Working Men's Associations was probably rather slight, but they represented a constructive form of recreation, and an alternative to the public house, and in this respect served a useful purpose.

The People's Hall was a larger institution than any of the working men's associations. It was established chiefly by the efforts of George Gill, who was also the founder of the People's College, and was designed to serve as a working-class version of the Mechanics' Institution, which Gill thought to be dominated by the middle class. It occupied a building on Heathcote Street and had a library and reading room. The hall also served as a meeting place for a number of societies not directly attached to the parent body, such as the Union Sick Club, the Oddfellows and the Young Men's Literary Association. The People's Hall was a disappointment from the start, probably because Gill died only a year after its opening. Membership declined from 460 in 1860 to 300 in 1869, and the Hall never made the impact which had been hoped for.

The 'Nottingham Town and Country Social Guild' was a similar institution with rather wider terms of reference, and which exemplifies the growth of social responsibility at this period. It was founded by the town clerk, S. G. Johnson, in 1875 and the aim was 'to improve the dwelling and surroundings of the working classes'. Education was only one aspect of its work, although not an unimportant one, and it ran adult classes in the three R's, singing, drawing, gymnastics, biblical and general literature, carpentry, and wood-carving. A girls' institute, opened a year or two later, offered the three R's, sewing, dictation, cookery, singing, drawing and botany. In addition the Guild paid a nurse for sick visiting, ran a

1 *Nottingham Review*, 27 January 1860.

window garden competition, helped the School Board provide penny dinners, and had a committee to supervise the boarding out of pauper children.[1]

One other institution was founded in this period, and this was undoubtedly the most important – the Nottingham Public Library. A permissive act of 1855 empowered corporations to spend public money upon public libraries, but it resulted in little action, and the Nottingham Corporation merely followed the majority in ignoring the act. As it happened, however, the Artizans' Library ran into financial trouble, and the committee offered it to the Corporation in return for the payment of outstanding debts of £120. At the same time the Nottingham Naturalists' Society offered its library and museum to the town.[2]

The library inherited 6,140 books from the Artizans' Library, and about 5,000 more were purchased with various donations. When the new public library opened its volumes were classified as follows:

theology and philosophy	661
history and biography, voyages and travel	3,270
science and art	1,115
law, politics, commerce	309
reference	150
miscellaneous literature	5,803

It was immediately apparent that reading habits had not changed very much since the days when the Mechanics' Institution complained of the neglect of serious study. In the library's first year of operation the total circulation of non-fiction books was 16,814, and of 'miscellaneous literature', 54,698.

The library increased rapidly in size and number of borrowers. By 1869 it had 5,505 members, whereas the Artizans' Library had been restricted to 400; in the following year 135,000 books were borrowed. The problem was that the library was still in the building on Thurland Street, which had served admirably for the 400 members of the Artizans' Library, but was now completely inadequate. It proved to be impossible to increase loans any further, and for some years there was a slight contraction. Some improvement was

[1] Wright's *Nottingham Directory*, 1893.

[2] Sources for the establishment of the Library are: *Reports of the Free Library and Museums Committee*, 1867–8 and following years; Beckett, *University College*, pp. 12 ff; E. T. Field, *Date Book of Nottingham*, Nottingham, 1884, part II, pp. 54 ff.

effected by opening branch libraries at Sneinton, Basford and Bulwell, but it was obvious that the only long-term solution was to provide a new building for the central library. This pressure upon the facilities of the library was one of the several factors which persuaded the Corporation to build University College.

The fourth period, from 1870 to 1900, saw a continuation of the philanthropic work in adult education which was a feature of the third phase. In fact the feeling among middle-class citizens of social responsibility was more marked than ever in this period; the continued work of the Town and Country Social Guild is an example, and university extension derived much of its drive from this source. But two other factors became important after 1870 and may be considered typical of the period, the intervention of local authorities and the demand of women for higher education. These issued in two major achievements, university extension and continuative evening schools. The evening schools are discussed in chapter 5, and attention will be concentrated here on the Nottingham contribution to the university extension movement.

It is difficult to disentangle the history of university extension from that of the foundation of University College, Nottingham, but in fact the establishment of University College was the result of a combination of four distinct motives. University extension was one of these, but it was reinforced by the demand for higher education of women, by the call for technical instruction for artisans, and by the appearance of the notion of an educational ladder leading from the elementary school to university. In this chapter the origin of the College will be considered from the point of view of university extension, but it will be necessary to refer briefly to the other aspects, which are treated in more detail elsewhere.

University extension was a further instalment of the attempt by the middle classes to carry liberal education to the masses, and it sprang from a realization that the classes offered at the Mechanics' Institution and elsewhere were too discontinuous and superficial to be of much value, and many of the lecturers inadequately qualified. The movement in Nottingham began with a meeting between the committee of the Mechanics' Institution and a number of representatives of working men with a view to selecting courses of lectures, which were delivered at the Institution early in 1873. By this time a powerful group had been formed to develop the idea of more organized adult education. The leaders were Richard Enfield, Canon Morse, vicar of St Mary's, and Dr J. B. Paton, principal of the Congregational College. Other prominent members were Edward Renals, secretary of the Mechanics' Institution, J. E. Denison, and Edward Goldschmidt, who was to play an important part in the movement as leader of the group within the town council which favoured municipal support for adult education.

At the annual meeting of the Mechanics' Institution in January 1873 it was agreed to send a memorial relating to university extension to the University of Cambridge, in support of similar memorials from other towns, including Rochdale, Crewe, Leeds and Birmingham. After referring to the meeting with the working men and the lectures which ensued, the memorial urged the University;[1]

(1) To appoint lecturers of approved eminence and skill who may conduct evening classes for working men in our large towns, and also at other times give lectures to the more educated in the same localities, so as to spread the advantages of university education throughout the country and to all classes.

(2) To form circuits of towns within which groups of lecturers might operate.

(3) To give distinction to those men who thus devote themselves to the higher education of the people by admitting them to share the titles and privileges of fellows in the Colleges equally with those who teach in the University.

It will be observed that Paton, who drew up the memorandum, took notice of the fact that the market for adult education was not restricted to the working class, which was its traditional field. In a speech delivered a month or two later he mentioned that he was influenced by the success enjoyed in other towns by lectures to women, and that he saw the advantages of combining several modes of approach.[2]

Progress from this point was rapid. A committee was formed which included the men previously mentioned together with the town clerk, the headmaster of the High School, several trades union representatives and several women. The trades unions promised to contribute towards the expenses of the courses, and Derby and Leicester were approached to form a circuit. The first extension classes opened in September 1873.

[1] *The Times*, 29 January 1873.
[2] *Nottingham Journal*, 2 April 1873.

University extension was not invented in Nottingham. The particular contribution of the Nottingham committee was to bring together a number of nebulous ideas and marry them into a practicable plan. The leaders of the extension movement gave full credit to the Nottingham Committee. Henry Sidgwick observed in September 1873 that, 'it was the definite, well-thought out character and practicability of the scheme presented by the Nottingham delegates which decided the Syndicate to take up the matter . . . The idea had existed for some time, but it would have remained an idea, but for the action taken by Nottingham'. At a later date Professor Stuart had much the same to say:

My principal help in bringing the matter before the University came from the town of Nottingham where a committee was formed of which the principal moving spirits were Mr Richard Enfield, Dr J. B. Paton and Canon Morse. These gentlemen were not only among those who memorialized the University but they cordially accepted the system proposed, and after the Syndicate was appointed, they gave evidence before it in which they stated they were prepared to organize classes for the various branches of the community, and to guarantee the funds necessary for the experiment.[1]

Three courses were laid on by the University for each of two terms of 12 weeks, the courses being aimed at, but not restricted to, (a) young ladies, who read English literature and physical geography; (b) young men engaged in business, who took force and motion, and astronomy; (c) working men, who read political economy and constitutional history. A University Certificate was awarded for attendance at one course, and a Vice-Chancellor's certificate for success in six courses in different terms.

The first series was a distinct success, all courses being well supported, the only drawback being that of 1,241 people who attended lectures only 143 presented themselves for the terminal examinations, 126 certificates being awarded. The financial situation was satisfactory. But the high hopes which accompanied the start of the scheme were soon disappointed. Attendance declined rapidly; by 1879–80 it had fallen to half the original figure, and the working-men's classes almost entirely ceased. Classes for young men and women continued with some success, but by the 1880s the classes were filled almost entirely by girls and women,

[1] Quoted by Beckett, *University College*, p. 29.

particularly from the local private schools. This was so even in subjects where men might be expected to predominate. In the session 1881-2, for example, two Vice-Chancellor's certificates were awarded, both to women, and there were 88 university certificates given, 67 to women. Women took certificates in French, German, geology, botany and mechanics, as well as the subjects more specifically aimed at a female audience like Shakespeare and Elizabethan literature.[1]

Once again a scheme for the adult education of the working class had missed its aim, and the reasons for the failure of the working men's classes were familiar: 'The fact was that the workers, ill equipped with only the most scanty elementary education, had not the background or knowledge to follow the courses or benefit by them ... One workman is reported to have said, "I'm all in a fog like – I don't known where I am and I don't know what he's talking about" '.[2]

Before the decline of the extension classes had seriously set in, however, the suggestion had been made that a permanent centre for the classes was needed, and this was joined by a suggestion that this centre should also include technical classes. Some at least of the sponsors of the classes were thinking in terms, either of an institution which would feed the existing universities, or even of a local university. Thus Canon Morse, reporting on the second session of the extension classes, said;[3]

it is now desirable to combine with this popular work more extended and more definite teaching in a larger number of smaller classes, so as not only to embrace the people as a whole, but to call out the most promising students of the larger audience ... the extension of this plan of classes will, it is hoped, prepare the way for the establishment of something like a fully equipped college in each town or district.

It was at this point that Richard Enfield wrote to the Town Clerk of Nottingham to inform him that an anonymous friend (assumed to be Lewis Heymann) was prepared to donate £10,000, the interest of which could be used for the payment of lecturers if the Corporation would provide premises which, he suggested, should include 'a lecture theatre seating about 500 or 600; two classrooms seating

[1] University College, Nottingham, Calendar, 1882.
[2] A. C. Wood, History of University College, Nottingham, Blackwell, 1953, p. 14.
[3] R. Enfield, Scrapbook, University College, Nottingham, 22 September 1875.

about 150 or 200; a small room for a library; a chemical laboratory and a residence for one resident lecturer . . .'. The response of the Corporation was unenthusiastic, and through the summer and autumn of 1875 there was much dispute in the council about whether to build the suggested college, and if so where and under what conditions. A strong party in the council preferred to use the money to build a new town hall, but the pro-college group eventually carried the day, the leading part on the college side being played by Edward Goldschmidt. After a suggestion to utilize the site of the Castle had been turned down by the donor, it was eventually determined to erect a building in what was then known as Horsefair Close to house the extension classes, the public library and the natural history museum, the foundation stone being laid in September 1877.

Already, however, adult education had become a decreasingly important part of the work envisaged for the 'first municipal college in England', and speakers at the laying of the foundation stone, who included Gladstone, were far more interested in the prospect of providing facilities for higher education, either liberal or technological, than in university extension work. At the same time the place of Cambridge as the mother university was being taken by London, which offered the attraction of external degrees. In 1878 the scheme of affiliation with Cambridge was drawn up whereby a two year course at Nottingham exempted a student from three terms at Cambridge. But few students took advantage of this; already a number of students were sitting for London Matriculation and higher examinations.

BIBLIOGRAPHY

There is no single source of material for the period 1800–70. Sunday schools are treated in some detail by W. B. Carter, who, writing in 1860, had personal knowledge of many of the events he describes. Nottingham Public Library has a comprehensive collection of local newspapers which give annual reports of schools, accounts of important events such as speech days and treats. Newspapers are also valuable sources of information about private schools, libraries and institutions of adult education. Guide books and directories are particularly informative upon private schools, but have to be used with caution as their material is often out of date. Glover's *History and Directory of the Town of Nottingham* of 1844 is much the most valuable of these and contains much information which is not recorded elsewhere. From 1839 the Minutes and Reports of the Committee of Privy Council on Education are of prime importance, the earlier volumes including much description as well as statistics.

A full set of the minutes of the School Board, together with many school log-books is in the Nottingham Record Office. Also preserved are the minutes of sub-committees of the council which were responsible for the Public Library and the University College.

Three collections of manuscripts are particularly valuable. The Standard Hill manuscripts record in detail the history of a private school. A scrapbook in Nottingham Public Library contains cuttings concerning the foundation of University College. Internal evidence suggests that it was assembled by Richard Enfield. Finally the High Pavement Collection (University of Nottingham) contains much material about the day to day working of High Pavement School.

A. PRIMARY MATERIAL

Newspapers: Selection of nineteenth-century local newspapers in Local History Library, Nottingham Public Libraries.
  Nottingham Journal 1784 onwards.
  Nottingham Review 1808 onwards.
Minutes of the Nottingham School Board, 1870–1903.
Printed Reports of the School Board and its Sub-Committees, 1877–89.
Free Library and Museum Committee, Reports 1867–80.
University College and Free Library Committee Reports, 1880 onwards.

Records of the Borough of Nottingham, 8 volumes, various editors, Nottingham, 1882–1951.

Scrapbook – The Origin of the First Municipal College in England – University College, Nottingham; Local History Library, Nottingham Public Libraries.

High Pavement Collection – Nottingham University Department of Manuscripts.

A Digest of the General Objects, Rules and Regulations of the People's College, Nottingham, Nottingham, 1846.

People's College, Annual Report, 1865, 1876.

University College, Nottingham, Calendar, 1881.

Standard Hill Manuscripts, Nottingham Public Library.

Minutes and Reports of the Committee of Privy Council on Education, 1845–69.

Abstracts of the Answers and Returns made Pursuant to an Address of the House of Commons, B.P.P., 1835, vols. XLI, XLII, XLIII.

Second Report of the Children's Employment Commission, 1842, B.P.P., 1843, vols. XIII, XIV, XV.

Second Report of the Commissioners for Inquiry into the State of Large Towns and Populous Places, B.P.P., 1845, vol. XIII.

1851 Census, Education, Report and Tables, B.P.P., 1852–3, vol. XL.

First Report of the Children's Employment Commission, 1862, B.P.P., 1863, vol. XVIII.

Second Report of the Royal Commissioners on Technical Education, B.P.P., 1884, vols. XIX, XXX, XXXI.

The History, Antiquities and Present State of the Town of Nottingham, Nottingham, 1807.

Nottingham Directory, 1815, Sutton and Sons, Nottingham.

Sutton, R., *The Stranger's Guide Through Nottingham,* Nottingham, 1827.

The Stranger's Guide Through Nottingham, Nottingham, 1848.

Dearden, W., *History and Topography of the Town of Nottingham,* Nottingham, 1834.

White's *History and Directory of Nottingham,* Sheffield, 1832, 1864.

Glover, S., *The History and Directory of the Town of Nottingham,* Nottingham, 1844.

Allen, *Illustrated Hand Book and Guide to all the Places of Interest in Nottingham and its Environs,* Nottingham, 1866.

Nottingham Directory, Wright, Nottingham, 1854; 1858; 1862; 1879; 1884; 1893.

Directory of the City of Nottingham, etc. Kelly, London, 1902.

Directory and Gazeteer of Nottinghamshire, Morris and Co., Nottingham, 1869, 1877.

Catlow, S., *Outlines of a Plan of Instruction adapted to the Various Purposes of Active Life,* Manchester, 1798.

Claxton, T., *Hints to Mechanics on Self Education and Mutual Instruction*, London, 1844.

Hill, M. D., *Plans for the Government and Liberal Instruction of Boys in Large Numbers, drawn from Experience*, 1822.

B. SECONDARY MATERIAL

I. *Local history – general*

A Century of Nottingham History, Nottingham University, 1952.

Armytage, W. H. G., *A. J. Mundella*, Benn, 1951.

Blackner, J., *The History of Nottingham*, Nottingham, 1815.

Briscoe, J. P., *Nottinghamshire and Derbyshire at the Opening of the Twentieth Century*, Brighton, 1901.

Brown, J., *A Memoir of Robert Blincoe*, Carlisle, 1822.

Chambers, J. D., *Modern Nottingham in the Making*, Nottingham, 1945.

Chapman, S. D., 'William Felkin, 1795–1874', M.A., Nottingham, 1960.

Church, R. A., 'The Social and Economic Development of Nottingham in the Nineteenth Century', Ph.D., Nottingham, 1961.

Erikson, C., *British Industrialists – Steel and Hosiery, 1850–1950*, C.U.P., 1959.

Field, H., *The Nottingham Date Book*, Nottingham, 1884.

Gray, D., *Nottingham – Settlement to City*, Nottingham, 1953.

Gray, D., *Nottingham through 500 Years*. Nottingham, 2nd ed., 1960.

Henderson, A. R., *History of Castle Gate Congregational Church*, London, 1905.

High Pavement Chronicle – articles March, April 1903; May, July 1914; February, June 1921.

Leeman, F. W., *History of the Nottingham Co-operative Society, 1863–1944*, Nottingham, 1944.

Lomax, J., *A History of Quakers in Nottingham*, Nottingham, 1948.

Marchant, J., *J. B. Paton*, London, 1909.

Mellors, R., *Men of Nottingham and Notts*, Bell, Nottingham. 2nd ed., 1924.

Orange, J., *History and Antiquities of Nottingham*, London, 1840.

Paton, J. L., *John Brown Paton*, Hodder and Stoughton, 1914.

Potter Briscoe, J., *Chapters of Nottinghamshire History*, Nottingham, 1908.

Russell, J., *A History of the Nottinghamshire Subscription Library*, Nottingham, 1916.

Snell, H., *Men, Movements and Myself*, Dent, 1936.

Warren, J. C., *The High Pavement Chapel, Nottingham*, Nottingham, 1932.

Wood, A. C., 'George, Lord Rancliffe', *Transactions of the Thoroton Society*, vol. LIX, 1955.

Wood, A. C., 'Nottingham 1835–1865', *Transactions of the Thoroton Society*, vol. LIX, 1955.
Wylie, W. H., *Old and New Nottingham*, Longman, 1853.

II. *Local history – educational*

Beckett, E. M., 'The Development of Education in Nottingham during the Nineteenth and the Early Twentieth Centuries, with Special Reference to the History of University College', Nottingham, M.A., London, 1922.
Beckett, E. M., *University College of Nottingham*, Nottingham, 1928.
Brettle, L., *A History of Queen Elizabeth's Grammar School for Boys, Mansfield*, 1961.
Briscoe, H. K., 'The History of Technical Education in Nottinghamshire, 1851–1902', M.A., Sheffield, 1952.
Carter, W. B., *History of the Nottingham Sunday School Union*, Nottingham, 1860.
Chapman, S. D., 'The Evangelical Revival and Education in Nottingham', *Transactions of the Thoroton Society*, vol. LXVI, 1962.
Granger, J., *Nottingham Mechanics' Institution – A Retrospect*, Nottingham, 1912.
History of the Nottingham Mechanics' Institution, 1837–1887, Nottingham, 1887.
Hugh, W., *Some Notes Historical and Educational Relative to the High Pavement Higher Elementary School*, 2nd ed., Nottingham, 1905.
Nottingham Mechanics' Institution; Fifteen Years Record, 1912–1927, Nottingham, 1928.
Taylor, F. W. V., *History of the Nottingham Bluecoat School, 1706–1956*, Nottingham, 1956.
Thomas, A. W., 'A Forgotten Nottingham Artist', *Transactions of the Thoroton Society*, 1954.
Thomas, A. W., *A History of Nottingham High School, 1513–1953*, Nottingham, 1957.
Thomas, A. W., 'The History of Nottingham High School, 1513–1901', Ph.D., Nottingham, 1956.
Wakerley, J. W., *A Centenary History of Wesley School, Nottingham*, Nottingham, 1915.
Wardle, D., 'The Work of the Nottingham School Board', M.Ed., Nottingham, 1961.
Wardle, D., 'The History of Education in Nottingham', Ph.D., Nottingham, 1965.
Wood, A. C., *A History of the University College, Nottingham*, Blackwell, 1953.

III. *Other works*

Altick, R. D., *The English Common Reader*, Chicago, 1957.

Beales, A. C. F., *Education under Penalty*, U.L.P., 1963.

Currie Martin, G., *The Adult School Movement*, National Adult School Union, 1924.

Dobbs, A. E., *Education and Social Movements, 1700–1850*, Longmans, Green, 1919.

Eaglesham, E. C., *From School Board to Local Authority*, Routledge and Kegan Paul, 1956.

Fletcher, A. E., *Cyclopaedia of Education*, Swan Sonnenschein, 1889.

Foden, F. E., 'A History of Technical Examinations in England, to 1918', Ph.D., Reading, 1961.

George, M. D., *England in Transition*, Pelican, 1953.

Greenberg, E. L., 'The Contribution made by Private Academies in the First Half of the Nineteenth Century to modern Curriculum and Methods', M.A., London, 1953.

Grobel, M. C., 'The Society for the Diffusion of Useful Knowledge', M.A., London, 1933.

Harrison, J. F. C., *Learning and Living, 1790–1960*, Routledge and Kegan Paul, 1961.

Hewitt, M., *Wives and Mothers in Victorian Industry*, Rockliff, 1958.

Holman, H., *English National Education*, Blackie, 1898.

Holt, R. V., *The Unitarian Contribution to Social Progress in England*, Lindsey Press, London, 2nd ed., 1952.

Hope, R. B., 'Education and Social Change in Manchester, 1780–1851', M.Ed., Manchester, 1955.

Jones, R. Alun, 'Knowledge Chartism', M.A., Birmingham, 1938.

Judges, A. V. (ed.), *Pioneers of English Education*, Faber, 1952.

Kay-Shuttleworth, J. P., *Public Education*, Longmans, 1853.

Lowndes, G. A. N., *The Silent Social Revolution*, O.U.P., 1937.

Magnus, L., *The Jubilee Book of the Girls' Public Day School Trust, 1873–1923*, C.U.P., 1923.

Magnus, P., *Educational Aims and Efforts*, Longmans, Green, 1910.

Maltby, S. E., *Manchester and the Movement for National Elementary Education, 1800–1870*, Manchester, 1918.

Moore-Smith, G. C., *The Story of the People's College, Sheffield*, Sheffield, 1912.

Newton, A. W., *The English Elementary School*, Longmans, 1919.

Peers, R., *Adult Education – A Comparative Study*, Routledge and Kegan Paul, 1958.

Philpott, H. B., *London at School*, Fisher Unwin, 1904.

Roberts, R. D. (ed.), *Education in the Nineteenth Century*, C.U.P., 1901.

Robson, A. H., *The Education of Children Engaged in Industry in England, 1833–1876*, Kegan Paul, 1931.

Sadler, M., *Continuation Schools in England and Elsewhere*, Manchester, 2nd ed., 1908.

Sangster, P., *Pity My Simplicity*, Epworth, 1963.

Simon, B., *Studies in the History of Education, 1780–1870*, Laurence and Wishart, 1960.

Simon, B., *Education and the Labour Movement, 1870–1920*, Laurence and Wishart, 1965.

Sneyd-Kinnersley, E. M., *H.M.I.*, Macmillan, 1913.

Spencer, F. H., *An Inspector's Testament*, E.U.P., 1938.

Tylecote, M., *The Mechanics Institutes of Lancashire and Yorkshire before 1851*, Manchester, 1957.

Wearmouth, R. F., *Methodism and the Working Class Movements of England, 1800–1850*, Epworth Press, 1937.

Wearmouth, R. F., *Some Working Class Movements of the Nineteenth Century*, Epworth Press, 1948.

Webb, R. K., *The British Working Class Reader, 1790–1848*, Allen and Unwin, 1955.

Webb, S., *London Education*, Longmans, 1904.

INDEX